Literature, Religion, and Postsecular Studies
Lori Branch, Series Editor

Victorian Women Writers, Radical Grandmothers, and the Gendering of God

GAIL TURLEY HOUSTON

THE OHIO STATE UNIVERSITY PRESS | COLUMBUS

Copyright © 2013 by The Ohio State University.
All rights reserved.

Library of Congress Cataloging-in-Publication Data

Houston, Gail Turley, 1950–
  Victorian women writers, radical grandmothers, and the gendering of God / Gail Turley Houston.
    p. cm. — (Literature, religion, and postsecular studies)
  Includes bibliographical references and index.
  ISBN 978-0-8142-1210-3 (cloth : alk. paper) — ISBN 978-0-8142-9312-6 (cd)
  1. English literature—Women authors—History and criticism. 2. English literature—19th century—History and criticism. 3. Women authors, English—19th century. 4. Religion and literature. 5. Religion in literature. 6. Goddess religion in literature. 7. Brontë, Charlotte, 1816-1855—Criticism and interpretation. 8. Jameson, Mrs. (Anna), 1794–1860—Criticism and interpretation. 9. Browning, Elizabeth Barrett, 1806–1861—Criticism and interpretation. 10. Nightingale, Florence, 1820–1910—Criticism and interpretation. 11. Eliot, George, 1819–1880—Criticism and interpretation. I. Title. II. Series: Literature, religion, and postsecular studies.
  PR115.H68 2013
  820.9'928709034—dc23
                    2012032539

Cover design by Mia Risberg
Text design by Juliet Williams
Type set in Adobe Garamond Pro and Delphin

∞ The paper used in this publication meets the minimum requirements of the American National Standard for Information Sciences—Permanence of Paper for Printed Library Materials. ANSI Z39.48–1992.

For my grandmothers

Divinity is what we [women] need to become free, autonomous, sovereign....

If women have no God, they are unable either to communicate or commune with one another.

—Luce Irigaray, *Sexes and Genealogies* 62

What does our great historical hunger signify . . . our consuming desire for knowledge, if not the loss of myth, of a mythic home, the mythic womb?

—Friedrich Nietzsche, *The Birth of Tragedy* 137

Contents

Acknowledgments ix
List of Abbreviations xi

Chapter 1 Introduction: Antecedents of the Victorian "Goddess Story" 1

Chapter 2 "Gods of the old mythology arise":
Charlotte Brontë's Vision of the "Goddess Story" 24

Chapter 3 Feminist Reincarnations of the Madonna:
Anna Jameson and Ecclesiastical Debates on the Immaculate Conception 49

Chapter 4 Invoking "all the godheads":
Elizabeth Barrett Browning's Polytheistic Aesthetic 73

Chapter 5 Eve, the Female Messiah, and the Virgin in
Florence Nightingale's Personal and Public Papers 98

Chapter 6 Ariadne and the Madonna:
The Hermeneutics of the Goddess in George Eliot's *Romola* 121

Afterword 143

Notes 145
Bibliography 155
Index 171

Acknowledgments

THERE ARE numerous people and institutions to be recognized for their assistance during the research, writing, and revision phases of this project. First of all, with funding from the University of New Mexico Feminist Research Institute and Research Allocations Committee, I was able to do research at the British Library, the J. P. Morgan Library, the Huntington Library, the Brontë Parsonage Museum Library, the New York Public Library, and the UCLA Library. The staff at these facilities were very generous and helpful. In particular, I must thank Michael St. John-Mcalester, Manuscripts Collections Cataloguing and Processing Manager at the British Library, for going beyond the call of duty in responding to my queries. The staff at the University of New Mexico Interlibrary Loan Office as well as Steven R. Harris, Director, Collections & Acquisitions, University Libraries at the University of New Mexico, also must be thanked for the resources they provided.

Colleagues who read or heard earlier versions of this manuscript and took the time to offer their insights provided immeasurable support during the writing process: they include Saree Makdisi, Anita Obermeier, Sarah Donaldson, Marissa Greenberg, Aeron Hunt, Scott Rode, and the dear departed Hector Torres. Stacey Kikendall and Ashley Carlson were meticulous and precise in the tasks they performed. The readers chosen by The Ohio State University Press provided scrupulous, painstaking critique, which inevitably informed the rewriting phase, helping me to crystallize and hone my ideas. John Hulse and Maggie Diehl made the production process as seamless as it could possibly be. Many kudos to them.

Finally, I want to express my admiration for my sister-in-law Nancy Freestone Turley, who has inspired my thoughts on the topic of gods and grandmothers over the years. And, once again, I thank my husband for his patience and support as I worked on this project. That I was blessed with two strong, independent, blunt-speaking grandmothers who watch over me from some supernal place surely impelled this work and my life.

Abbreviations

BL	British Library
BPM	Brontë Parsonage Museum
CB	Charlotte Brontë
EBB	Elizabeth Barrett Browning
EN	Ellen Nussey
FN	Florence Nightingale
GE	George Eliot
GEL	George Eliot Letters
HM	Huntington Museum
JPM	Morgan Library
MRM	Mary Russell Mitford
NP	Nightingale Papers
NYPL	New York Public Library

1
Introduction

ANTECEDENTS OF THE VICTORIAN "GODDESS STORY"

England has had many learned women, not merely readers but writers of the learned languages, in Elizabeth's [page break] time and afterwards—women of deeper acquirements than are common now in the greater diffusion of letters; and yet where were the poetesses? The divine breath . . . why did it never pass, even in the lyrical form, over the lips of a woman? How strange! And can we deny that it was so? I look everywhere for grandmothers and see none. It is not in the filial spirit I am deficient, I do assure you—witness my reverent love of the grandfathers!

—*The Letters of Elizabeth Barrett Browning,* edited by Frederic G. Kenyon, 1:231–32

I felt a mother-want about the world[.]
—Elizabeth Barrett Browning, *Aurora Leigh* 1:40

IF VICTORIAN WOMEN WRITERS yearned for authorial forebears, or, in Elizabeth Barrett Browning's words, for "grandmothers," perhaps that longing had something to do with what Barrett referred to as "mother-want," a sense of the actual and metaphorical absence of a maternal entity (*Letters of EBB* 1:232).[1] While a multitude of orphans crowd the pages of Victorian fiction, anecdotal and statistical evidence testify to the all-too-common incidence of mothers felled by childbirth. But, as this study shall show, "mother-want" is also inextricably connected to what I call "mother-god-want." Indeed, the lack so keenly indicated in the phrase "mother-want" exacerbated the need for a Mother in Heaven, which Victorian Protestantism was unprepared to supply. The women writers taken up here—Barrett Browning, Charlotte Brontë, Florence Nightingale, Anna Jameson, and George Eliot—responded to this lack by imagining symbolic female divinities that allowed them to acquire the authorial legitimacy patriarchal culture denied them.

If these writers confronted a want of earthly and divine mothers, I suggest that there were grandmothers who, in the late eighteenth and early nineteenth centuries, envisioned powerful female divinities that would reconfigure society in dramatic ways. These millenarians and socialist feminists felt that the time had come for women to bring about the earthly paradise that patriarchal institutions had failed to establish. Recuperating a symbolic divine in the form of the Great Mother—a pagan Virgin Mary, a female messiah, and a titanic Eve—Joanna Southcott, Eliza Sharples, Frances Wright, and others set the stage for Victorian women writers to envision and impart emanations of puissant Christian and pagan goddesses. Though the Victorian authors I study often mask progressive rhetoric, even in some cases seeming to reject these foremothers, their radical genealogy appears in mystic, metaphysical revisions of divinity.

Marianne Thormählen remarks that it is a disservice to imagine Victorian religious life as anything less than variable and complex, perhaps more so for the female adherent (2). In keeping with this insight, I assume that while the patriarchal language of Christian God talk was omnipresent in the nineteenth century, it did not prevent the strong agency of women who utilized Christian dogma for progressive purposes.[2] Indeed, though from the Althusserian and Foucauldian perspective religion may be viewed as a disciplinary apparatus, it is also true that women who were profoundly engaged in institutionalized religion were not merely automatons reproducing patriarchal religious systems, for women's involvement in radical spirituality has historically been aligned with demands for their rights (Rickard 143; Braude xv; Knight 8–9).

Recognizing that patriarchal Christianity is powerful but not monolithic, I couple analysis of the historical record with respect for the writer's intellectual labor and spiritual—even mystical—pursuit of knowledge. I should firmly state here that my purpose is not to argue that a maternal deity exists. Nor am I interested in debates about matriarchy and goddess worship as precursors of patriarchy or in their contributions to what is called the modern "goddess movement." While this study provides historical background for the "goddess movement," I am more drawn to the tantalizing relationship between nineteenth-century British women's radical politics and the woman writer's tortuous engagements in gender politics vis-à-vis her professions as writer and believer.[3] My aim is to show that the rhetorical concept of a female god is important to a number of major, mid-century Victorian women writers who revise Christian and classical mythology to create alternative mythoi that subversively critique nineteenth-century gender politics.

To accept that religion provides culture with a myth system regarding gender also requires the scholar to confine the term "God" to its always already metaphorical representations. Nineteenth-century literati understood this. In *Literature and Dogma* Matthew Arnold captures the linguistic turn concerning the ontology of deity when asserting that "the word 'God' is used in most cases as by no means a term of science or exact knowledge, but a term of poetry and eloquence, a term *thrown out,* so to speak, at a not fully grasped object of the speaker's consciousness, a *literary* term, in short; and mankind mean different things by it as their consciousness differs" (Arnold 10–11). Likewise, Nietzsche notes that what we call "truth" is merely a "mobile army of metaphors, metonyms, and anthropomorphisms" ("On Truth and Lie" 46). In the twentieth century, feminist religious studies scholar Elizabeth Schussler Fiorenza repeats this refrain, cautioning that the Bible allows the reader to converse about deity only in "metaphorical, symbolic, mythological, analogical language" (Fiorenzi, "G*d" 116; see also E. Johnson).

In this study, I generally refer to 'feminist symbolic deities' as god and use the capitalized version, "God," to refer to the Christian metaphor for deity. But since this study cannot be an analysis of God or of knowing God, I gravitate to Martin Bidney's method for studying literary epiphanies, which he views as analogous to "traditional theophanies or appearances of the divine." Thus, rather than attempting to describe the divine, Bidney focuses on the "*observed structures*" inherent to the genre of epiphany (1, 9). Such an approach recognizes that although analyzing the writer's inner feelings and individual personal characteristics alone is problematic, textual remainders can be historicized and analyzed through attentive close reading of a range of rhetorical and textual signs.

The Epistemology of Mysticism

Of the writers I study, all but Jameson depict spiritual and aesthetic trance-like experiences—in fact, the agnostic Eliot had an encounter with a painting of the Madonna that was all too immanent, sending the great writer into momentary hysteria. Analyzing such epiphanies requires scholarly consciousness of the body's intelligence, that is, its ability to represent internal states through intensities of "mood, feeling, sensibility, affectivity" (Code

148).⁴ Analyzing phenomenologist Maurice Merleau-Ponty's discussion of the body's hermeneutic aptitudes, Carol Bigwood explains that *only* the connatural body (the body immersed in the physical world around it) is capable of knowing the world, meaning that all metaphysical knowledge bears physical reminders of the body, and vice versa (Bigwood 108). The connatural body, Rudolph Otto avers, has intuitions that are "*cognitions*" in a cosmos that is always deeply mysterious (147). Gloria Anzaldúa's aesthetic might be described as graphically phenomenological when she asserts that literary language actually affects blood pressure, heart rate, and muscles (77). Clearly, the above-named thinkers struggle to find a language to describe the dynamic relation between identity, emotion, the physical world, and the body. Likewise, they share the belief that knowledge is created, transferred, shared, and analyzed by and through complex physical entities that participate in, influence, and are acted upon by physical, psychological, and cultural phenomena. To ignore the body's knowledge, if that were even possible, would be to negate the original site of knowledge gathering and processing.

If Barrett Browning, Brontë, Nightingale, and Eliot were in some ways mystics, it is important to grapple with the epistemology of mysticism. I turn to descriptions of thirteenth-century medieval Beguine mystics because they exhibited so many similarities with the writers studied here and because these mystics were dependent upon the body's knowledge. As Alvilda Petroff remarks, in the visions of Beguines Hadewijch and Beatrijs "knowing is performed . . . by the whole person—body, soul, and heart" (61). A strong influence on the Beguines, medieval theologian William of Thierry believes that love was "the only faculty capable of leading" to divine knowledge (Brunn and Epiney-Burgard xxviii). As Emilie Zum Brunn and Georgette Epiney-Burgard explain, "It is Love herself that becomes knowledge," since "Love alone is able to reach God's depths which transcend the intellect" (xviii). William of Thierry asserts further that reason can understand God only by examining what He is not, whereas "Love is content to rest in what He is" (qtd. in Brunn and Epiney-Burgard xxviii). In letter 9, Hadewijch illustrates this understanding in her avowal that mystic love can occur only through relationality, in which two beings are "wholly in the other, and yet each one . . . will always remain himself" (qtd. in Petroff 61).

Beatrijs of Nazareth's treatise titled *Seven Manners of Loving* describes the phases of spiritual love that begin with a yearning for caritas founded on a desire for perfection and then moves to a recognition of the mortal's inability to love perfectly. This is followed by the experience of "*Excess*" and "*violence*" coming from the suffering invoked by attempting to love divinely (Petroff 58). Having submitted to violence and torment, the seeker is malleable enough to be "'lovingly embraced'" by God (qtd. in Petroff 58). In the penultimate phases the return of torture converts the soul in the "crucible of desire" so that the seeker experiences serenity when desire is no longer the "object of knowing but a way of knowing" (Petroff 59). In the seventh and final phase the perfected soul awaits being received into heaven by the "'limitless abyss of Divinity'" (qtd. in Petroff 59). What is so astonishing in these writings is that the mystic's adoration of the human ability to love almost surpasses her love for God. As Hadewijch writes, "'Love holds God's divinity captive in its nature'" (qtd. in Petroff 61). Though each maintained a profound relation with the Christian God, the nineteenth-century writers I examine yearned for a more expansive, loving concept of divinity than they found in the patriarchal God of their fathers.

The writings of at least one medieval female mystic were translated during the Victorian period. Originally published in 1640, Julian of Norwich's *Sixteen Revelations of Divine Love* was reissued in England in 1843. In the preface, the Victorian editor confesses that it was impossible to judge "how far these Revelations may be imputed to a fevered imagination," surely an indication of how essential it was for women writers to manage and mask their own epiphanies (vi–vii).[5] Nevertheless, the publication of Julian's visions suggests that the age was ripening to the idea of female visionaries and female gods. Seeking metaphors for the excess that the word "God" cannot describe, Julian writes that "the high might of the Trinity is our Father, and the deep wisdom of the Trinity is our Mother, and the great love of the Trinity is our Lord" (*Sixteen Revelations* 14:58). Julian expands upon the female aspect of the Trinity, saying, "I saw that the Second Person which is our Mother substancially, the same deer worthy person is now become our mother sensual; for we be double of Gods making; that is to say, substancial and sensual. Our substance is the higher party which we have in our Father God Almighty: and the Second Person of the Trinity is our Mother in kind, in our substancial making, in whom we be grounded and rooted: and he is our Mother of mercy, in our sensuality" and "in our Mother Christ we profit and encrease" (145).

These excerpts from Julian's "showings" illustrate the irony that human beings are capable of incorporating the sum total of the Trinity's qualities, whereas the ostensibly perfect Christian God's character must be divided into three parts. In addition, like her nineteenth-century descendants, the mystic of Norwich could not conceive of God without imagining a feminine element alongside the implied social ("sensual") good that such a divine materiality would produce. Mixing gender designations, Julian implies that masculinity cannot account for all that is divine and that an amorphous gender may be more characteristic of deity and humankind. As I show in the chapter on Anna Jameson, Victorian debates about the Immaculate Conception articulate the subliminal fear that a male God cannot fully comprehend all creation. Uncannily, too, Julian's depiction of Mother Christ is reminiscent of Florence Nightingale's longing for a female savior as well as of Barrett Browning's image of the double-breasted Victorian Age and of the double-seeing female poet who sings a song of a male and female God in *Aurora Leigh*.

Resacralizing the Feminine:
Romanticism and Anthropology

Distinctive metaphors for female divinity were not born Athena-like out of the minds of the writers I study. Though "God" is an abstraction, my approach to that concept is of necessity materialist, for the writers I examine embody the concept of a female god for the purpose of imagining substantive improvements in the world in general and for women in particular. Hence, I now turn to historicizing the dynamics of mother-god-want to show that the Victorians were at the cusp of a number of heritages from the Romantic period that influenced the production of goddess imagery. I consider the Romantic concept of Mother Nature and poetic creativity; nineteenth-century anthropological debates about the origins of the family and its relationship to the gender of deity; and Victorian interest in Britain's own polytheistic pagan roots. I shall conclude by discussing utopian feminists and millenarians, whose depictions of a female divine foreshadow the mythologies imagined by the women writers I study.

Thomas Vargish argues that prior to publication of George Eliot's novels, fictional inscriptions of providence unified the English novel, meaning that for most early Victorians the universe was a "moral theater" in which history was explained by a Christian deity (3). Providing unity and order, cosmogonies featured deities overcoming chaos and explaining the origins of the universe as well as its historical cycles (Prickett 128). Though polytheism held sway in the ancient world, with the rise of Judaism and Christianity in the West the idea of God became that of a single, unchanging being (Gunton 24). The problem with monotheistic religions, as Colin A. Gunton suggests, is that they often underwrite monolithic political positions (24). These attitudes are apparent in *The Mythology of Ancient Greece and Italy* (1838), when the historian and Trinity College alumnus Thomas Keightley stated that while polytheism is the religion of "unenlightened," feeble "tribes," Christian monotheism is the apex of civilization (2–3).

Despite such imperial attitudes, the major male Romantics had revised the literary tradition through what Northrop Frye refers to as a "polytheistic imagination," given Wordsworth's sanctification of Mother Nature; Keats's vow to ensure that the "heathen Goddess" Psyche is not "neglected"; Blake's extraordinary parallel universe of Ossian-like gods; and Byron's depictions of Astarte, among other pagans (Frye 16; Keats, *Poetical Works* 7:289–90).[6] With a polytheistic classical tradition that was central to the British cultural and educational apparatus, England itself was rife with variant mythologies, bearing as it did the Celtic heritage so apparent in British landscape and history. Thus, there were more goddesses than one knew what to do with, and it would be surprising if women writers had not been piqued by the female figures represented in sacred and profane texts. Indeed, unlike many of their sister writers, Barrett, Nightingale, Brontë, and Eliot were themselves immersed in classical and Christian mythologies.[7]

If the Romantics were in the process of resacralizing nature, as Kate Rigby argues, we see this exhibited in Rousseau's *Émile*, which states that only one book is "open to every one—the book of nature," a declaration subordinating the Bible as the most sacred text (Rigby 24; Rousseau 259). But even the venerable Bible participates in its own deconstruction. Mired in doublespeak, the gloss in the Brontë family Bible regarding multiple gods in the Genesis ur-text reads as follows: "It is plain from many other texts, as well as from the nature and reason of the thing, that God alone is man's Creator; and it is no less plain from this text than from diverse other places, that man had more Creators than one person."[8] To annotate a self-proclaimed monotheistic text thusly certainly does not inspire the faith the annotator intended. Hardly monolithic, then, the jealous male Jewish God and his adherents constantly refer to other gods and goddesses who are the enemy of monotheism. There are at least forty places in the Old Testament referring to Jews' participation in goddess worship (Davis 67).[9] For example, Jeremiah records that Jewish women worshipped Ishtar, burning "'incense to the queen of heaven'" and pouring out "'drink offerings to her'" (Jer. 44:17; Parrinder 195). Likewise, the papyri of Elephantiné (a Jewish military colony) report on the worship of "Yahweh but also of other gods of whom one, Anathyahu, bore the name of the female deity Anath" (Parrinder 195).

For all its masculinism, the Bible also teems with feminine images of God, including those of the female pelican, mother bear, female homemaker, and other similar tropes (Mollenkott 44–48, 49–53, 60–68). Furthermore, the Virgin Mary's ambiguous power troubles the patriarchal Law of the Father, as will be discussed more fully in the chapters on Jameson, Nightingale, and Eliot. Victorian scholars suggest that the early Christian Church would not have obtained its hegemony if it had not bowed to the hoi polloi's desire to worship the Virgin. For instance, Dean of St. Paul's Cathedral Henry Hart Milman admits in *History of Christianity* (1840) that the early Church was able to obtain and continue its mainstream status only by becoming polytheistic (3:424). Regarding schisms in the early Church, Milman eschews the idea that "our colder European reason" would accept the intolerable Gnostic fiction of a God who had a "female associate, personating the male and female Energies or Intelligences of the Deity" (2:49). Nevertheless, he adds that debates about the Trinity (always itself polytheistic) and the essence of Christ's divinity led to the worship of the Virgin, angels, and saints (3:424).

For all Milman's grumbling, the Victorian period was immersed in popular renditions of the Madonna. As Eric Trudgill's study shows, at mid-century it became a fad to call women "Madonna," with Margaret Oliphant among those bearing the moniker (258, 259). Apparently, G. H. Lewes referred to George Eliot as "Madonna," and some of her friends dubbed her "Our Lady" (Gilbert and Gubar 476). Many fictional characters also were signified with the term "Madonna," including Eliot's own cast of characters. *Scenes of Clerical Life* (1858) features Mrs. Amos Barton as "'a large, fair, gentle Madonna'," and there is a Virgin Mary motif in *Adam Bede, Middlemarch,* and *Romola* (1:24; qtd. in Trudgill 263).[10] Charles Kingsley's *Yeast* depicts a Freudian rationale for the lure of the heroine as Virgin *avant la lettre* when a High Church curate who contemplates going over to Romanism querulously asks, "'Would you have me try to be a Prometheus, while I am longing to be once more an infant on a mother's breast? . . . . Will you reproach me, because when I see a soft cradle lying open for me . . . with a Virgin Mother's face smiling down all woman's love about it . . . I long to crawl into it and sleep awhile?'" (qtd. in Trudgill 260).

Such fictional renditions of mother-god-want live up to John Ruskin's dictum that "All beautiful fiction is of the Madonna, whether the Virgin of Athens or of Judah—Pan-Athenaic always" (267). Ruskin's reference to the "Pan-Athenaic" confesses Christianity's immersion in classicism and its gods, and if we return to Milman's history, there, too, he acknowledges and adulates the "beautiful anthropomorphism of the Greeks," praising the way in which "The cumbrous and multiform idol, in which wisdom, or power, or fertility, was represented by innumerable heads or arms or breasts, as in the Ephesian Diana, was refined into a being, only distinguished from human nature by its preterhuman development of the noblest physical qualities of man." As Milman asserts, moving away from depicting gods in female form, "The imagination here took" a "nobler course" and "by degrees deities became men, and men deities" (1:24–25). As we see in this extract, the Western patriarchal tendency was to disavow "multiform" goddesses because their "breasts" and "fertility" were viewed as barbaric in contrast to the ostensibly "grander," unified, godlike male form.

While Romantic writers revised the culture's mythoi, they also brought Britain's Celtic heritage to the fore. Matthew Arnold viewed the Romantics—Keats in particular—as the high point of the Celtic strain of "natural magic" in British literature (*Complete Works* 9:214; see also "Study of Celtic Literature" 4:123). With the study of Stonehenge and its provenance, late eighteenth- and early nineteenth-century historians feverishly recuperated indigenous remains.[11] In his work, eccentric amateur archaeologist Godfrey Higgins refers to a female progenitor of the gods ("Eire, Eirin, Eirean, Eirinn") (169), while Welsh writer Edward Davies references "*Dwy-vach*" as "the mother of mankind," analogous to the "*Magna Mater* of antiquity" (105). Theosophist Madame Blavatsky would later consult Higgins's study when she wrote *Isis Unveiled*. Walter Scott's recuperation of Scottish artifacts and Thomas Macpherson's *Ossian* fueled interest in the gods and goddesses of the Celts for decades.[12] Reviling the polytheism practiced by Druids in the area and describing their worship of the goddess Onvana, Cornish antiquarian H. J. Whitfield conceded that the "rude sublimity" of Druid worship "impressed itself upon nature, and a thousand years have passed over, but not eradicated it" (52).[13]

Likewise, Arnold describes how the English bear a physical and primordial mark on their bodies and souls from the Celts' rude sublimity. Prescribing Celtic literature as the cure for Victorian malaise and Mammonism, he exclaims that even though *Ossian* was a forgery, its Celtic Titanism spread "like a flood of lava through Europe" and inspired writers thereafter (Arnold, "Study of Celtic Literature" pt. 4:116).[14] He goes so far as to assert that nothing England might do for the Celts could surpass what the Celts had done for England, for English literature received its passion and "*Titanism,*" a là Byron, from these forebears (Arnold, "Study" pt. 4:116, 117, 118). Contending that the Celtic imagination glories in nature, Arnold also concludes that the Celts' "feminine idiosyncrasy" caused their deep connection to "the secret of natural beauty and natural magic" and their need to "be close to it, to half-divine it" (Arnold, "Study" pt. 3:545–46).

In these passages, Arnold could well have been describing the wild-hearted Scotsman Thomas Carlyle. Unmoved by moribund Christianity,

Carlyle's Teufelsdrockh asserts in "The Everlasting Yea" that it was crucial to "'embody the divine Spirit of that [Christian] Religion in a new Mythus, in a new vehicle and vesture'" (*Sartor Resartus*). Carlyle explicitly pays tribute to Nature as god's sartorial garment of choice, when Teufelsdrockh, ecstatically receiving his longed for vision, exclaims, "'O Nature!—Or what is Nature? Ha! why do I not name thee GOD? Art not thou the 'Living Garment of God'?" Like other Romantics, Carlyle was deeply moved by Goethe's representation of the "Eternal Feminine" in *Faust*. In "Goethe's Helena," Carlyle quotes the climactic moment where Helena enfolds Faust and "*her Body melts away,*" while her "*Garment and Veil remain in his arms.*" At this point, Phorcyas interprets the sign to Faust, saying, "Hold fast, what now alone remains to thee. / That Garment quit not," for "*The goddess is it not,* whom thou hast lost, / Yet godlike is it. See thou use aright / The priceless high bequest, and soar aloft" (emphasis added). The stage directions read: "*HELENA'S Garments unfold into Clouds, encircle FAUST, raise him aloft, and float away with him*" (215). In this revelation, Faust learns that the garment of god is more truly the garment of the goddess. In deconstructionist splendor, Carlyle comments of this moment that "symbol and thing signified are no longer clearly distinguished" (217).

Heavily influencing the English Romantics, Continental writers conceived an extraordinary interest in the feminine divine. In the chapter on George Eliot, I discuss Ludwig Feuerbach and Auguste Comte's representations of the all-but-divine goddess. Here, though, I will mention Novalis's *Henry von Ofterdingen,* which features a sacrament in which lovers partake of a drink mixed with the ashes of a goddess. Those who imbibe the potation immediately experience a "pleasant greeting of the mother with ineffable joy" for "She was present to each one there, and her mysterious presence seemed to transfigure all" (144). Friedrich Schiller also genders Nature in "On Naïve and Sentimental Poetry," writing that "We see then in nature devoid of reason only a fortunate sister, who remained behind in the maternal home, out of which we stormed in the high spirits of our freedom to foreign lands. With painful desire we long to return thence so soon as we've begun to experience the distress of culture and hear in the foreign country of art, the moving voice of the mother" ("On Naive and Sentimental Poetry").

But then, counterintuitively, Schiller warns the reader to resist nature's siren call. Rather than desiring to exchange places with nature, Schiller contends that men must "take it into thyself and strive to wed its infinite advantage with thine own infinite prerogative and to produce the divine from both" ("On Naive and Sentimental Poetry"). Thus, Schiller only imagines the feminine (Nature) as an inferior imago of the rational, male divine, which, nonetheless, has hold on man because of its primal, prelinguistic associations. Imposing masculine will ("prerogative") upon nature's fertility is the only way to make her almost vulgar fructifying powers serve the higher intellectual purposes of men. Carlyle makes a similar shift in *Sartor Resartus,* asserting that nature is at once spectacularly and *merely* the garment that mediates for and protects mortals from the dazzling, superior masculine divinity. In fact, when Teufelsdrockh conceives of the ultimate deity he avers that "The Universe is not dead and demoniacal, a charnel-house with spectres; but godlike and my Father's!" Though condescending about the female aspect of God, Teufelsdrockh recognizes that he cannot approach the Father God without encountering and loving "'The poor Earth'" who is "'my needy Mother'" (*Sartor Resartus*).

And, in fact, for all the attention paid to Mother Nature as female deity, masculinity is still the natural denominator of creative energy in Romantic mythology and aesthetics. As Frye explains, prior to the Romantic period, God was viewed as the only originating actor in the universe. But, boldly asserting that the human mind was a creative agent, male Romantic poets saw themselves as like God in their ability to create sacred texts (37, 157). J. Hillis Miller describes the sacramental heritage the Romantics hoped to revitalize: insisting that the bread and wine *are* literally God's body, the Catholic sacrament depends profoundly upon the presence of God (3). Likewise, poetry was seen to "incarnate[s]" the objects it named in the same way that the texts of the sacred Mass were seen as part of the "transformation they evoked" (Miller 3, 6; see also Vargish 22). In contrast, later Protestant understanding of the Eucharist transmogrified the sacredness inherent to literature, for as modern "reference at a distance" replaced medieval symbolism that conceived a web of cosmic connections, so did the Protestant Eucharist illustrate the vast distance between deity and humanity (Miller 6). In response to this dynamic, the Romantics asserted that the poet could create a secular sacrament that would return God, humanity, and Nature to their pre-lapsarian unity (Miller 13–14). Thus, the canonical male Romantics yearned for uncanny, defamiliarized manifestations of Mother Nature.

The increase of women's political, social, and artistic power during the nineteenth century occurred in conjunction with subliminal mother-god-want. The accession of the professional female author and a long-lived queen, and the establishment of a potent domestic ideology sanctifying the mother, reverberated with the idea of a female divine. Certainly the deaths of so many Victorian women in childbirth—making them actual Mothers in Heaven—and the notion of the Angel in the House partially divinized women, while Queen Victoria's rule could easily be analogized to that of the

Queen of Heaven. Elsewhere I examine the concerns of mainstream male writers who were apprehensive about the advent of a formidable female sovereign because they worried she would emasculate the age.[15] In fact, in what hardly seems a coincidence given Queen Victoria's large family, in the nineteenth century historians debated whether the original social system was matriarchal or patriarchal (see Rosalind Coward). Historian J. J. Bachofen was the leading supporter of the hypothesis that matriarchy preceded patriarchy. In his introduction to *Mother Right,* Bachofen asserts that he aimed to describe the trajectory of the matriarchal age and "the primordial character of mother right" (69, 88). Established prior to the classical and Judeo-Christian patriarchal systems, mother right was traced through archaeological symbols from past civilizations that may have worshipped goddesses (xvii).

But if the Romantic age opened a space for viewing divinity as in part female, were professional women writers included in the belief that authors were a special class of mortals who metonymically participated in God's imaginative powers and spoke to and for that entity? Noting that the Romantics analogized God's creativity with the poet's visionary powers, M. H. Abrams suggests that the artist was a creator, who is "likest God because he creates according to those patterns on which God himself has modeled the universe" (42). Attending to the pronoun in this statement illustrates the assumption that divinity and the bard share an essential masculinity. Claims that the male writer's imaginative powers are metonyms of God's creativity, then, elide the woman writer's potential for being viewed as sharing in God's mental or physical parts (think: Milman's comment that the male body is symbolic of God while the ostensibly gross female form could not be associated with deity). If, as Hillis Miller comments, the Romantics represented the artist as the "creator" of "hitherto unapprehended symbols . . . which establish a new relation" between "man and God" (13), I argue that it is essential for women writers to suture the gap that still figures humanity as man and God as Father.

The difficulty faced by the Victorian female writer is apparent in Barry Qualls's discussion of *Jane Eyre* and *Sartor Resartus*. Comparing Brontë's and Carlyle's bildungsromans, Qualls contends that feminine nature is not the answer to Jane Eyre's needs and that she must achieve a higher, Carlylean understanding that "the universe is godlike and my Father's" (64, 65). Participating in the blind spot of many male Romantics, this analysis suggests that imagining a divine female archetype is an illusory flight into quietism while acceptance of the masculine metaphor for God provides sanity. Indeed, though Carlyle sought a new language for nature and referred to it as "Mother," his approach was not as radical as it could have been, and neither did male, and most female, Romantics consider retailoring culture with female equality in mind. Unable to commit to imagining a potent, sacred feminine underlying the universe that would make the metaphor of God new again, the Romantics end up reinscribing the masculine divine. Hence, the longing for Mother Nature featured in Romantic texts, especially those by male writers, produced a trope for God that elides the very entity Romantic texts attempt to descry.

This study of mother-god-want could not have been written without feminist intellectual grandmothers whom I cite throughout this work. At this point, I should note that many feminist scholars have pointed out how problematic the trope of Mother Nature was for nineteenth-century women writers. Margaret Homans argues that the Western canon rejects the mother's material body and replaces it with "powerless figurative substitutes" (*Bearing the Word* 160).[16] Likewise, Nancy Goslee contends that in male Romantic poetry, women obtain power only as muses rather than as powerful speakers (3–4). Mary K. DeShazer finds that when the muse appears to the Romantics in the form of Mother Nature, the poet, as Mother Nature's son, co-opts her creative power in order to "'give birth'" metaphorically to his opus (17). As we have seen, the co-optation of nature is evident in Schiller's and Carlyle's writings. But regardless of the exploitation of nature as trope, there were Romantic writers who did change the language for god. As this study will argue, radical early nineteenth-century feminists as well as Brontë and Barrett Browning used Mother Nature as an emblem for a woman-centered mythology featuring the biological, political, and linguistic potency of classical goddesses, a titanic Eve, and a female savior.

Pamela Sue Anderson's deft feminist epistemology helps explain the mythologies these writers created. Suggesting that the term "exists" may refer to aspirations that we strive to achieve as well as to material, verifiable entities, Anderson argues that although the ideal exists as a "fiction" to be achieved, it can also be understood as a paradigm providing material meaning and identity for individuals and groups (118). Sites of intense desire (such as mother-god-want) or mysticism in women's religious texts might be seen, then, as eruptive traces of a suppressed desire for actualizing an ideal female deity (100). Anderson calls for feminists interested in religion to create "mythical configurations of their own sex" in new narratives for women (158). By recuperating a symbolic female divine, feminists acknowledge the "legitimacy of female power" and make available women's "divine horizon," that is, her highest potentiality (Christ 277; Jantzen 65). Thus the revaluation of the term "God" by Romantic women millenarians and radicals goes a long way toward reversing the patriarchal effects of imagining god, agency, and the ideal as always and only male, and this revaluation establishes a genealogy for such imagining on the part of the nineteenth-century British women writers I examine in this study.

Frantz Fanon suggests that "Mastery of language affords remarkable power. Paul Valéry knew this, for he called language 'the god gone astray in the flesh'" (18; Valéry, qtd. in Fanon 18). This astounding statement is useful for describing Victorian women writers who attempted to deconstruct the world established by the master's language. Not to put too fine a point on it, in the Victorian period, even though the Christian God was "necrophilia[c]," as Grace M. Jantzen suggests, He was hard to kill off even with the advent of the Crisis of Faith. His proxy was written into every institution through legal language, sacred and profane ritual, and metaphorical governance (8).[17] The women writers I study wrestle with "the god[dess] gone astray" from literary language and, in eruptive moments, return her to the flesh and to discourse. By expanding the divine metaphor to include women as omnipotent beings, they critique the culture's mood regarding women's rights and, in the early stages of the first wave of feminism, uncover an absent center of late Western patriarchy: mother-god-want. I would argue that this desire for the existence of a female mythology and a female divine helped to bring about an extraordinary paradigm shift so that women's rights gradually became normalized.

Utopian Feminists and Millenarians

In this section, I outline connections between the Victorian women writers I study and some of their grandmothers. I direct attention first to the prophetic voices of religious women of the late eighteenth century whose radical beliefs may have resonated with later Victorian women writers. I then discuss Romantic-era socialist feminists whose tropes reappear in the work of Brontë, Barrett Browning, Eliot, Jameson, and Nightingale.

Asserting the importance of genealogical ties between different generations of women, Christine L. Krueger recuperates early nineteenth-century women preachers such as Joanna Southcott and Mary Bosanquet Fletcher as antecedents of women writers previously believed to be "originary" (Krueger 11; see also Showalter, *A Literature of Their Own* 7). Krueger suggests that for a brief time in the late eighteenth and early nineteenth centuries, the masculine rhetoric of the evangelical movement abated, and a space opened up for women to use the "authoritative language of scripture." During this period, women preachers feminized evangelical rhetoric and were able to end many patriarchal evangelical practices and discourses. As will be illustrated presently, millenarians Southcott, Luckie Buchan, and Ann Lee mastered what Krueger calls the "evangelical ideolect" and used it to recuperate potent symbolic female divinities. By doing so, they endowed the next generation of women writers with this rhetoric as well as with the "camouflage" necessary to make protofeminist demands safely and subversively (5, 6, 9).

Women preachers who claimed to be part of the Christian godhead were, by and large, from the lower classes. Hailing from Glasgow, the much-reviled Elspeth Simpson (1738–91) came to be known as Mrs. Luckie Buchan. Claiming to be the Holy Ghost, Buchan prophesied that the Second Coming was imminent and that she, along with her adherents, would be "translated direct to Heaven" when Christ reappeared ("The Buchanites" 363). As the third member of the Trinity, she was gifted with the ability to grace others with the Holy Spirit simply by breathing on them. Buchan's politics merged with her heretical theology. Known for their egalitarian ways, Buchan's adherents ate together at the same table, except for "Mother" Buchan, who helped serve the food to the gathered assembly (Harrison, *Second Coming* 35). Referring to herself as "mother" and "god," Buchan appealed to the mother-god-want of those who viewed mainstream patriarchal Christianity as unresponsive to their needs. The Buchanites were a relatively small group who came to a parting of the ways when it became financially impossible to support the communal life style.

From Manchester, Ann Lee was also referred to as "Mother" by her followers ("Extract from Dr. Holley's Review"). Because Jesus had manifested his godhood in masculine form at his first advent, the Shakers reasoned that Christ's second appearance would be in female form as Mother Lee. Thus her motherhood also referred to the Shaker belief that Lee was "the Mother Spirit in the Godhead" (Evans 11, 14). Under Lee's aegis, the Shakers gloried in the feminization of the age and the possibilities for political reform. Adherent William Leonard, for example, expresses the community's joy that the whole earth was feeling the "emanation" of the redeemer in the form of "increasing agitation upon the subject of the *Rights of Woman,* the Rights of Marriage, the Rights of Property,—the *Rights of Man.*" Exhibiting a strong mother-god-want, the Shakers hoped that this agitation would culminate in the millennial revelation of the "true order of the *Godhead* as Male and Female,—'the *Eternal Heavenly Father,* and an *Eternal Heavenly Mother*'" (Leonard 55). In keeping with a rather literal attempt at gender equity, some Shakers also looked forward to the coming of "the first-born Daughter" of God as a balance for the Son (Evans 14, 24).

Beginning in 1792 and lasting until her death in 1814, another female preacher, Joanna Southcott, received spiritual manifestations based upon what she saw as three important moments in the Bible when women changed the course of spiritual history: Eve participated in the Fall, Mary engendered the Savior and thus the redemption of the world, and "'a woman clothed with the sun'" would initiate the Second Coming, as Revelation 12 foretold, (Balleine 23). As Southcott claimed in numerous revelations, salvation would occur only through a female descendant of Eve, who would overcome Satan's power and make way for the establishment of God's Kingdom on earth (Matthews 59–60). Uniting the entities of the "'woman clothed with the sun'" and the "Bride of the Lamb" mentioned in Revelation 19, Southcott's Voice claimed that *she* was "The true and faithful Bride" spoken of in the Bible and that the world would be reborn only when it acknowledged her as the Bride who warned the people of Christ's return (Balleine 23; *Communications to Joanna Southcott beginning 1801,* 7). Repeatedly she noted that Christ's intention was for Southcott to redeem woman from the censure and subordination she had endured as a result of the Fall (Harrison, *Second Coming* 108). Making woman central to Christ's return—if not replacing him in his own Second Coming—Southcott revealed that the Savior's return would cause the world to "see the truth": that Eve was the conduit through which Christ's "Gospel first did come" [original underline] (*Communications to Joanna Southcott beginning 1801,* 7).

Southcott's heretical notions about salvation focused on a female as savior, thus suggesting that women had not been included in the mainstream Christian narrative. Her obsessive focus on Eve also implied that Christ's sacrifice fell short of paying the cosmic price of evil—a semidivine woman had to participate in the atonement. Concomitantly, asserting that Adam was a coward who had defamed Eve, Southcott's Voice declared that the first man initiated sin and that it was evil to hold Eve solely responsible for the Fall (Communication of September 21 and 22; BL Add. 32633 f.98). Southcott also exhorted the world to understand that men could "not be freed ["be freed" is double underlined] from the Condemnation of the fall, before the Woman be made free" (undated letter of Add. 32633, *Communications to Joanna Southcott* 1:37–40). Hammering men's misogyny, the spirit tells Southcott that Christ would "burst" upon the men who "despise[d]" Eve and Joanna (BL Add. 32636 f.18). Hence, Southcott's prophecies suggest that Christ's greatest accomplishment was to redeem his all-but-divinized Mother Eve through one of her divinized daughters.

Many feminist socialists implicitly believed that a secular Millennium would occur when, as Eliza Sharples exulted in 1832, "woman shall reign, and the kingdom of the man shall be no more" ("The Second Person of the Trinity" 615–16). We know that a feminist trajectory to the utopian movements occurred during the social upheavals accompanying the French Revolution and its aftermath (Goldstein 93).[18] Charles Fourier famously stated, "*Social progress and changes of period are brought about by*" the "*progress of women towards liberty,*" and, as Leslie Goldstein reminds us, he was perhaps the first to use the term "feministe" (qtd. in B. Taylor, *Eve* 29; see also Goldstein 92). Prominent between 1826 and 1834, the Saint-Simonians, like Fourier, advocated for women's equality and believed that "the feminization of the world was imminent" (Goldstein 96). Influenced by the Saint-Simonians, socialist Robert Owen also believed in female equality (B. Taylor, *Eve* xiii, 45–46). As "Signs of the Times," an article in Owen's *The Crisis,* suggests, the increase of self-appointed messiahs foretold the precipitous disintegration of the ancien regime's political ideologies (*The Crisis* 4:10 [Saturday, June 14, 1834]: 77).[19]

Owen's associate James Elishma Smith suggested that the female prophets appearing in England in the early 1800s were "'forerunners of a great change'" (*The Crisis* 31 Aug 1833; qtd. in B. Taylor, *Eve* 168). Smith also proclaimed that "Hitherto God has been worshipped as a man; let us now worship the female God" (*The Crisis* 4 May 1833; qtd. in Taylor, *Eve* 168). In 1834 two St. Simonian missionaries announced "the advent of the Mother" and a "new Church, wherein the spirit of emancipated women will unfold its germs of moral feelings and be instrumental in building up the new heaven and the new earth" ("St. Simonism in London by Fontana and Prati Chief and Preacher of St. Simonism in London" 1834; qtd. in B. Taylor, "Woman-Power" 127). Similarly, in 1842 Pontiffarch of the Communist Church John Goodwyn Barmby circulated a paean titled "Venus Rising from the Sea: An Ode to the Woman Power," featuring the following lines: "Woman-Saviour now we muster / To await thy advent sure, / In the cluster of thy lustre, / Come and leave the earth no more" (*Promethean* 1.1 [Jan 1842]).

The boundary between millenarians and radicals was surprisingly porous, for heretical beliefs in a female savior and millenarian sects led by women accompanied the call for women's rights and socialist agendas (B. Taylor, "Woman-Power" 122; see also Harrison, *Second Coming* 222–23).[20] In fact, J. F. C. Harrison asserts that the two groups were "aspects of the same phenomenon" rather than distinct entities (Harrison, "Paine" 80). The connections are fascinating. In their sermons, freethinkers the Reverends Erasmus Perkins and Robert Wedderburn fused Thomas Paine's ideas with millenarianism. Freethinker Richard Carlile, who had published Paine, also had a strong connection to Zion Ward's millenarian followers (Harrison, "Paine" 83). A significant minority of millenarians were political radicals, including William Blake and William Sharp (76, 82). François Piquet argues that

Blake, Coleridge, and Shelley were millenarian in their hope that the French Revolution would result in a new heaven and earth, while Ernest L. Tuveson suggests that Marx should be viewed through the lens of millenarianism, for Marxist thought included the precept that violent revolution was a purifying force culminating in a secular millennium (Piquet 30, 31, 35; Tuveson 329). And, if George Eliot was enamored of Feuerbach, it should be recalled that Marx recognized him as the first philosopher to undermine Hegel's idealism and thus facilitate the philosophical foundations of Marxism. Completing the circle of influence, Marxism was profoundly influenced by the radical utopians Saint-Simon, Owen, and Fourier.

For that matter, we can include Barrett Browning, Brontë, Nightingale, and Eliot in the fold of a broader form of millenarianism, for these authors imagined an imminent new heaven and earth, which they would help bring to pass, in part through sublimated incarnations of a feminine divine. Indeed, *Aurora Leigh* ends with Aurora invoking a quasi-secular millennium based on Revelation; Nightingale seeks a female messiah to provide sanitation in the hellish English slums; Brontë imagines a titanic goddess who initiates a form of love that encompasses lords and Luddites; and Eliot analogizes the millennial politics of Victorian Britain with the apocalyptic radicalism of quattrocento Florence, which her heroine oversees. It should be remembered, too, that these writers commented on socialist and millenarian agendas to friends, and at least two of these writers had associations with socialists and millenarians: Barrett and her father were obsessed with millenarian Edward Irving, and after hearing his sermons, she declared that "As a Preacher, he affected me more than anyone I ever heard" (EBB to Mr. Boyd 38; see also *Browning's Correspondence* 281, 293, 298). Meanwhile, Eliot received at least one social call from Robert Owen, who discussed his political agenda with her.[21]

Whether early nineteenth-century socialists were atheists or believers, they sought a secular Eden in the here-and-now. Feminist socialist Eliza Sharples, for example, sounds much like Southcott in the myth system she proposes:

> This is the time, when woman shall reign, and the kingdom of the man shall be no more. The man and the woman are the two Messiahs of the Bible....
> Woman is the bride—the lamb's wife, and the Bible says that she comes, when the millennium begins. ("Second Person" 615–16)

Along with her common-law husband Richard Carlile, Sharples published the short-lived journal *The Isis* in 1832. Using Christian rhetoric for socialist ends, Sharples firmly links the Savior's return with feminist goals, describing the Second Coming as a time of "republicanism and happiness" (614). Secularizing the Madonna, Sharples declares that "the virgin is the personification of wisdom, so personified throughout the Bible, and so personified under the names of Pallas and Minerva in the Pagan Mythology; and the son to be brought forth is . . . *Jesus Christ,* or *Reason,* which is the virgin-born principle" ("Sixteenth Discourse" 228). Blasting the all-male Trinity, she declares, "The Pagan had the good sense to find a Juno for their Jupiter, and to perceive the dual quality in the great first cause" ("Tenth Discourse" 131).

Given such proclivities, it is not surprising that Sharples decided she would revere—and name herself after—"Isis Omnia" as well as Eve, both of whom represented for her the highest aspiration for women, the search for knowledge ("To Correspondents" 190; "Editor's Response" 128). In the inaugural issue of *The Isis,* Sharples defies gender norms by discoursing publicly on politics. As she notes, many would protest, "Politics from a woman!" Her response is rousing: "YES, I will set before my sex the example of asserting an equality for them with their present . . . masters, and strive to teach all . . . that the undue submission, which constitutes slavery, is honourable to none; while the mutual submission, which leads to mutual good, is to all alike dignified and honourable" ("First Discourse" 1). This passage acknowledges the virtual impossibility that women will be taken seriously as political pundits. But, unlike so many nineteenth-century female writers, Sharples eschews wearing a mask or apologizing for her audacious entry into male territory. Perhaps this explains why her writing could not make headway with a majority of the male and female audience, and thus why her oeuvre is all but unknown today.

Like Southcott, Sharples also recuperates Eve as a semi-divine figure. In a poem in *The Isis* that merges the eponymous goddess with Sybil and Eve, the writer appeals to Isis because the "Father, Son, and Holy Ghost have fail'd" ("To the Lady of the Rotunda" 112). Denouncing the fallacious Christian myth of the Fall, the poem notes that the religion of Isis includes no trees that "bring forth *forbidden fruit.*" In Isis's renewal of the earth, ignorance would be driven from the land, and the primordial divinity, Nature, would not menace human beings with a fictional hell ("To the Lady of the Rotunda" 112). Rewriting the myth of Eve's Fall, Sharples blasphemes a God that bars women from knowledge. Imagining a different cosmic beginning, she praises Eve, for if hers "were a fall," it "was a glorious fall, and such a fall as is now wanted" ("Tenth Discourse" 132). The rest of this rather long disquisition is worth repeating:

> I will be such an Eve, so bright a picture of liberty! . . . I will . . . distribute the fruit of the tree of knowledge. How much better would the Bible have read, if, in the introductory part of it, *God* had been represented as saying to his new-made man: 'Of every tree of the garden thou mayest eat freely; and by thy studies get knowledge; but in the midst of the garden there is a gaudy creation for the shelter of superstition. . . . Beware that thou dost not enter there'. . . . Such a caution as that would have been god-like; and man might rationally have worshipped in wonder, love, and praise. No such thing now. ("The Tenth Discourse" 132–33)

In this astonishing passage, Sharples deftly utilizes the Christian myth to underscore her secular vision of a new world order and of the potentialities and ideals that could exist for women. Turning the Christian God's cosmology on its head, Sharples's brilliant discourse makes Eve the only divine *and* rational being in the garden—while also advancing a more spiritually fulfilling and just atheism. This rewriting of the Fall is at once bracing, passionate, and intellectually acute. Such rhetoric, it would seem, would call forth an exhilarating response from women who felt unjustly and irrationally condemned for participating in a quest for knowledge apparently allowed only to men. Likewise, Sharples's deconstruction of the biblical Fall would seem to free her male readers to conceive of and support the logical conclusion of the call for the rights of man.

The wry Scots socialist feminist and freethinker Frances Wright engaged her audience through a revision rather than an absolute rejection of the Christian Fall. Dismayed by the current "ignorance of our sex," Wright notes that the modern "Eve puts not forth her hand to gather the fair fruit of knowledge" because the "wily serpent . . . beguileth her *not* to eat" ("Lecture I" 38), Pleading with believers not to offend their maker by "imagining him armed with thunders to protect the tree of knowledge from approach," Wright exhorts her sisters that if they believe they were made by a divine being they must honor him by "employ[ing] his first best gift—your reason" ("Lecture III" 76).[22] Another radical feminist reiterates the same theme, suggesting that if the Fall had been written by a woman, "we should have had a very different version of it" because it would have been written to show that Eve's "great folly" was not the eating of the apple but, rather, in sharing it with Adam (*New Moral World* 19 July 1845; qtd. in B. Taylor, *Eve* 146).

Buchan, Lee, Southcott, and Sharples faced a brutal press and public, which could not have been lost on women writers who came after them. Buchan was depicted as an "absurd woman" for figuring herself as the "Third

Person in the Godhead" (Rev. "*The Buchanites, from First to Last,*" *Tait's* 61). One journal jeered at her followers for giving her the Virgin's moniker of "Our Lady" (Rev. "*The Buchanites, from First to Last,*" *New York Observer* 28). Robert Burns leeringly complained that Buchan's spiritual breathings on her flock were performed with "postures and practices that are scandalously indecent," reminding one of Milman's horror of the always already debased female body (Burns; qtd. in "Superstition and Folly" 978). *Chambers's Edinburgh Journal* also brayed that in attending to her spiritual ministry, Buchan neglected her housework, and, worse, she affirmed the doctrine that marriage was heretical ("The Buchanites" 363). For these blasphemies this "witch-wife" was, on at least one occasion, the victim of mob violence. Dragged through the streets "nearly in a state of nudity," Buchan was eventually let go when the crowd decided that her husband was the proper authority to murder her if "'he pleases when he gets home'" ("Superstition and Folly" 977).

Similarly, an exposé of the Shakers deplores Ann Lee for declaring, "that she was greater than Jesus; that he came to suffer and die, but she should never die" (Dyer 18). Former Shaker William J. Haskett whined in his tell-all that Lee's refusal to have sex with her husband, even though he was an "inebriat[e]" lout, illustrated her "sarcastic" "misanthrophy" [*sic*] (15). Meanwhile, the famous critic Francis Jeffrey wrote of Southcott that her "tedious" communications were "ravings" and "unintelligible trash," while Dickens's *Tale of Two Cities* derisively links her with séances and the "Cocklane ghost" ("Review" 455, 454, 461; Dickens 35). And as to the socialist feminists, an article in *Fraser's Magazine* titled "Women and the Social System" (1840) lays out the epithets they had to endure: These dissolute "Gorgons" are "plunged into abandoned debauchery" with "libidinous young men" (700, 699, 701).

It is not surprising, then, to learn that a viable movement dedicated to Owenite feminism did not occur. Apparently, as Gail Malmgreen points out, joining socialism with the emancipation of women did not appeal strongly enough to lower-class Owenites (20). Malmgreen argues that this failure negatively influenced later feminist activism and, combined with emerging Victorian domestic ideology, helped tamp down lower-class radical feminist goals (20). Thus, if, as Krueger speculates, women writers gained cover from the evangelical rhetoric their female forebears passed on, they also made the strategic decision to defuse as much as possible discussion of the culture's misogyny. If, as Amy Christine Billone remarks, Victorian women writers had "to mask what they were articulating" (6), the writers I study were, in Rita Felski's words, "skilled in the art of deception and concealment, in putting on masks and performing in elaborate disguise" for political and personal reasons (Felski qtd. in Billone 7).

The following chapters will show how the rhetorical choices made by Barrett, Brontë, Nightingale, Jameson, and Eliot bear and mask traces of the grandmothers I have described in the last few pages. Ann Taves suggests that first-person narrative allows historians to access material reality as well as "the links between experience and the bodily knowledges, cultural traditions, and social relations" that form individual experience (361). In the remainder of this study, I examine the works, first-person and otherwise, of women writers vis-à-vis cultural artifacts to identify how these writers created profound mythoi while also authorizing spiritual desire. As a scholar engaged in always historicizing—in this case historicizing what I call mother-god-want and its repressions—I put a range of Victorian texts in conversation, closely reading biographies, journals, and other personal documents in relation to Victorian sociocultural texts about religion. I also consider engagements with mother-god-want through analysis of the physical condition of the writers' manuscripts and handwriting, as well as the author's hermeneutic praxis vis-à-vis her descriptions of bodily effects resulting from trances and revelations.

The chapters of this study are organized chronologically, according to publication date, or, in Nightingale's case, the date of writing, of the text focused on: Brontë's *Shirley* (1849), Jameson's *Legends of the Madonna* (1852), Barrett Browning's *Aurora Leigh* (1856), Nightingale's *Cassandra* (1860), and Eliot's *Romola* (1863). In the second chapter, I show that mother-god-want appears in Brontë's early writings that feature a "Great Mother" who acts as a precursor to an amorphous female deity in *Jane Eyre* and *Shirley*. By examining Brontë's juvenilia, letters, journals, handwriting, and editing practices in the fair copy of *Shirley*, I analyze her evolving metaphor of the divine and argue that her recuperation of Eve as a mother of the gods is not only in keeping with Romantic aesthetics; it is also an extension of early nineteenth-century radical feminist socialists and millenarians' rhetorical challenges to the biblical devaluation of Eve.

In chapter 3, I examine Anna Jameson's *Legends of the Madonna*, published in 1852, vis-à-vis Victorian debates about the Papal Bull that officially sanctified the Virgin's Immaculate Conception. As many feminist scholars have shown, the figure of the Madonna acts as a lightning rod for understanding a culture's constructions of gender, and for this reason alone the Victorian media mêlée surrounding the official institution of the Immaculate Conception is telling. I shall argue that Jameson's depictions of the Madonna are so daring that they are reminiscent of the audacious millenarians and radical feminists of the generation that preceded her.

In chapter 4, I take up Barrett's polytheism. Delineating mother-god-want in her work, I contend that she combines the Christian God with disturbing images of the gods of Greece, primal descriptions of god as mother, and Swedenborgian notions that the spiritual and material worlds are inseparable. I argue that in the spirit of the utopian feminists, Barrett's tropes upend gender classifications in a poetics that enlarges the notion of god and human identity. I suggest, too, that Aurora Leigh's need to resolve the degrading effects of poverty through divine poetry must be seen in light of the utopian politics she explicitly sees as the context of her epic.

Florence Nightingale is the focus of chapter 5. A polytheistic reader, Nightingale was dedicated to her own rendition of mystical Christianity. I note the rhetorical similarities between Nightingale's rendition of a female savior in "Cassandra," Sharples's references to Isis and the Savior, and Southcott's recuperation of Eve as a godlike being. A mystic like Southcott and Julian of Norwich, from an early age Nightingale communicated with God through a "Voice." In this chapter, I examine her written descriptions of these manifestations, particularly her absorption in images of the Virgin Mary, a female Savior, and the desire to be those divinities. I suggest that when Nightingale refers to the female messiah in the feminist classic "Cassandra," she co-opts this utopian trope from early nineteenth-century radical feminists and re-envisions it (and the figure of Eve and the Virgin Mary) for her own private and semipublic engagements with gender and class politics.

In the final chapter, I study George Eliot's *Romola* in light of the author's disturbing encounter with Raphael's *Sistine Madonna*. I will argue that Eliot's choice of setting in *Romola* allowed utopian opportunities for the heroine that are reminiscent of those called for by radical feminists in the early nineteenth century. As I will show, the unique quattrocento combination of worship of the Virgin, Renaissance research on the pagan archives, and the establishment of the first republic founded on Christian principles provided the dynamic with which Eliot could fuse the Madonna's value system with that of the pagan goddess Ariadne in order to make Utopia available through the political acts of wise, loving women in the public sphere.

2

"Gods of the old mythology arise"

CHARLOTTE BRONTË'S VISION OF
THE "GODDESS STORY"

[Y]our gods are not my gods.
—Charlotte Brontë, *Shirley,* Clarendon Press edition, 632

[Brontë] attempts to discover new modes by which the soul may be realized through the self, indeed a new synthesis of the old religion and Romanticism.
—Barry Qualls, *The Secular Pilgrims of Victorian Fiction* 52

CHARLOTTE BRONTË was fourteen when she wrote "The Violet," spoken by her Angrian hero, the Marquis of Douro. Cataloguing famed classical writers, the Marquis desires to be numbered in a modern "Parnassas." When Douro asks Nature to reveal herself, she appears as a goddess with raiment made from "mountain hoar," "plume-like trees," and an "azure river." After a description of the sartorial flair exhibited by the "'Mighty Mother,'" the deity grants the Marquis's request for eternal renown (CB, *Poems* #51; MS. Bonnell 127, poem 102).[1] In 1837 in another version of the Great Mother motif, Brontë wrote a lyric poem under the guise of Thomas Aird, a Scotsman and sometime contributor to *Blackwood's Magazine.* The young Charlotte portrays Aird as a bounder who begins the poem with a hair-raising apostrophe: "Gods of the old mythology, arise in gloom and storm" (*Poems* #90). As Brontë imagines him, the scandalous Aird bellows that he will not allow pagan deities such as Baal and the "sons of Anakim" to intimidate him when he meets them in hell after his demise (*Poems* #90). Then, more respectfully, he appeals to the goddesses Ashtaroth and Semele to "Picture forth thy Goddess story" (CB, *Poems* #90).

Marianne Thormählen astutely argues that Brontë's treatment of religion is so dynamic and ambiguous that critics need not "'rea[d] against the grain'" (5). I suggest, however, that Brontë's writing is dynamic because, despite trying to suppress it, she herself wrote against the grain of Christian patriarchy, calling forth the "goddess-story" in one form or another all her life.[2] As "The Violet" and "Gods of the old mythology" reveal, however, by the age of ten, she knew that wearing a male mask would aid her in telling the "goddess" and other stories. As Christine Alexander points out, the adolescent Brontë created a sophisticated repertoire of male voices that afforded her vicarious access to masculine privilege, aiding her in becoming a keen competitor with the brotherhood of authors (*Early Writings* 227; "Autobiography and Juvenilia" 154–55).[3] But notwithstanding the young writer's use of the male mask, while "The Violet" is written in the voice of the Marquis of Douro, at the end of the lyric the teenage prodigy boldly signs her own name as the author of that persona *and* his oeuvre. As with "The Violet," Brontë's own outsized personality exceeds the male persona's masculinity in "Gods of the old mythology."

The use of a male mask, of course, held over into the novels Brontë published as an adult—she remained concealed behind the pseudonym of "Currer Bell" as long as she could and was angry when G. H. Lewes publicly revealed her identity.[4] Brontë received a striking example of masking from her father, who described to Elizabeth Gaskell a pedagogical tool he had used with the children when they were very young. Believing that they "'knew more than I had yet discovered, in order to make them speak with less timidity, I deemed that if they were put under a sort of cover I might gain my end; and happening to have a mask in the house, I told them all to stand and speak boldly from under cover of the mask'" (Gaskell 48). Catechizing Brontë, he queried, "'what [is] the best book in the world,'" to which she replied, "'The Bible.'" He directed her to name "'the next best'" and she answered with Romantic precision, "'The Book of Nature'" (48). Gaskell remarks of this experiment on the sisters, "Wild, strong hearts, and powerful minds, were hidden under an enforced propriety and regularity of demeanour and expression, just as their faces had been concealed by their father, under his stiff, unchanging mask" (61). Gaskell's statement is telling in its reflexivity as well as its understanding of this odd example of Patrick Brontë's patriarchy.

Recognizing that Brontë's reasons for using a male mask are manifold, I suggest that Brontë vicariously presented herself as one capable of calling forth the gods ("Gods") and receiving power from them ("The Violet"). Indeed, Victor A. Neufeldt opines that "The Violet" is an obvious rendition of Brontë's artistic aims (CB, *Poems* #401). In keeping with Alexander's argument that as an adolescent Brontë was a "self-conscious author," I surmise that "The Violet" and "Gods of the old mythology" are metonymic expressions of a pattern in her writing that crosses over into her adult writing, usually in more muted form (Alexander, *Early Writings* 231). If the adult author feelingly portrays the oppressed condition of women in Victorian culture, Brontë's novels are grounded in her adolescent writings that feature pagan mythologies, including powerful goddesses whose stories have been suppressed and are in need of recuperation. Thus, although Brontë was temperamentally incapable of rejecting traditional Christian mythologies outright, she reinvigorated the Christian cosmogony with pre-Christian mythoi featuring women in empowered roles. "The Violet," especially, suggests that Brontë believed that the ambition to be an author had to be legitimized metaphorically by an omnipotent feminine essence that understood and extolled her unique genius.[5]

Her belief is particularly astonishing because, as the daughter of a perpetual cleric, the adolescent author was immersed in the daily negations of patriarchal language. Brontë understood that nineteenth-century Protestantism worshipped a male God that was demanding and disciplinary toward women. Ruth Y. Jenkins argues that although the individual Victorian woman might generally have experienced a fulfilling private spiritual life, "institutionalized religions severely restricted, even denied, her a voice in the dialogues that shaped theological doctrines and informed secular mores." As to the specific conditions affecting Brontë, Jenkins asserts that her demanding father and the provincial West Riding district in which she was reared made it all but impossible to live up to evangelical expectations (Jenkins, *Reclaiming Myths* 16, 66). Thormählen, however, persuasively argues that Patrick Brontë had friendly relationships with Nonconformists and that since his daughters constantly shifted in their allegiance to Catholic, evangelical, and High Church dogma, it is all but impossible to pin down their ambiguous approaches to spirituality and religion (2). Thormählen stops short of calling Brontë a thoroughgoing radical, conjecturing instead that the author's fierceness is the "heroism of the pilgrim rather than the wrath of the rebel" (8). I suggest that attending to the heroic and wrathful stories in the juvenilia, with their evocation of pagan gods and Mother Nature, helps the reader navigate the eruptions of non-Christian matter and savage intensity in Brontë's adult narratives.

If Brontë regularly uses nature images as "'objective correlatives' of subjective states," she also was deeply influenced by George Sand, whose fiction, according to Pam Hirsch, is inundated with "'mother-want'" for which

Nature serves as the replacement (Lindner 126; Hirsch 214).[6] On the most primal level, mother-want is found throughout Brontë's work because she lost her own mother at such a young age. But her astute close reading of Victorian culture also made the author sensitive to the disparagement of women. One of Brontë's comments about the Woman Question indicates her recognition of how difficult it was to get at the roots of misogyny. Responding to the argument that women were responsible for their subordinate condition, she concurred that "'there are evils which our own efforts will best reach.'" Nevertheless, she remarked that "'there are other evils—deep-rooted in the foundations of the social system—which no efforts of ours can touch; of which we cannot complain; of which it is advisable not too often to think'" (qtd. in Gaskell 356). In this statement, Brontë previews, avant la lettre, Frantz Fanon's understanding that if the minority group "is a neurotic society, . . . we are driven from the individual back to the social structure. If there is a taint, it lies not in the 'soul' of the individual but rather in that of the environment" (Fanon 213). I would argue that the traces of a female divine in Brontë's oeuvre helped heal the misogyny the author saw incised on the Victorian female body by a network of institutional interdictions. Concomitantly, Brontë's ambitious enactment of authority as a female writer endowed by God with hierophantic powers resisted patriarchal gender ideology.

Swinburne, Gaskell, May Sinclair, and Brontë scholars comment in passing on the author's description of a female divinity, while others recognize a pagan female Nature worship in her writing. But when describing this divine female, said critics assert that Brontë was only representing her sister Emily's experience rather than limning her own unique vision.[7] Janet L. Larson briefly mentions Brontë's use of "female messianism" in *Shirley*, but her major focus is on how Brontë used and defied the male bardic heritage (72). In her classic study, *Holy Ghosts: The Male Muses of Emily and Charlotte Brontë*, Irene Taylor examines Brontë's use of a "Mighty Mother" to fulfill the need to narrate her own genius, but Taylor admits that Brontë probably saw the *Magna Mater* as a created being and not a life-giving goddess (139–40, 171, 185). Taylor concludes that the God Brontë sought was male because the author was caught between wanting to *be* her ambitious father and wanting his love (7–17, 292). Kate Lawson sees the vision of "Mother/Eve/Nature" as the heart of "feminist dissent" and suggests that *Shirley* offers an alternative Trinity of Gaea, Eve, and Mother Nature. However, Lawson sees this view as a weak inversion of the patriarchal God story ("Dissenting Voice" 737; "Imagining Eve" 415-16). Thus, there has been no in-depth analysis of the difference that Brontë's feminine metaphor for the divine makes to feminist or Victorian scholarship.

Temperamentally a Romantic, Brontë viewed literary genius as the sacred mediator of the divine. In "Reflections on the fate of neglected Genius," fourteen-year-old Brontë (who referred to herself in the Angrian saga as the Chief "Genii") claimed that God, or "Genius," raised its followers' minds to "mightier worlds" (*Poems* #56).[8] In a letter to G. H. Lewes in 1847, the mature Brontë still makes special pleading for the imagination, saying that it is "a strong, restless faculty," and she worries that restraints on women might force her to "be quite deaf to her [imagination's] cry" (Letter to G. H. Lewes 6 Nov. 1847; qtd. in Gaskell 268). Apparently Brontë was not deaf to the cry of genius, for, on at least one occasion, she insisted that she heard a voice dictating poetry to her, and one scholar suggests that from a young age Brontë wrote her fiction "spontaneously," even in a "trancelike state" (Gaskell 100, 111; see also Lonoff in CB, *Belgian Essays* 243). For example, in a prose manuscript attached to the poem "Look into thought & say what dost thou see," written at Roe Head in 1836, Brontë describes a voice that "wakens me up" and reveals "the divine, silent, unseen land of thought, dim now & indefinite as the dream of a dream the shadow of a shade." This voice arouses a "dormant power," she analogizes to a wind "pouring in impetuous current the air, sounding wildly unremittingly from hour, to hour, deepening its tone as the night advances, coming not in gusts, but with a rapid gathering stormy swell" (CB, *Poems* #117). Elsewhere, she describes how a "trance seemed to descend on a sudden" at the crepuscular hour when a "still small voice" enraptured her and "whirled me away like heath in the wilderness for five seconds of ecstasy" ("Well, here I am at Roe Head"). She also complains about students interrupting her reveries and analogizes herself with God in the process, saying, "I fulfil my duties strictly & well," adding, "I, so to speak,—if the illustration be not profane,—as God was not in the . . . wind, nor the earth-quake, so neither is my heart in the task" ("Well, here I am at Roe Head").[9] On another occasion at Roe Head, she is "ecstatic" because "All this day I have been in a dream" that "showed almost in the vivid light of reality the ongoings of the infernal world" ("All this day").

Brontë's script is revealing, particularly in "Well, here I am at Roehead." Usually, her handwriting is neat, regular, and steady, with neither an up- nor a downhill slant. But in this trance, the punctuation and capitalization are inconsistent. Where her writing is normally very even-keeled and legible, in the transcription of her vision one line of writing will often merge with a previous or following line, almost making the words illegible as the writing undulates across the page. The script also seems hastily put to paper, and many words are lined or blotted out, which is uncharacteristic of the usually tidy author. Although I do not intend to overstate the difference between her normal penmanship and the handwriting that limns her visionary states, I do believe it to be another element that should be considered when studying Brontë's writing practices, particularly in regard to the goddess story.[10]

Grace M. Jantzen imagines a "feminist symbolic" of "becoming divine" that sustains the imagination, values birth, and centers on life and spirituality, in contrast to what she calls the "necrophilia[c]" Christian religion that focuses on punishment and death (4, 8, 95). Jantzen understands feminist spirituality as focusing on human potentialities or "horizons" for divinity rather than on spiritual deities who expect to be worshipped. As Jantzen explains, "becoming divine is understood at least partly as being divine for one another" (94). Certainly Brontë's literary imagination is attached to a feminist religious symbolic, but she was also wracked by an internal battle between creative polytheism and the demanding Christian God with which she was saddled. Her dual spiritual praxis—the two gods contending in her very flesh, if you will—was mirrored in her emotional life. Like Lucy Snowe, who was torn between masochistic "Reason"—which in *Villette* is a synonym for repression—and self-indulgent passion or imagination, Brontë teetered between obsessive and complete immersion in the passionate world of Angria and the too-often-deadening self-discipline Christianity proffered (*Villette* 251). Sadly, much of Brontë's writing is a casebook for Jantzen's delineation of the Christian God as a "disembod[ied], omnipoten[t], and omniscien[t]" male who expects His adherents to be obsessed with justice, self-renunciation, sadism, and death (10, 2).

Brontë often berated herself for her inability to sacrifice herself to such a God. For example, in a letter to Ellen Nussey on 6 December 1836, she worries that she cannot fulfill the demands of the Church: although she wishes to practice "self-denial," she worries because she inevitably returns to the "gratification of my own desires." Acknowledging her "evil wandering thoughts," Brontë desires holiness but confesses that she will "*never, never* obtain" it (Bonnell 162 BPM). Entrenched in Christian self-abnegation, Brontë dutifully admits, "The right path is that which necessitates the greatest sacrifice of self-interest" (qtd. in Gaskell 238). Thus, in crippling grief after the deaths of her three remaining siblings within nine months, leaving her as the last living child in the family, Brontë felt "tamed down and broken" and focused intently on "recalling my thoughts, cropping their wings, drilling them into correct discipline" (qtd. in Gaskell 212, 348). Brontë certainly may have attended to the "drilling" she found in the family library, wherein Jeremy Taylor's manual for Christian living (1655) exhorts his reader not to "faint in the labours of mortification, and austerities of repentance: for in hell, one hour is more intolerable than a hundred years in the house of repentance" (45).[11]

Although I do not have the space here to discuss the many poems in the juvenilia that illustrate Brontë's ritual summons of the divine, it is important to outline their structure.[12] In the Angrian saga, the poems are often spoken in the first person by Brontë's fictional characters, but I agree with Neufeldt that Brontë is also finding her own voice in these poems. In these verses, Brontë conceives of a numinous veiled entity that must be approached through ritualistic stages. Often the epiphany is of a fairy world, but at other times the poem's persona merges with a more profound fundament. In one verse fragment, for example, a vision occurs when radiant beings "Cras[h] through the firmament." The poem ends with the onset of a trance, "veil[ing] my eyes with a holy fear / For the coming visions no mortal may bear" (CB, *Poems* #41). Typically these visions feature the luminous transformation from day to night presided over by the moon, which acts as a metaphorical eye–I watching and mediating the vision.[13] If the moon is a recurring emblem in Brontë's writing, it is associated with the fact that Brontë could indulge in her fantasy world only in the evening after her dull daytime duties were done. When she specifically genders the moon, it is always designated as female, while the sun is always male.[14] At the start of the visions, the moon is often veiled but then throws off obscuring clouds as the speaker moves closer to an epiphany. The moonlight mystifies and brilliantly radiates the world in ways the sun's light cannot, revealing a heightened, sacred state. For example, in Brontë's essay "The Immensity of God," the "majestic" moon shows "nature under a new aspect," as "more artistically arranged than when the sun shone on it" (*Belgian Essays* 48).

An article prominently featuring the moon was published in 1830 in *Blackwood's Edinburgh Magazine,* one no doubt the Brontë children read, especially since the essayist repeatedly refers to his companion named "O'Bronte." The piece, titled "The Moors," describes a trek through northern England and Scotland and features a mystical description of the moon that must have appealed to Brontë:

> And, lo, and behold! There is Diana—but not crescent—for round and broad is she as the sun himself—shining in the south, with as yet a needless light—for daylight has not gone down in the west—and we can hardly call it gloaming. Chaste and cold though she seem, a nunlike luminary who has just taken the veil—a transparent veil of fine fleecy clouds—yet, alas! . . . and now, though Day is still lingering, we feel that it is Night. When the one comes and when the other goes, what eye can note, what

tongue can tell—but what heart feels not in the dewy hush divine, as the power of the beauty of earth decays over us, and a still dream descends upon us in the power of the beauty of heaven! (604)

The writer also limns the "moonlight" as "carr[ying] the imagination on—on—on—into inland recesses that seem to lose at last all connexion with the forgotton sea," for "All at once the moon is like a ghost;—and we believe devoutly—heaven knows why—in the authenticity of Ossian's Poems" (Wilson 605). Such Romantic rhetoric indicates not only the powerful influence of *Ossian* but also how important moon imagery was in this infamous text. Of *Ossian*, Hugh Blair wrote, "The sun, the moon, and the stars . . . form the circle, within which Ossian's comparisons generally run" (qtd. in Thacker 105).[15] We know that *Ossian* had a great influence on the impressionable, Brontë children, who glossed and critiqued their copy of the poem, while also writing essays about it in their hand-made journals (BPM 206 [1222H]).

The epiphany in Brontë's early poetry is not a manifestation of dogma. Rather, the vision may facilitate a brief merging of the mortal with a supernal entity that brings knowledge of supernal love, somewhat similar to what the Beguine mystics experienced. Indeed, more often than not, relationality *with* the divine as well as the human potential to be divine *is* the feminist matter of Brontë's epiphanies. I am thinking, too, of Jantzen's feminist theology in which humans "become God for one another" by being a God *for* rather than over others (93). In "The Violet," the moon's link to a "Mighty Mother" is not only part of a ritual setting for accession of the divine; it is the metonymic talisman of a female deity. We see this spirituality associated with the moon in Brontë's non-Angrian juvenile poems as well.[16] "The Vision," for example, describes the moon as a "glorious gem" watching over an incandescent group of immortals who "Dazzl[e]" the poet (CB, *Poems* #28). Likewise, "When thou sleepest" features a landscape "Robed in moonlight," wherein the poem's speaker flies on the "spirit's waiting wings" to see "'mld transcendency" that "Star to star was mutely telling / Heaven's resolve & fate's decree" (CB, *Poems* #128).

The depiction of the moon in *Jane Eyre* also alludes to a divine presence. The famous red room scene features a "preternatural voice" or "haloed face" that will later appear as her mother in the guise of the moon (48). The vision occurs at a liminal moment when day is turning to night. Recalling that her child self saw an ethereal light gleaming on the wall and ceiling of the room, the adult Jane notes that "I can now conjecture readily that this streak of light was, in all likelihood, a gleam from a lantern" outside (49). Yet the mature narrator has it both ways—as a mundane and a mystical manifestation. She recalls that the young Jane thought the light "herald[ed]" a "coming vision from another world" and that only later did she understand that what seemed to be "the rushing of wings" and something descending upon her was just the feeling of "oppress[ion]" from being in the frightening room (49). However, although the adult Jane gives rational reasons for the "vision," the text uses the same language the young Charlotte Brontë had used to describe her trances in poetic and diary form. Jane's later "vision" of light that "was such as the moon imparts to vapours she is about to sever" also bears strong resemblance to Brontë's trances. In fact, Jane's vision cribs from Brontë: "I watched her come—watched with the strangest anticipation; as though some word of doom were to be written on her disk. She broke forth as never moon yet burst from cloud." At this point, the moon becomes a gynomorphic God with a "glorious brow," who "gazed and gazed on me" and "spoke to my spirit" (346).

Brontë's personal trances conform to the ritual she describes in the poems and novels: a subject moves from the mundane world into an epiphanic state brought about by hypersensitive awareness of nature during a liminal moment, usually that between day and night.[17] On 11 August 1836, having spent the morning teaching "fat-headed oafs" the difference between an "article and a substantive," Brontë was overcome by the thought that her life was to consist of this kind of "wretched bondage" forever ("All this day"). When Brontë finished teaching the students that day, she experienced a reverie, with the "murmur" of her charges studying acting as a hypnotic chora. Gazing out the window, she hears an "uncertain sound of inexpressible sweetness." Watching a mist on the hills, Brontë hears a "liquid" sound that comes from the nearby church bells. Like a Proustian madeleine, the sound initiates a vision of "the mighty phantasm," causing Brontë to realize that "this had conjured from nothing,—from nothing to a system strange as some religious creeds" ("All this day"). Brontë reveals that when the afternoon turns to dusk, she actually sees her fictional characters in the flesh with her "bodily eyes" ("All this day").

Under the influence of her visions, Brontë speaks like an ineluctable force in a poem describing the process of writing about Angria: "Succeeding fast and faster still / Scenes that no words can give, / And gathering strength from every thrill / They stir, the[y] breathe, they live. / They live! They gather round in bands, / They speak, I hear the tone; / The earnest look, the beckoning hands, / And am I *now* alone?" (qtd. in Alexander, *The Early Writings* 141) Living a double life in which her imaginary characters live with more vitality than the real students and teachers she works with every day, Brontë is not *in* the moment when she is teaching at Roe Head.

She throws off enervation only when god enters her flesh and, godlike, her imagination is as "quick as thought." Feeling that she could write about the Angrian world "gloriously" if she could escape from classroom drudgery, Brontë asserts that the result would be "some narrative better at least than anything I ever produced before." But, of course, "just then a dolt came up with a lesson" ("All this day"). Brontë is unfailingly bitter about the price of teaching, commenting, "I thought I should have vomited" ("All this day").

Having examined excerpts from the juvenilia, I suggest that the trope of a female god in *Jane Eyre* and *Shirley* is not just an outlier but rather a continuation of Brontë's supple aesthetic. I focus the remainder of this chapter on *Shirley*, which features subliminal and explicit manifestations of mother-god-want, including 1) a masked or cross-dressed narrator and heroine; 2) trances or epiphanies initiated by a supernal moon; and 3) a revision of the Eve mythos that mirrors the radical voices of Southcott, Sharples, and Wright.

The most intense vision of a mother god in *Shirley* appears in the middle of the novel. It acts as an entr'acte amid severe conflicts between lower-class weavers and the nouveau riche manufacturers that transpired during the Luddite revolts near Haworth in the 1820s. The class combat is duplicated in the warfare between the "misogamist[s]" who view women as inferior and the "womenites" who see them as intelligent human beings who desire more than just to marry (*Shirley*, Penguin 176, 175). Shirley's trance occurs during the liminal time when Mother Nature is "at her evening prayers" after a long day in which the town's Anglicans celebrate their dominance in the community (314). Tired after the day's festivities, Shirley asks her friend Caroline to remain outside with her. She refuses to go into the chapel to hear the sermon given by Caroline's uncle, whose speech she knows will reiterate the communal norms of patriarchal Christian society. If this is a political book dealing alternately with the Condition of England and the Woman Question, I suggest that it politicizes the culture's metaphor for God, intimating that how a society constructs the divine will have implications for all sociocultural manifestations. Ruth Yeazell's argument that the social problem novel quickly changes to a love story when the narrative can no longer suture the intractable wounds inherent to a class society should be revised to acknowledge the ties between women and class unrest (Yeazell). Indeed, it is important to recognize that Shirley's vision is so incendiary that although it seems to burst out of nowhere like an opium dream, it is more revolutionary than the coming skirmish between the Luddites and the manufacturers. Thus, Brontë defuses the provocative implications of a divine female *with* the entrance of the radical Luddites and their opponents.

As laid out in chapter 1, many feminist utopians and millenarians referred to a female messiah and a mighty Eve who supported the establishment of a new political order (B. Taylor, *Eve* 161–63).[18] These radical revelations of a divine female commingled with progressive politics when, for example, the heretical notion of the female savior occurred among women in the egalitarian English Civil War sects (B. Taylor, "Woman-Power," 122)."[19] We know that the notion of a female messiah was revived at the end of the eighteenth century in response to the French Revolution, when the rhetorical apotheosis of a female savior and millenarian sects led by women went hand-in-hand with a relatively small but intense movement advocating women's rights and socialist agendas (B. Taylor, "Woman-Power" 122). Feminist utopian socialists such as Eliza Sharples, as we have seen, recuperated Eve as a powerful, semi-divine figure, as did the millenarian prophetess Southcott. Sharples applauded an Eve who gladly eats the fruit, declaring, "*well done woman! LIBERTY FOR EVER!* [new paragraph] If that was a fall, sirs, it was a glorious fall, and such a fall as is now wanted" ("Tenth Discourse" 132). Similarly, another radical writer known as "Syrtis" declared that if the Fall had been written by a woman, "we should have had a very different version of it" because it would have been written so that Eve's "great folly" would have been not the eating of the apple but sharing it with Adam (qtd. in B. Taylor, "Woman-Power" 143n73). Meanwhile, republican Frances Wright laments the fact that modern Eves have been warned by the Christian church against seeking the "fair fruit of knowledge," and she implores them to utilize God's "first best gift—your reason" (Wright, "Lecture I" 38, 76).

That Brontë might have had knowledge of these radicals is a possibility: in the early 1800s Southcott visited the West Riding near Haworth, and many weavers in that area became followers (Balleine 45; Harrison, *Second Coming* 222).[20] It would not be improbable that Brontë ran across this information during her research in preparation for writing the novel.[21] Her father had been the prelate at Dewsbury and knew many of the Luddites, and since Roe Head was located in the middle of the area that experienced the Luddite revolts, Brontë's teacher from Roe Head, Margaret Wooler, also might have told her of the struggles (Alexander, *Oxford Companion* 100, 465). Brontë might have learned about these earlier radicals from her friend Mary Taylor, whose family held radical republican views (Alexander, *Oxford Companion* 490). Since Patrick Brontë subscribed to *Fraser's Magazine* after 1830 and the children avidly read it, Brontë may have read an article in it attacking Owenite feminism titled "Woman and the Social System" (1840). But whether Brontë was aware of the millenarian and feminist efforts to recuperate Eve, her own evocation of a female deity uncannily mirrors the rhetoric of these grandmothers. The linking of heretical incarnations of a female deity with republican politics during the Luddite insurrections certainly goes a long way toward explaining what others find inexplicable in Brontë's Condition of England novel: that is, how does the titanic Eve figure in a tale ostensibly about the management of radical socialist politics?

In fact, cross-dressing in her gender designation, Shirley crosses class lines when she openly espouses her love for the bourgeois Louis Moore rather than the effete aristocrat Sir Philip Nunnely. The title and the placement of the chapter featuring Eve mirror the disruption of class lines. Set in the very center of *Shirley*, the vision of Mother Eve is masked by the physical bulk of the chapters surrounding the epiphany. The ironic chapter title reiterates the Invisible made visible: "Which the Genteel Reader is Recommended to Skip, Low Persons being Here Introduced" (*Shirley*, Penguin 314). This titular mot appears to advise the reader to pass over the chapter yet also entices with its seeming reference to "low" doings. Implying that the chapter will be about the working classes, in fact, it begins with a vision of a divine Mother Eve in rebellion against the Anglican sermon being preached in the nearby church. Thus the narrator associates Shirley with the rebellious Luddites who contend with a traditional class hierarchy.

A radical in a mask, Brontë's narrator ironically asks her audience not to read the subversive chapter on Eve, thus putting the reader in Eve's position, requiring that she/we desire the forbidden fruit of knowledge. When the reader accepts the challenge to partake, she obtains the knowledge that a female divinity acts upon and underlies the cosmos. Putting forward a "feminist challenge to patriarchally privileged hermeneutics" by making a mother god visible, Brontë's writing is simultaneously heretical and eminently practical (Jenkins, *Reclaiming Myths* 80). Indeed, as Kathryn Bond Stockton suggests, Brontë's tendency to take Romantic and Christian doctrines literally leads to surprisingly subversive revisions of the letter of the law (Stockton 116–17) Indeed, Brontë's hardheaded literalism and insistence on experiential connections to the deity cause her to imagine Nature as a real mother, for no father, even a God, could procreate without a woman (116–17). I would suggest that the subliminal anxiety is most intense at this point in the novel because of the interlineation of rebellious causes—political and religious, gendered and classed. In fact, the vision of Eve, which shatters the generic conventions of the novel, marches side-by-side with the convention-busting workers, creating an ecstatic feminist social(ist) rapture at the text's center.

Brontë's brilliant use of masking is intrinsic to her characterization of the heroine. Like Brontë, who was still going by the pseudonym Currer

Bell and the narrator of the novel *Shirley,* the eponymous heroine is a crossdresser. Although she regards the Luddite rebellion as a personal insult to her class standing, she recognizes that she is also a "rebel" (*Shirley* MS. BL [674/101]). The stubborn conservative Mr. Helstone playfully suggests that she may be a "'Jacobin'" and "'free-thinker'" (*Shirley,* Penguin 210). Shirley understands that her female body contradicts mainstream patriarchal religious and political codes, and her masculine pretensions amplify that disruption. An aristocratic, young, unmarried woman without parents or other close family to restrict her, she styles herself as "gentlemanlike," "Captain," "Esquire," and county leader (213, 217, 247, 273, 274, 326). Repeatedly referring to herself in the masculine third-person pronoun, Shirley knows that even her Christian name is the "same masculine family cognomen [her parents] would have bestowed on a boy" (211).

Jill Liddington convincingly suggests that Shirley may be based on Anne Lister, a young unmarried aristocrat who was the heir to Shibden Hall, which was just ten miles away from where the Brontës lived in Haworth. The lesbian Lister regularly wore mannish-looking clothing and referred to herself in masculine terms. Emily Brontë would almost certainly have known of Lister from her time as a teacher at Law Hill School in 1838 because Shibden Hall was not far from the school (see Liddington). Throughout *Shirley,* Brontë consistently and approvingly figures its heroine as being guided by "feeling," particularly about her culture's "misogam[y]" (*Shirley,* Penguin 176, 226, 313, 359, 374, 387). In many ways, then, Shirley and her vision of a female deity recuperate the radical feminists of the early nineteenth century, although Brontë adds an aristocratic cast to her "womanism."

A number of scenes in the novel feature the moon as harbinger of the visionary.[22] The narrative, for example, explains that before the age of eighteen, "our world is heroic; its inhabitants half-divine or semi-demon; its scenes are dream-scenes. . . . What a moon we gaze on before that time! How the trembling of our hearts at her aspect bears witness to its unutterable beauty! As to our sun, it is a burning heaven—the world of gods" (121). In another rendition of the moon's importance, while the eponymous protagonist is reading, a light suddenly streams in through the window and illuminates the pages she peruses. She looks up to see that the lunar body is the source of the light (373, 374). The moonlight causes her to go into a "trance," because the "'sweet regent,' new throned and glorious" is capable of making "earth an Eden, life a poem" (374). The narrator evokes a Romantic vision, asserting that the transcendent moon provides Shirley with "the pure gift of God" and "the free dower of Nature," which gives her "experience of a genii-life" (374). The reference to the "genii" is, of course, Brontë's own private reminder that she herself was the Chief Genii, Tallii, in the Angrian saga, who, like a God, could create and kill off fictional characters at will. Thus we might gather that Brontë's narrator links Shirley to the Romantic writer's divine powers and foreshadows her receptivity to visions that might make earth an Eden through the creation of new kinds of human relations and new ethical systems.

In another epiphany associated with the moon, the novel highlights mother-want and later links it to the protagonist's mother-god-want. Shirley's companion, Mrs. Pryor, is an unsociable character who conceives a warm interest in the orphaned Caroline. Late in the narrative, Mrs. Pryor nurses and saves Caroline from grave illness, thereby providing her with a kind of rebirth. She then dramatically reveals to Caroline that she is her long-lost mother. The narrator describes the moment before Mrs. Pryor makes this sublime revelation: "She threw back the curtain to admit the moonlight more freely" (409). Without knowledge of Brontë's repeated linking of the moon with a female divine in the juvenilia, the reader would not gather the implications of the imagery. The narrative further strengthens the association of the moon with mother-god-want because in the major vision of a mother god, Caroline's desire to know her real earthly mother merges with Shirley's description of Mother Eve.

As Shirley's vision of the goddess ends, the narrator states that the word "'mother'" "suggested to Caroline's imagination not the mighty and mystical parent of Shirley's visions, but a gentle human form—the form she ascribed to her own mother; unknown, unloved, but not unlonged-for" (316). If, as Jenkins suggests, "Caroline's mother is the physical, earthly counterpart to Shirley's maternal creation stories," Brontë creates a female god that is human, divine, and ultimately relational (Jenkins, *Reclaiming Myths* 87). After all, the narrator's point *is* that the titan Eve *created* all the gods and the human race, thus implicitly creating others with whom to associate intimately. Indeed, occurring when the township is celebrating its Christian heritage, the "Pagan" mythos Shirley professes explicates the class and gender warfare in which England is embroiled, melding the orphan Caroline's mother-want with Shirley's mother-god-want (*Shirley*, Penguin 315).

As Pamela Sue Anderson notes, in the patriarchal version of the Adam and Eve story, Adam, by virtue of his masculinity, has a different, more sacred relation with God, while Eve, as woman, is prohibited from the highest form of communion with deity (152). Brontë's novel defies this mythology. In rhetoric similar to that used by feminists like Sharples and Wright, Shirley explicitly reviles Milton's version of Eve, saying,

> I would beg to remind him [Milton] that the first men of the earth were Titans, and that Eve was their mother: from her sprang Saturn, Hyperion, Oceanus; she bore Prometheus. . . .
>
> I say, there were giants on the earth in those days; giants that strove to scale heaven. The first woman's breast that heaved with life on this world yielded the daring which could contend with Omnipotence. . . . The first woman was heaven-born: vast was the heart whence gushed the well-spring of the blood of nations; and grand the undegenerate head where rested the consort-crown of creation." (*Shirley,* Penguin 315)

Here Brontë retailors the Christian view of Eve, merging the Judeo-Christian and polytheistic traditions to show that Eve was the foremother to all things, including the gods. A "woman-Titan" and "mighty and mystical parent" who comes before what were thought of as the original gods of Western civilization, Brontë's Eve is a primeval force powerful enough to give birth to "all living."

According to the staid Caroline, Shirley's vision is "a hash of Scripture and mythology" (315). Imagining the primal scene of the cosmos as female generated, Shirley's "hash" limns the titan Eve as Mother Earth herself, much in the same way she is depicted in "The Violet." Exclaiming "I see her! and I will tell you what she is like," Shirley presents the pagan gods as more primal and powerful than the Christian divinity (314). Thormahlën points out that in Brontë's fiction the heroines often receive spiritual inspiration in Nature, but never inside a church (68). And, in fact, when timid Caroline suggests that they should go to the parish church, Shirley declares that they are already in a holy place: "I will stay out here with my mother Eve, in these days called Nature. I love her—undying, mighty being! . . . She is taking me to her bosom, and showing me her heart" (*Shirley,* Penguin 316). At the heart of the universe, there is no longer a possibility for words as Brontë's cross-dressing goddess and heroine magnify the mystic moment. For a brief time in the center of the novel, the mannish heroine undresses the masculine representation of God to find that the Holy of Holies is female, and the reader obtains the forbidden knowledge that male depictions of deity were just a garment after all.

A later iteration of this revolutionary vision occurs when Louis Moore, in another form of cross-dressing, recites from memory a devoir Shirley had written when he was her tutor. Titled "La Première Femme Savante?" the essay is based on the biblical passage that reads, "And it came to pass when men began to multiply on the face of the earth, and daughters were born unto them, that the sons of God saw the daughters of men that they were fair; and they took them wives of all which they chose" (Gen. vi.1–2). Mixing religious myth traditions, Brontë rewrites the fall by turning Eve into a more pagan "Eva," who, like the early nineteenth-century socialist feminists, makes no apology for seeking knowledge. Eva marries a son of God to whom she exclaims ecstatically, "Oh, take me! Oh, claim me! This is a god." "[C]hosen" by this Christ-like titan-man, she obtains the status of "'Seraph.'" A typical Brontëan liminal setting appears at the beginning of the essay: "before the Flood," Eva finds herself alone watching day turn into night. The rising of the moon signals the oncoming trance: "The Evening flushed full of hope: the Air panted; the Moon-rising before—ascended large" (*Shirley,* Penguin 457–59). As evening approaches, Eva thrills to the "boundlessly mighty" cosmos. In the same situation as Brontë had been at Roe Head, Eva desperately hopes that her life will not be "waste[d]." In response to her "agony," the cosmos rejoins,

> as if Silence spoke. There was no language, no word, only a tone.
> Again—a fine, full lofty tone, a deep, soft sound, like a storm whispering, made twilight undulate. (457–58)

Christ then speaks to her, but in thoroughly Romantic terms, with no hint of a curse upon Eva for eating of the tree of knowledge:

> Such was the bridal-hour of Genius and Humanity. Who shall rehearse the tale of their after-union? . . . Who shall tell how He, between whom and the Woman God put enmity, forged deadly plots to break the bond or defile its purity? Who shall record the long strife between Serpent and Seraph? . . . [page break] this faithful Seraph [Eve] fought for Humanity a good fight through time; and, when Time's course closed, and Death was encountered at the end, barring with fleshless arm the portals of Eternity, how Genius still held close his dying bride, sustained her through the agony of the passage, bore her triumphant into his own home—Heaven; restored her, redeemed, to Jehovah—her Maker; and at last, before Angel and Archangel, crowned her with the crown of Immortality. (459–60)

As representative of the capitalized "Humanity," Eva fills a liminal role as both divinity and mortal. She is married to "Genius," a Romantic term for God (and reminiscent of Brontë's childhood pseudonym, "Genii," thus suggesting that it may be her own artistic genius that saves her). Rather than being punished for seeking knowledge, Eva is a monumental heroine and protector of mortals. All but equal to the man-God Christ, she makes it possible for mortals to receive "the crown of Immortality," hence repeating Southcott's blasphemy that salvation could be made available only through Eve as initiator. In Brontë's version, Eva is "faithful," not fallen, and she fights "a good fight," braving Death to bring humankind through "the portals of Eternity."

The fair copy of these two scenes suggests their importance and Brontë's need to manifest and mask the female deity. The introduction to the Clarendon edition notes that there are more alterations to the fair copy of *Shirley* than there were to *Jane Eyre*, with volume three of the former including the most changes to the text. There are 271 changes in volume one, 458 in volume two, and 707 in volume three (*Shirley*, Clarendon xxvi). The Clarendon editors, Herbert Rosengarten and Margaret Smith, explain that the revisions increased in volumes two and three because they were written "during the 'dark and desolate' period of bereavement" after Emily and Anne died. Hence, Brontë's writing shows "greater uncertainty of composition and more laborious revision" (xxvi). The scene of the colossal woman Eve occurs at the beginning of the second volume, which features "fourteen actual excisions, varying from [page break] three lines to half a leaf, many extensively altered passages, and a number of phrases so heavily cancelled as to be almost indecipherable" (xxvi–xxvii). Rosengarten and Smith assert that most of these excisions have to do with Shirley's character and speeches, which, they argue, are based upon the recently deceased Emily. They write that the "painful, even raw, reality" of this tragic, enigmatic sister could not "easily be adapted into the fictional framework" (xxvii).

But it should be added that the heaviest changes occur in the scene depicting Shirley's vision in volume two and in Shirley's devoir describing "Eva" (xxvii). Thus one also must consider the matter of Shirley's vision and devoir in order to understand why they are so heavily amended. Having examined the fair copy at the British Library, I conclude that the changes are indicative of aesthetic and ideological concerns as much as of Brontë's supposed loss of creative control due to the deaths of her siblings. The large excisions from and careful small incisions into the pages having to do with the vision contrast sharply with the first volume of *Shirley*, which is seldom marred by such edits. The physical look of these pages is like a literal suturing, with paper seemingly glued over the cuts. I suggest that the incisions highlight the tensions and double-duty of the rhetoric. Indeed, the fair copy simultaneously exhibits the experience of the trance state while also illustrating Brontë's conscious aesthetic. That she so heavily edited the scenes describing a divine female, in contrast with the very slight editing elsewhere, indicates that she was very conscious of her choices, however painful they may have been.

John Bryant observes that revisions of manuscripts, whether by author or by publisher, indicate "hot spots of cultural contestation" (1044). To my mind the alterations to the chapter on Eve show that Brontë knew that the intense visionary nature of these scenes would be problematic to her readers, but, like Shirley, she cannot fully collude with patriarchal religion. Hence, replacing "My Eve" [strikethroughs in original] with the phrase "That Eve," she expands the concept of a female god from Shirley's (or the author's) own personal icon to that of a more universal entity (*Shirley* ms. BL Smith Bequest). Brontë also replaces the term "dream" with "trance" to describe Shirley's apparition, figuring it as resembling more a revelation than a hallucination (ibid.). At the end of the trance in the fair copy, Brontë squeezes in the sentence "She is very vague and visionary!" spoken by Caroline (ibid.). This editorial afterthought perhaps indicates Brontë's savvy understanding that the goddess could be boldly revealed to Shirley only if there were also a female character who undermined that vision. Caroline acts as that mask through this comment and when she immediately adds, "Come, Shirley, we ought to go into church" (*Shirley*, Penguin 316).

I argue, too, that the changes to the fair copy may indicate that originally Brontë described a more radical divinity. After "And that is not Milton's Eve, Shirley," as Rosengarten and Smith correctly point out, "the remainder—just over half—of f.157 is cut off" and the "word 'Juno' is visible above the cut" (*Shirley*, Clarendon 359n4). It appears, too, that possibly Brontë was trying to connect the word "milk[?]" to "the first woman's breast that heaved with life on this world" (*Shirley* ms. BL Smith Bequest). Did Brontë originally include a paragraph on an Eve merged with Juno? Was she going to include an image, similar to Barrett Browning's, of a gigantic female figure whose breasts the universe sucks for informing energy and life (*Aurora Leigh* 5:213–22)? A few lines later, the rest of f.159 is cut away, and the first 8 lines of f.160 are also excised (*Shirley*, Clarendon 360). More than any other section in the fair copy, Shirley's vision, then, is heavily redacted, with some sections completely excised and other phrases blackened out.

Why waste the ink to blacken out words when in other places Brontë merely lines through the matter she wishes to delete? Why spend laborious amounts of time cutting and pasting when she could have lined the offending paragraph out? Certainly the careful changes speak to the author's habit of neatness. But might Brontë have seen this passage as so central to her vision of the numinous while at the same time she knew it was so blasphemous about the Christian God that it required masking of the deep structure of divine feminine effulgence? When Caroline begs Shirley to return to the chapel, Shirley resists because the sermon would be "all sense for the Church, and all causticity for Schism," with schism carrying radical connotations about the heroine (*Shirley*, Penguin 314). Or perhaps the vision Brontë describes is just the dying ember of the prophetic apparition she originally conceived. In any case, critics have not considered in any depth why the normally precise writer makes a hodgepodge of this scene in the fair copy. To my mind, not to analyze the importance of the woman titan at the center of this text is to rend and score the very material garment with which the narrator-author addresses and redresses her.

Similarly, in volume three, chapter 26 ("Le Cheval"), which includes Shirley's devoir on Eva, the editing is heavier than that in the rest of the fair copy, with the exception of Shirley's vision of Eve. The beginning section of the devoir is neatly written and includes only minor changes. But on page 672/99 the top half of the page is cut away, and it is clear from marks around that excision that this deleted half-page included writing. More importantly, perhaps, the excised section comes immediately after the question, "Who shall, of these things, write the chronicle?" This question leaves the reader to wonder about the entity described in the answer. The passage after the half-page excision on page 672/99 reads: "'I never could correct that composition,' observed Shirley." The heroine adds, "'Your censor-pencil scored it with condemnatory lines whose signification I strove vainly to fathom.'"

Only the fair copy makes the irony of the editing choices apparent: Brontë censored her fictional heroine who complained that her male tutor censored her vision of a female quasi-deity. Thus, the question "Who shall, of these things, write the chronicle?" will never be answered. The material deleted will never be known. But given the surrounding text and its incisions, presumably "these things" refers to an even more expansive vision of Eva and Shirley's trance-like powers to reveal her. The visionary Brontë, I suggest, recognizes that this more visible depiction of deity as female was too revolutionary for her audience. If she had allowed "these things" to remain in the text, she risked being viewed as a ridiculous, even mad, woman preacher, creating her own religion, like the ostensibly loony Southcott.

On the following page (673/100) the editing is more substantive: two-thirds of the page is cut out, and the markings around the cut indicate that there is text missing. This excision comes after Moore explains that he was not censoring Shirley:

"I never said that the lines I drew were indications of faults at all. You would have it that such was the case, and I refrained from contradiction."

"What else did they denote?"

"No matter now."

And quite literally there is no matter now—the text following this statement is deleted. Just after the large section that has been excised, it reads: "'Mr. Moore,' cried Henry, ~~suddenly wrenching the discourse from its present bent.~~ 'Make Shirley repeat some of the pieces she used to say so well by heart'" (Smith Bequest BL 673/100). Henry's attempt to begin a new conversation hints that the deleted matter was unseemly and that Henry was trying to steer the conversation to a more conventional topic.

On the very next page (674/101), Shirley exclaims, "Certainly, I was a rebel!" which suggests that explicit descriptions of her rebellious views must have been what was cut out. Given that her mythic devoir regarding Eva initiates this scene, it is not unlikely that Shirley's "rebellion" has to do with belief in a female deity and that Brontë decided that such radical views needed to be masked. Given the similarities in subject matter and the fact that these are the most heavily redacted sections in the novel, I contend that the excisions in chapter 26 very likely have to do with Shirley's "Schism[atic]" visions of a female divine. My sense is also that Brontë's handwriting is different in these redacted scenes. As with the diary entries at Roe Head, in which Brontë describes her trance experiences, her handwriting loses its characteristic neatness. In the scenes describing Eve and Eva, the pressure on the page seems heavier, the letters darker and more intense, and the script larger and more passionate.

Brontë inserts another goddess story when Louis Moore soliloquizes about Shirley, whom he believes he is losing to Sir Philip Nunnely. He exclaims,

> I think of the fable of Semele reversed.
>
> It is not the daughter of Cadmus I see: nor do I realize her fatal longing to look on Jove in the majesty of his god-head. It is a priest of Juno that stands before me, watching late and lone at a shrine in an Argive temple. For years of solitary ministry, he has lived on dreams: there is divine madness upon him: he loves the idol he serves, and prays day and night that his frenzy may be fed, . . . She has heard; she will be propitious. . . . The doors of the temple are shut: the priest waits at the altar. (*Shirley*, Penguin 491)

Then, while the whole city sleeps, a bolt from heaven "wrapt in sudden light" crashes "Through the roof—through the rent, wide-yawning, vast, white-blazing blue of heaven above, pours a wonderous descent—dread as the down-rushing of stars." The light blinds the priest, and an "insufferable glory burning terribly between the pillars" destroys the temple of Juno (491).

The next morning all that is left is a "shivered" shrine. Only the statue of Saturnia is left untouched. At her feet lie the ashes of the priest who worshipped her (491–92). This last iteration of the goddess is an objective correlative for Louis's seemingly unrequited love for Shirley. But Brontë's use of this trope should be aligned with the whole of her oeuvre, from the juvenilia onward. Each rendition reverses, if you will, the myth tradition associating godhood with masculinity. Likewise, it seems important to Brontë to have the hero, on at least two occasions (here and when he recites Shirley's devoir on Eva), vocally reciting the goddess story, as though he is memorizing a new scripture. Whether she uses Moore as a mask for her own persona, as she was wont to do with male characters in the juvenilia, or whether she believes Shirley's theology would be rendered more valid in the readers' eyes because it is spoken by a man, Brontë subliminally uses the mask to validate the goddess story.

But can *Shirley*'s subliminal goddess story resolve the disjunctive narrative?[23] The story of the Yorkshire weaver's revolt against the manufacturers combined with a minute description of the literal death by boredom of the Victorian middle-class woman is not, according to many critics, of a piece. Philip Rogers rejects the notion that "Brontë's proto-feminism" equates with progressive politics, contending instead that *Shirley* represents Brontë's "antidemocratic" leanings (146). Albert D. Pionke argues that Brontë's novel uses Luddism as a palimpsest through which to comment on the 1848 Chartist threats to the status quo (Pionke 82; see also Zlotnick 284). I suggest, however, that the Eve at the novel's center acts as the mediating device ensuring that the two stories—the Condition of England and the Woman Question—intersect. This mediation illustrates that the scenes in the women's private sphere are inseparable from the social struggles of which the domestic sphere was a central component. Thus, despite Brontë's "Wellington panegyrics" and seeming contempt for radical unrest, one should be alert to *Shirley*'s similarities with the rhetoric of millenarians and feminist socialists (Rogers 144).

Mirroring the arc of these radical groups, *Shirley*'s rebellions against patriarchy and the Industrial Revolution reach an ecstatic crisis only to end with the subordination of women in marriage and lower-class submission to the owners, a plot that undermines the insurgencies of the novel and ostensibly heals the communal rupture they have caused. Yet the association of heretical incarnations of Eve with radical politics acts as a subliminal counterbalance to the novel's ostensibly reactionary proclivities, especially when we realize that Brontë's revisions to the sections that describe Eve are considerable in an otherwise clean fair copy. Furthermore, as Tim Dolan points out, "in *Shirley* the sexual-provincial counter-discourse endeavours to re-define the territories of Victorian fiction and challenge the voices of territorial sovereignty over them" so that even though Luddite revolt seems to vanish, "nonetheless the novel's passionate allegiance to its own—to the north and to the woman novelist—never abates" (201, 212). Dolin's insights remind us just how much there is that *is* rebellious in *Shirley* and how much Brontë was risking as a woman writer from Northern England when she placed it before the public.

In fact, although Brontë's solution to class warfare is underwritten by Victorian horror of mob violence as well as Shirley's tendentiousness, Brontë structures the chapter describing the titanic Eve so that it concludes with a conversation about gender and class between Shirley and the lower-class William Farren and Joe Scott. Shirley's engagements with Eve must not, then, be separated out from the Luddite rebellion. Indeed, when Shirley, like Moses, comes down to earth after having seen divinity, the chapter insists on examining Shirley's interactions with the lower classes to see whether there is any hope for a level playing field between men and women, the lower and middle classes. This section reads as though Brontë wanted to see if the feminist deity Shirley has evoked can make any difference in the material reality of "low persons introduced" of the chapter's title. It is a move reminiscent of feminist republican Sharples, who requires Christianity to make a real difference. The structure of this chapter suggests that if a feminist religion is needed to forestall class warfare, the negotiations for peace must occur in a practical dialogue between diverse entities.

Joe Scott works as Moore's trusted manufacturing hand and is one of the chief "misogamists" in the novel. William Farren, Moore's former employee, had been out of work for three months and his family on the brink of starvation when Moore finds him a job as gardener, after which he is able to raise the family's standard of living. Thus Shirley speaks with a member of the lower class who is loyal to his betters (Scott) and one (Farren) who was on the verge of becoming a "'rebel—a radical—an insurrectionist'" (*Shirley,* Penguin 319). Just after her trance, Shirley meets William coming out of the church, and he complains that the preacher talks "to poor folk fair as if they thought they were beneath them" (318). Shirley agrees with his estimation but insists that William has his own class pride. Nonetheless, she asks him about lower-class suffering and sympathizes when he asserts that "'starving folk [page break] cannot be satisfied or settled'" and thus "'The country's not in a safe condition'" (319–20). She asks him what more she can do to help, and William avers that she has done everything she can by giving her money to the poor.

In fact, he notes earlier that it was when she came to give him money that he thought of becoming an "insurrectionist" because "'I thought it shameful that, willing and able as I was to work, I suld be i' such a condition that a young cratur . . . suld think it needful to come and offer me her bit o' brass'" (319). William's lower-class "misogamy" and Shirley's and Brontë's inability to fully engage with the need for class equality weigh down the conversation. However, given Brontë's Tory tendencies and the usual move by the middle-class Victorian writer to quash eruptions of lower-class desire, I argue that this conversation indicates the author's recognition that such interclass, intergender dialogues must occur in order for the culture to solve working-class distress *and* woman's need for purposeful work. The earlier vision of Eve impels the tentative solution: the classes and genders must be psychically, spiritually, emotionally, and politically willing to see each other in their material reality.

At this point, Joe Scott appears and Shirley asks about his political leanings, remarking that she did not know whether he was Tory or Whig (321). Joe asserts that the Tories "'carries on the war and ruins trade'" and that "'I'm of that which is most favourable to peace, and, by consequence, to the mercantile interests of this here land'" (321). Shirley responds boldly, "'So am I, Joe.'" Joe does not label himself a Whig, and neither does Shirley identify herself as a Tory. Rather, Brontë seeks a way to find common ground between them by eliding labels that divide the classes. But here again, Joe's sexism gets in the way of converse, and Shirley responds with frustration, saying, "'do you seriously think all the wisdom in the world is lodged in male skulls?'" Scott's reaction returns the reader to the beginning of the chapter and its focus on Eve. "'Let the woman learn in silence, with all subjection,'" he proclaims, and "'suffer not a woman to teach, nor to usurp authority over the man; . . . For Adam was first formed, then Eve'" (321–22). Seeking communion, Caroline asks whether he believes in "'the right of private judgment,'" which Joe enthusiastically affirms. Caroline responds that women have the right to such "private judgment," but he disagrees, asserting that they should "'take their husbands' opinion, both in politics and religion'" (323).

Exasperated, the far-from-feminist Caroline sets forth a revolutionary credo, as another rebellion occurs in the novel. Indeed, if the long-suffering

Caroline can find feminist common cause with the fiery Shirley, there may be hope for a dialogical engagement with the bull-headed misogamist Joe. Speaking as though she herself is filled with the rapture with which Shirley began the chapter, Caroline invites Scott to abandon Pauline views of women: "'he wrote that chapter for a particular congregation of Christians, under peculiar circumstances,'" she declares, and "'besides, I dare say, if I could read the original Greek, I should find that many of the words have been wrongly translated, perhaps misapprehended altogether.'" Then Caroline's oracular speech is filled with *jouissance* as she articulates the rebel's (and utopian feminist and millenarian) translation of Paul. "'It would be possible,'" she avows, to make the passage say, "'Let the woman speak out whenever she sees fit to make an objection;'—'it is permitted to a woman to teach and to exercise authority as much as may be. Man, meantime, cannot do better than hold his peace'" (323). In this moment, the usually conventional Caroline makes a "contrary turn" in her own gendered behavior (323).

When Joe scoffs at her, Caroline fumes that he is "'a thoroughly dogmatical person.'" Shirley mediates the angry exchange, noting, "'Joe is well enough in his own house,'" for there is not a "'better nor a kinder husband in Briarfield. He does not dogmatize to his wife'" (323). Calibrating Joe's politics, Shirley recognizes that the personal is political and that Joe's actions toward his wife in the domestic sphere compensate greatly for his rant about women in the public sphere. But, brutally realistic, Brontë does not leave it there. In his rejoinder to Shirley's gracious words, Joe complains that women like Caroline and Shirley are full of "'superficial sort o' vanities'" and cannot be counted upon to understand the world as men do (324). Shirley, though, has the last word of the chapter, brusquely telling Joe that he is a "'real slanderer.'" "'I would give you your answer,'" she says, "'only the people are coming out of church.'" And one must wonder what those words would have been if Brontë had decided to write them in a novel that already had so many politically motivated deletions. But Shirley's last words to him are telling enough: "'Man of prejudice, good-bye'" (324).

Having carried on an intelligent exchange, on their side, with Joe about gender and class politics, Shirley and Caroline cannot pursue a monological and therefore futile conversation. Yet the protagonist does not give up her efforts to achieve what Brontë would have seen as a mediating conclusion to their discussion about class, even though Joe undermines the mutual understanding established between the genders. Symbolically and literally leaving the door open for further exchange, she turns to William's children and utters the last words of the chapter: "'come up to Fieldhead to-morrow, and you shall choose what you like best out of Mrs. Gill's store-room'" (324).

Although patronizing, this response implies that it is for less-oppressed and less-prejudiced future generations to pick up the short-circuited conversation between the classes and genders, a future Brontë seems to have hoped that her own novel might help make possible. What she did make possible was the deconstruction of gendered notions about who may be a writer and who might be God. Further, *Shirley* puts the reader into the habit (dress) of thinking fluidly and nonconventionally, of imagining and knowing the world through a trope for god that is, at least in part, symbolically feminine, and that was available in the voices of her sister millenarians and republican feminists.

3

Feminist Reincarnations of the Madonna

ANNA JAMESON AND ECCLESIASTICAL DEBATES ON THE IMMACULATE CONCEPTION

APART from the horrors and calamities of war, unquestionably the leading topic of the day is the new Romish dogma—the Immaculate Conception of the Blessed Virgin Mary: "the event of the nineteenth century," as the Dublin *Telegraph* most correctly calls it.

—Edward Maguire, *The New Romish Dogma of the Immaculate Conception* v

All by Mary: nothing except by Mary.

—Qtd. in *"Histoire de l'Eglise de France"* 428 ("Observateur Catholique")

[T]here she stands—the transfigured woman, at once completely human and completely divine, an abstraction of power, purity, and love, poised on the empurpled air, and requiring no other support.

—Anna Jameson, *Legends of the Madonna* xliv

CHARLOTTE BRONTË'S *Villette* is one of the major fictional venues depicting Victorian Protestant fascination with and repulsion for the Catholic Church. In the fair copy of *Shirley* Brontë deletes the words "by the hallowed Virgin Mary" in the vision of the titanic Eve (ms. BL Smith Bequest). In the arguments between Protestants and Catholics in Victorian Britain, one figure stands out as causing the most disagreement—the Virgin Mary. On 8 December 1854, Pope Pius IX formally gave his blessing to the unofficial dogma that not only was the Madonna a virgin at Christ's conception but she was also born without sin.[1] Referred to by Catholics as the "Marian age," the period between 1850 and 1950 saw the official establishment of the Immaculate Conception, the rise in devotion to the Madonna, and an increase in accounts of the Virgin's appearance to lay adherents. The period closed in 1950 when the doctrine of the Assumption was proclaimed (Herringer 11). In Victorian Britain, arguments about the Virgin—a sacred version of the Angel in the House—always filtered ideological concerns about gender. Thus it is no surprise that after centuries of relative calm, such debates reached a zenith during the nineteenth century, although conflicts between Protestants and Catholics in England were ever-present from the sixteenth century onward (Herringer 4, 20, 2, 19; see also O'Malley 7). Men were the main participants in the public brouhaha between Protestants and Catholics that centered on the Immaculate Conception, and their disputes more often than not ended up reiterating the proper behaviors expected of women. Indeed, as Carol Herringer points out, the virulent colloquy about the Madonna's identity duplicated questions about women's morality, maternity, and virginity (26).

In this chapter, I will examine these debates vis-à-vis Anna Jameson's *Legends of the Madonna* and suggest that given the vehement male responses to the Immaculate Conception, Jameson's participation in the discussion is astonishing, masked though it is behind analyses of artworks depicting the Virgin. I assert that the gender ideology ensconced in *Legends* and other writings by Jameson contains traces of the audacious mythoi articulated by female millenarians and socialist feminists from earlier in the century. If it can be argued that Mary put Christian concepts about gender and godhood under interrogation, I shall analyze how the dogma of the Immaculate Conception aggravated anxieties about the sexuality (read: sexual fallenness) of mothers; panic about women's attainment of power over men, concomitant with concerns that divine justice should include no exceptions, especially for women; worries that strict boundaries were not intrinsic to the ontology separating God and human beings; and fears that God's masculine ontology might not universally encompass all of creation, particularly the female.

In the Victorian period, Catholic and Protestant interpretations of the Madonna differed starkly. On the one hand, Catholic construal of Mary undermined parts of the dominant Victorian gender ideology in that Catholics saw her as morally superior *and* powerful in both the private and public spheres. That superiority was founded on the idea that a woman's chastity held the highest moral premium, a principle that was, as Marina Warner notes, the most significant and unique concept that early Christianity appended to older myth systems (48). Warner adds that the Madonna's "miraculous virginity" was the most palpable topic in writings by the Church Fathers and heavily influenced ideas about mortal women (67). Indeed, the image of Mary always implicitly disciplines mortal women for being anything but celibate, and although mystified as few other women have been, the Virgin occupies a category of the ideal that no woman can achieve (Kristeva, "Stabat Mater" 327; Warner xxi, xxv, 104, 153, 159).

Many Protestants believed that any devotion to the Virgin was a step toward paganism, for the worship of Mary seemed analogous to the worship of the goddesses Isis, Juno, and Astarte (Herringer 97). As the *Pall Mall Gazette* noted, "The belief that there is to be a Goddess as well as a God for Christians" should be met with "contemptuous silence" (10). Unlike Catholics, Protestants in general believed that Mary was a mortal woman who was good but not necessarily morally superior. This led to the idea that the Virgin and women in general had no moral superiority (or power) over men, thus creating inconsistency in the ideal of the Angel in the House (64, 78). Protestants were also anxious about the Catholic belief in Mary's eternal virginity and were concerned that women who remained celibate achieved a form of independence that upset the categories of gender (88). For example, Charles Kingsley represented the fear that sexual abstinence virtually "'unsexed'" men and women by feminizing both sexes. As such, the dogma of celibacy denied the sexes the erotic desires that Kingsley saw as inherent to Christian devotion (qtd. in Griffin 123). Clearly, the Virgin was a controversial figure from almost any viewpoint. Thus she acted as a touchstone for anxieties about gender and power.[2]

Henry Hart Milman's *History of Christianity* (1840) illustrates the subversive nature of the Virgin in Church history. Deriding the early Church's inclusion of paganism, Milman remarked that the Church Fathers' fierce battles over the nature of the Trinity and of Christ's essence refocused devotional attention onto the gentler images of the Virgin (3:424).[3] He also argued that Mary's maternity and chastity were appealing because men had the highest regard for these qualities in women. Making a case for man's inborn chivalry toward the opposite sex, Milman contended that women "deified" Mary as the ideal example of womanhood, thus ensuring that women's status would increase (430). At the end of his three-volume tome, Milman wrote that worship of Mary offers "humane feeling" to the Christian religion, allowing it to increase its membership rather than having it dwindle away (436). But to end a text on the history of the *Christ*ian Church and its all-male Trinity by invoking the Virgin as the most powerful entity in that religion hardly met the aims of Milman's digest. After all, he averred in his preface that his goal was to defend Christ's divinity against Renan and

Strauss (1:vi). Here, as elsewhere, the concept of the Madonna outmaneuvered gestures toward its subordination.

Milman's commentary is predictive of gender concerns that underlay debates about the Immaculate Conception. In such debates in print media during the 1850s and '60s, Tory, Whig, and radical media reviled the *Bull Ineffabilis* for its "heretical harlequenadings" ("Mary—, the Rise, Progress, and Development of a Theological Illusion" 26). Even before the pronouncement, the *Rambler* complained that worship of Mary was one of the many "impieties" of the Italian Church ("The Doctrine of the Immaculate Conception" 547). After the official Bull was proclaimed, the *London Review* grumbled that it undid everything ever prophesied about the immutable kingdom of God ("The 'London Review' Irish Church Commission" 616–19). Meanwhile, the Tractarian *Christian Remembrancer* panned Alphonsus de Ligouri's "The Glories of Mary," deeming the Bible and early Church Fathers as spurious sources for the doctrine ("The Glories of Mary" 417–67). The Tory *Quarterly Review* decried the new doctrine for being an insulting addendum to the "heterogeneous mass of fiction" the Catholic Church had already perpetrated on its followers ("La Croyance à l'immaculée Conception" 148). Elsewhere, Richard Carlile, editor of the radical *Republican* and paramour of Eliza Sharples, lamented the dogma as a "stultifying" doctrine turning men from reason toward superstition (495).

When the *Wesleyan-Methodist Magazine* queried, "How came Divine honours to be rendered to the mother of our Lord?" a number of responses were given ("'Immaculate Conception' of the Virgin Mary" 13 [July 1867]: 597). Fears that papal aggression would overturn national sovereignty appeared in coverage of the decree. French Gallicans (nationalists) and Ultramontists (who believed that Church sovereignty was superior to State sovereignty) clashed over the doctrine, as though Mary were a site of a new French Revolution. Reviewing L'Abbé Guettée's *"Histoire de l'Eglise de France,"* the *Christian Remembrancer* worried that Ultramontist beliefs held "sway" in France and that the contention between Ultramontists and Gallicans threatened the fall of the Gallican Church (423). The *Quarterly Review* warned that the schism within the Church over the new doctrine was a palimpsest for French revolutionary inclinations. The writer fretted that the "violent" Ultramontists paid homage to the doctrine not out of love for the Virgin. Rather, the conservative *Quarterly* was horrified that the new dogma might represent victory of "controversialist" over temperate Gallicans (172).

Apprehension that the Bull afforded the Virgin a higher status than God also reverberated in the public discussion. The *Wesleyan-Methodist* sneered,

"Every knee bows to Mary" while the Savior became "less loved" ("'Immaculate Conception' of the Virgin Mary" 600). Likewise, the *London Review* bristled at the Virgin becoming the omnipotent mediator, which, according to the Protestant Church, was the right of the Savior only ("The 'London Review' Irish Church" 616). Censuring the propaganda supporting the *Bull Ineffabilis* another journalist reviled the sacrilegious ideas that God the Father obeyed the all-powerful Mary; and that it was by "'Mary that the virtue of grace, and the ineffable blessings of the Most High descend.'" The writer fumed that the new dogma instituted Mary as a higher being than God because she exhibited "infinite goodness," which could reside in only one deity. Thus, if Mary was infinitely good, God must then have been stripped of His "essential attribute" when Mary replaced Jesus as the sacred go-between (qtd. in *"Histoire de l'Eglise"* 428). The binary logic mimicked the antisuffrage rationale that if women received the vote, men would be divested of a power essentially their own, and it also assumed that power is indivisible and therefore must always and only reside in the male, whether mortal or divine.

Concerns about God's omnipotence also registered anxiety that He might not encompass the identity of female creation. Put simply, if the male Christian God could not fathom half of human creation, His power and omniscience were lacking. For example, the review of "The Glories of Mary" quotes William Gladstone, who worries that allowing Mary to be the intermediary with the Son because of her "tenderness and intensity of feminine sympathies" only "disguises a reality of infinite danger" (466). The review ends with a curious musing: "'As if the Maker of woman did not possess in inexhaustible abundance those treasures of tenderness from and out of whose overflow it is that He has adorned the loveliest of His works'" (467). This caveat suggests the concern that perhaps a male God might not be capable of imagining and embodying female qualities without encompassing those very qualities, thus undermining the supposed essence of Christian godhood as an all-encompassing and omnipotent masculinity. Gender slippage is imminent and Immanent in this subliminal alarm. Likewise, the Immaculate Conception creates slippage between what is considered human and divine. If a woman could attain Godhood in her mortal state, what was to stop Christian principles from being overthrown wholesale? And what might that mean for earthly constructions of political and spiritual power that reproduce Christian patriarchy?

The notion that Mary obtained her heavenly station through feminine wiles underwrites another Protestant response to the Bull. Signaling distaste for the Virgin, the *London Review* argues that she availed herself to the utmost of a source of attraction which has been in all ages most powerful with the heart of man. In woman he beholds the most beautiful object in creation, one whose form excites his admiration, whose trusting tenderness and devoted attachment inspire him with love, whose virgin purity he holds to be sacred, whose affection as a wife and a mother fills his heart with the ... most grateful esteem. The Mother of Jesus appears in the Church of Rome invested with all those sweet, endearing attributes exhalted, intensified, etherealized in the highest possible degree. ("The 'London Review' Irish Church Commission" 617)

This writer imagines a Mary who engineers ("availed herself") her dominance over the Catholic laity and clergy through her devious sexual and maternal attraction, which she cleverly "intensifie[s]" and "etherealize[s]." As the "object" of man's worship, in part because of her sexual attraction, she makes men slavering devotees. What attractions the Virgin might have for the female believer are of no concern to the writer. But there is another tension implied: that God did not create humanity. Instead, male yearning for the erotic and maternal created the Madonna. Furthermore, even the all-powerful male God is inept at creating such intense worship in the hearts of His believers; without any effort whatsoever, the glamorous Mary aggregates adoration to herself and away from the Father, who continually grouses that his devotees do not adore Him enough. Thus the only spiritual relationship described takes place between passive men and a deified woman who need not seek omnipotence because men naturally cede it to her.

Remarks from the pulpit fueled antagonisms toward the Virgin. William Bernard Ullathorne, Catholic Bishop of Birmingham (and an acquaintance of George Eliot), metaphorically viewed Mary as the sacred earth (temple) from which Christ was made: in the same way the "Divine Artist" had made man's body from Mother Earth, God had created Mary in "body as from earth and in soul as from Heaven to be a Mother for His Son" (34). Hence, Ullathorne made reproduction woman's spiritual essence and in doing so admitted that the male Trinity lacked the power to engender. In his view, women need a model of perfection that mothers biologically and spiritually, which is impossible for men to achieve. The Bishop concluded that the "supreme excellence of woman as the type and head of womanhood" is to be found only in the Madonna. In answer to the question "what place is she assigned in the grand scale of the creation?" Ullathorne answers that Mary receives the "ministry" of the "divine maternity" (51, 52). He also gives highest place to Mary as a "spiritual paradise" of the second Adam, Jesus: that is, after the Fall, God created a new heaven and earth within which the second

Adam, Christ, was created, and Mary was that new paradise (18, 25).[4] Here again, the ever-scheming Mary accumulates cosmic universality; she is everything and everything is she, and she automatically deprives the supposedly masterful male God of her own vast energy and self-containment.

Protestants also worried that God's justice could not be fulfilled if one mortal became the exception to the rule that all humanity was born in sin. In a sermon titled "The Recent Decree on the Immaculate Conception of the Blessed Virgin Mary" preached on Christmas Day 1854, a cleric (name unknown) explained that by establishing the doctrine of the Immaculate Conception, Catholicism had undone the foundational concept of the Incarnation. In other words, if one mortal woman could be exempted from Christ's salvific act, then the supposedly unchanging Christian God was inconsistent. Likewise, the Bull negated the concept that since all mortals, including Mary, were born in sin, all had to be redeemed by the Savior. Further, the sermon expounded, the Immaculate Conception obviated the doctrine that Jesus became mortal so that humans could see his graphic suffering and thus feel more unified with Him and more capable of believing in the possibility of their own redemption.

Predictably, in "The Recent Decree" the "man" in "humanity" has rhetorical currency: "God's purpose lies in man, . . . and He will not fulfil it otherwise than by man. He will not put in subjection unto the angels the world that is yet to come—He will subject it to man" and "man shall reign over it" (2). The cleric was almost sniveling about the insult to masculinity: If the "blessed Virgin Mary . . . attained to perfect and unspotted holiness in the flesh previous to the Incarnation, then, proof . . . has been afforded that the act of Incarnation, and the work of redemption consequent thereupon, were not necessary or indispensable in order to attain that end" ("The Recent Decree" 6). Thus the writer views Mary's Immaculate Conception not as the sublime exception that proves the rule but rather as the one exemption illustrating the male Trinity's lack of absolute power over human salvation.

Ten years later in his *Eirenicon*,[5] the High Church cleric E. B. Pusey sought a merger of the Anglican and Catholic churches. But strangely undermining his own line of reasoning, he laid out the issues that interfered with his proposal, the Roman Catholic worship of the Virgin chief among them. English Protestants, he asserted, would never reconcile with Catholicism because it gave Mary precedence over Christ and God the Father. This argument created another theological dustup. Asserting that he looked forward to the "intercommunion" between Catholic and Protestant churches, Pusey offered a solution for the schism. That is why it was so bizarre when he laid out the reasons why such a hoped-for event could not occur, and his *Eireni-*

con essentially remains trapped in that aporia. In speech worthy of a modern political campaign, Pusey averred that the two sects were separated by a "vast practical system" that supported doctrines with only "quasi-authority" (43). The most important dogma blocking union was the "special 'crux' of the Roman system," or the "vast system as to the Blessed Virgin" (44). Pusey was most troubled by the fact that Mary was now seen as the "'Co-Redemptress'" between the Church and Jesus (67). Not only did Mary's "vastness" trouble Pusey; her cosmic universality and demand for the full attention of her worshippers stymied the reunion of the homosocial, male-dominated Christian religion.

Pusey's litany of the accretions to the Catholic Church under the false doctrine of Mariolotry is comprehensive:

> '[I]t is morally impossible for those to be saved who neglect the devotion to the Blessed Virgin;' that 'it is the will of God that all graces should pass through her hands;' . . . that Jesus has, in fact, said, 'no one shall be partaker of My Blood, unless through the intercession of My mother;' . . . that 'God granted all the pardons in the Old Testament absolutely for the reverence and love of this Blessed Virgin;' . . . that God is 'subject to the command of Mary;' that 'God has resigned into her hands . . . His omnipotence in the sphere of grace;' 'that it is safer to seek salvation through her than directly from Jesus. (45)

Thus, with the advent of the Immaculate Conception, Mary's power was consolidated because the "Cultus" of the Virgin was authorized through official imprimatur. Pusey also worried that the doctrine would allow this "Cultus" to grow ineluctably (50). So, for example, the former Tractarian abhorred the practice of naming churches after Mary and scorned the gigantic statues of the Virgin placed near the altars of the Roman Church (47). Most galling was Mary's accession to divinity on a par with and even above God. Pusey loathed the Catholic endorsement of the idea that *Mary* so "'loved the world, that she gave her only begotten Son,'" culminating in the concept that only Mary could provide salvation to all mankind (69, 70). Pusey specified his fears clearly: Christ's relationship to Mary as a "naturally inferior" son guarantees that, as a mother, the Virgin is therefore "superior to God," with God Himself being "her subject" (71). Here again, Mary causes rupture in Christianity. She makes unity impossible between the Catholic, Protestant, and Greek Orthodox churches. She also creates a gap that cannot be explained: in other words, how was it that a mortal female could attain the mode of godhood when Christianity was rooted in the patriarchal concept of God's Fatherhood and Sonship? Mary, it appeared, irrationally imposes the notion of divine motherhood upon that holy, impregnable male twosome.

Following Pusey's public display of disaffection from the Virgin, Cardinal John Henry Newman entered the fray. In his public response to his old friend, Newman acknowledged his lack of enthusiasm for Mariolatry. Explaining that he had always wondered why the fallen Eve was called the "Mother of all living," Newman asserted that it was from Mary that "Life itself was born in the world" and that where Eve brought about the death of mankind, Mary had brought about its salvation (43). Pointing out the "national good sense" of the English, Newman rejected Pusey's claim that Mary had become the centerpiece of the Catholic Church. English Catholicism, he avowed, is not subject to the "extravagances" found in other countries because the English disdained "curiosities of thought" that appealed to the "undisciplined imaginations" and "grovelling hearts" of non-English nations. Thus the English would avoid the histrionics that less-educated countries might exhibit (105). Distinguishing between "healthy" and "artificial" worship, Newman asserted that it is possible to revere Mary as mother and virgin without undermining the Trinity. This pragmatic type of devotion, he proudly proclaimed, is "the English style" in its "Christian good sense" (105).

Newman responded in kind to Pusey's litany, asserting that he and other English Catholics never practiced the scurrilous Mariolatry that Protestants loved to claim the Roman Church indulged in:

> God has resigned into her hands His omnipotence; that . . . it is safer to seek her than her Son; that the Blessed Virgin is superior to God; that He is (simply) subject to her command; that . . . Mary takes His place as an Advocate with Father and Son; [page break] . . . that, as the Incarnate God bore the image of His Father, so He bore the image of His Mother; . . . that His Body and Blood in the Eucharist are truly hers and appertain to her; . . . that the Holy Ghost brings into fruitfulness his action by her, . . . that the kingdom of God in our souls, as our Lord speaks, is really the kingdom of Mary in the soul." (118–19)

The Cardinal bitingly concluded, "Sentiments such as these I never knew of till I read your [Pusey's] book, nor, as I think, do the vast majority of English Catholics know them" (119).

If Newman was rich in rhetorical flourish and righteous anger, he was poor in substance, for he had nothing to fill the lack produced by Mary's ostensible coup. Strangely, in seeking to show that Mary was not invincible, the English Cardinal concluded his rejoinder to Pusey by discussing the imminent approach of the Feast of the Immaculate Conception, followed by Christmas. Noting that Christmas focuses on Christ's birth, Newman accepted that the Nativity cannot help pointing the worshipper's attention to the "peculiar prominence" of the Virgin. Unlike the Easter season, when Mary remains safely behind the scenes, at Christmas she is the intermediary who "brings Him to us in her arms." Thus, Mary is inexorably imprinted on one of the holiest Catholic holidays (123).

Having previously derided notions of Mary's preeminence over Christ, Newman began and ended his depiction of the Christmas season with Mary, noting that her ineluctable "image is upon it." Despite the astonishing disjunction, he called for unity, saying, "May the sacred influences of this time bring us all together in unity! May it destroy all bitterness on your side and ours! . . . May that bright and gentle Lady, the Blessed Virgin Mary, [page break] overcome you with her sweetness, and revenge herself on her foes by interceding effectually for their conversion!" (123–24)[6] Unable to elide the rhetoric about Mary that he abjured, Newman must link her to any negotiation of Christian unity between Protestant and Catholic. Registering her virtual omnipotence, Newman pictured the Virgin as the only God able to "overcome" the very schism she seems to have created. Like the confounding God of the Old Testament, she creates the very conundrums she is meant to resolve.

Tropes about the "Immaculate" nature of the Madonna's sexuality were, one might say, bloodcurdling. If Cardinal Newman could not erase Mary's pesky influence, Bishop Ullathorne was awkwardly enmeshed in her ambiguous sexuality. Quoting St. Proclus's view of Mary, spoken in 429 A.D., Ullathorne reminded his audience that "'we celebrate her, who is the argument for chastity and the glory of her sex; her [page break] who is Mother at once and Virgin. Lovely and wonderful is this union'" (14–15). Fears of the sexualized woman/mother were gratified and appeased in Mary's erotic ambiguity, with which the good Bishop was infatuated: "She is a mother without man's concurrence. She is mother of God and man at once. She is a mother whilst she remains a virgin. She is exempted from the curse of Eve, that fruit of [page break] original sin, and brings forth her Son without pain or sorrow. Her child is born, whilst her virginal integrity is preserved. She nourishes God at her breast. She commands Him by her words, and He is subject to her" (40–41). The conspicuous lack of discussion about the Father's and Son's sexual purity, coupled with Ullathorne's need to "preserv[e]" Mary's "virginal integrity" (to keep her intact), virtually acts as the sole basis for her accession to a divine state.

The centuries-long attempts by Church Fathers to preserve Mary's virginal integrity led to tortuous deliberations like Ullathorne's. Each theologian who entered the debate was tasked with pinpointing the exact moment that Mary became immaculate. As Nancy Mayberry points out, "The confusion was the result of the belief that sin was passed on to each generation through the act of concupiscence," and thus the question was, did she become immaculate "at her conception, in the womb, at birth, at the Annunciation, or in the mind of God before her conception" (211).[7] With this confusion, even a convert to Catholicism and devotee of the Virgin would become distressed by her female stain on Christ's purity. Obsessed with the sex act and procreation, Frederick William Faber worried about the sharing of blood when Christ was in Mary's womb. He remarked that it was impossible to believe that "the matter of the Precious Blood had ever been itself corrupted with the taint of sin" but fretted that "what was to supply the free price of our redemption was once enslaved to God's darkest, foulest enemy" (Faber 29; qtd. in Herringer 124). Satan, of course, is that "enemy," but the implication is that the mortal Virgin's tainted blood might have corrupted the Savior's blood during pregnancy, when all his physical functions transpired through intermixture with Mary's bodily functions.

Similarly, Protestant Edward Maguire focused on Mary's postpartum cleanliness. Asking whether Mary "observed the law of *Purification*" after Christ's birth, Maguire asserted that all "uncleanness, ceremonial or moral, is connected with *sin*" (21). One gathers that he assumed the biblical horror of female blood, that is, that the shedding of blood after the birth process was unclean and sinful and thus a mode of being that could not be associated with the Mother of God. This might explain the *Eclectic Review*'s dismay about the new dogma: one of the "More monstrous" implications is that "we have not only the transubstantiation of the body and blood of Christ in the Eucharist. We have Mary's too" ("Doctor Pusey's Eirenicon" 83). One cannot help wondering whether this writer is alluding to the different forms of blood that Jesus and Mary shed—the Virgin's post-puerperal, supposedly "unclean," matter that always reiterates the menses and women's fertility. The *Eclectic Review* seemed to ask how males could identify with such a bleeding deity. Again Milman's inability to connect the female reproductive anatomy with noble Godhood enters the equation. It is obvious that woman's need to identify with deity was ignored, along with what might be her query: how could women identify with a procreative deity who did *not* bleed as Mary did?

Viewing Protestantism as sturdy, British, rational, and manly, and Catholicism as effete, Continental, irrational, and feminine, many Protestants believed that because Catholicism appealed to women, it was "'feminized'" (Herringer 4, 56; LaMonaca 2, 3). In one instance, the debates about the Bull evoked a withering interrogation of the masculinity of a Catholic who reverenced this vexing female deity. While the Protestant press admired Cardinal Newman, perhaps because of his so-called rational English refusal to divinize Mary, it could not abide Cardinal Manning's enthusiasm for the Madonna. In its critique of the official doctrine, the *British Quarterly Review* highhandedly attacked Manning for his devotion to the Virgin and for being "too effeminate" himself, thus suggesting that by worshipping a female divinity, male adherents became feminized (Dale 289). Maligning Manning's virility, the High Church journal complained that while the Cardinal's sermons were "severe without being robust," his preachments lacked "depth and vigour." The Protestant writer did not stop there in questioning the cleric's manhood, adding that although the "sentiment" of Manning's homilies may be "delicious," they lacked "passion," "sinew," and "logic" (289). "Vigour" and "sinew" are, of course, code words for masculinity, which, this journalist snidely implied, Manning had not properly displayed, making him and his Church not only "effeminate" and "powerless" but also implicitly perverse (289).

The debates between the male laity and patriarchs over the Virgin's role were similar to Victorian commentary by males on the Woman Question: in both discussions, any hint of equality between the sexes raised fears that women would supersede their male counterparts in power. Further, there was an anxious desire to remind women that their central meaning to men and the Christian patriarchy was sexual: they must be virginal while also fulfilling woman's "essential" function of motherhood. Likewise, the generic meaning of the term "man" as a universal marker for both sexes implicitly comes into question when distinctions are made between inherent male and female roles, duties, and characteristics. In the rigidly gendered Victorian culture, the iconic Virgin automatically put the male God into question; that is, without male involvement she biologically conceived and thus created the *summum bonum* of God's plan, the Savior. Indeed, Mary's role *is* a recognition that God cannot do without woman in the creative act—the divine not being generative without an earthly female in the process. As I have also shown, obsessive fears about masculinity, female purity, and bodily functions hovered subliminally in these debates between men.

But while many Catholic and Protestant clerics agreed that woman's inherent duty was simultaneously motherhood and chastity, Catholicism provided more of a horizon, if a troubled one, for divine womanhood. In arguing that religion must offer women a model of perfection, Bishop Ullathorne declared that Jesus is the "head and type of all human excellence," being the "one perfect man." But he then asked, "where shall we look [page break] for the highest form and example of excellence in woman?" This being, of course, was Mary, who had "a nearer resemblance to God than all others, and a greater union with God than all others" (51–52). Offering woman vicarious divinity, Ullathorne's approach implies that the fully male Trinity cannot act as the absolute sign of divine perfection. In suggesting that the generic term "man" could not cover the woman, the Bishop intimated that the generic male Trinity was also lacking in the feminine graces and thus incapable of modeling and encompassing perfect womanhood.

Herringer points out that while Protestant attacks on Mary were based on the belief that women were limited in their divine and earthly emanations, Catholic representations of a powerful Virgin implied that the very "virtues that were intended to restrict women to the domestic sphere were a means by which to access the public sphere" (25). Both Maria LaMonaca and Ruth Vanita assert that Protestant Victorian women writers subversively used Catholicism to undermine and protest Victorian "sacred cows" by examining Victorian culture through Catholic "tropes." Most importantly, the Madonna becomes "a site of free signification" for these writers (Vanita 19; qtd. in LaMonaca 3, 4). When mainstream Victorian women writers publicly responded to the Woman Question and discussions about the Virgin Mary, the rhetoric was usually more carefully calibrated than the debates between men. This does not necessarily mean that their analysis is feeble; it suggests that in order to retain a voice in the culture, they often had to resort to masked, convoluted discourse.

If the official establishment of the Immaculate Conception offered a new potentiality for divine womanhood, the feminist American journal *The UNA: a paper devoted to the elevation of woman* (1855) fearlessly stated its opinion about the historic pronouncement. Much in the vein of early socialist feminists, *The UNA* proclaimed that the Bull did not complete a much-needed revolution in thought. In an article titled "The New Catholic *Goddess*," the writer (unknown) argued in Carlylean tropes that she expected that the *Bull Ineffabilis* "would be something more than a new metaphysical patch on an old metaphysical garment." Looking for the "revelation of some fact that would stretch the faith of Christendom up to a higher measure or a broader compass," the journalist expressed her wish that the Church had sanctified a "quartet divinity" by adding Mary as the "fourth" member of the erstwhile male Trinity rather than leaving her on her own private, ambiguous pedestal in limbo. Yet the writer was optimistic, believing that eventually Mary would have equal standing with the Trinity, and womanhood would be "reinstated in the functions which were superseded during the dark and barbarous ages" ("New Catholic Goddess" 41–42).

Derrida's definition of empirical events facilitates the understanding that paradigmatic occurrences are always in process rather than hypostatized as a fait accompli. As he remarks, "one thinks at the same time the impossibility of predicting an event necessarily without horizon, [and] the singular coming of the other" [Tel partage suppose aussi qu'on pense à la fois l'imprévisibilité d'un événement nécessairement sans horizon, la venue singulière de l'autre, et par consequent une *force faible*] (qtd. in Callinicos 84). Likewise, as Pamela Sue Anderson argues of the mythoi surrounding the Virgin, the maternal is an "ambivalent unnameable principle" since it is both "outside of the paternal social-symbolic order and a condition of that order" (157). Coupling Derrida's and Anderson's insights with the optimism of the writer of "The New Catholic Goddess," one might say that in the face of historic fatality about the maleness of God, imagining a feminine divinity may be made possible by patriarchy. Nevertheless, the female divinity also brings into view what Grace Jantzen refers to as the "divine horizon" of potentiality for women and the concomitant possibility for real historic change (65).

One of the few mid-Victorian women who publicly took men to task about the Woman Question, Anna Jameson remarks that when women "presume" to question male "rights and privileges," or intimate the "horrors and moral disorders to which they give rise," those same women are viewed as "unfeminine," for it:

> shocks the nice delicacy of "her protector, 'man'" and yet the assumption that the woman consults the decorum of her sex by appearing not to know that which she does know—that which all the world *knows* that she knows—the common . . . most fatal assumption, that women have "*nothing to do*" with certain questions lying deep at the very root and core of society, has falsehood on the very face of it; but no one dares to look it in the face, and show its heartlessness . . . ! If woman has nothing to do with what concerns the fidelity of her husband, the health and virtue of her sons, the . . . honour of her daughters,—with what, in heaven's name, *has* she to do?" ("Woman's Mission" 243)

Here Jameson brilliantly captures the double standard regarding women who dare to discuss the double standard. Hence Jameson's statement offers an explanation for why few women publicly engaged in the ideological meanings of the Immaculate Conception in terms of the Woman Question, even though the Madonna might offer them the perfect opportunity to imagine divine femininity.

Similarly, Jameson's final words in "Woman's Mission" are a gauntlet flung at a culture that trivializes women's work:

> The question must be settled one way or another; either let the man in all the relations of life be held the natural guardian of the woman—constrained to fulfil that trust—responsible to society for her well being and her maintenance; or if she be liable to be thrust from the sanctuary of home to provide for herself through the exercise of such faculties as God has given her, let her at least have fair play; let it not be avowed in the same breath, that protection is necessary to her, and that it is refused to her; and while we send [page break] her forth into the desert, and bind the burthen on her back, and put the staff into her hand,—let not her steps be beset, her limbs fettered, and her eyes blindfolded. (247–48)

Jameson's heated words should be juxtaposed with her remembrance of a possibly trancelike existence, when "from ten years old to fourteen or fifteen, I lived a double existence; one outward, linking me with the external sensible world, the other inward, creating a world to and for itself, conscious to itself only. I carried on for whole years a series of actions, scenes, and adventures; one springing out of another, and coloured and modified by increasing knowledge. This habit grew so upon me, that there were moments—as when I am to some crisis in my imaginary adventures,—when I was not more awake to outward things than in sleep,—scarcely took cognisance of the beings around me" (*Commonplace* 131). In this passage, Jameson poignantly recalls that during this period her "reveries were my real life" and that it was an "unhealthy state of things" (132). She asserts that "Employment!" was the answer to her dis-ease as well as to the brutal "fetter[ing]" and "blindfold[ing]" of girls (*Commonplace* 133; "Woman's Mission" 247–48).

An advocate of women using their god-given intellectual and other talents, a point Nightingale would later strongly support, Jameson matter-of-factly writes that "according to the diversity of the gifts which God has bestowed," all should offer the "best that is in us, and lay it a reverend offering on the altar of humanity, to burn and enlighten" ("Woman's Mission" 211). Jameson's own rhetorical gifts enlighten others on the need for women's rights, which, she recognizes, must begin by dismantling arcane notions about gender, particularly as manifest in Christianity and its Victorian secular formations. Her brassy rhetoric well deserves to be set against the radical utopians who preceded her, for Jameson bracingly derides the cult of domesticity. Archly, she remarks that the "beautiful theory of the woman's existence" so long portrayed by moralists and poets became socially acceptable in all lands even in the "teeth of fact and experience!" (217). In a sharply satirical section, Jameson derides the "trite" notion that while man should be the "bread-winner," woman should be relegated to the domestic sphere because is "she not *the mother?*—highest, holiest, dearest title to the respect and the tenderness of her 'protector *Man!*'" (217)

Jameson's stern attacks on Victorian verities about motherhood, the cult of womanhood, and the Angel in the House must be taken into account when turning to her views on Eve and Mary as models of femininity. Born during the French Revolution, Jameson bears traces of the socialist feminists who recuperated the first Eve. She figures the second Eve, the Madonna, as a fluid entity that expands and elides boundaries, while also modeling for mortal women their divine potentiality here and now. Jameson's *Legends of the Madonna* (1852) precedes by two years the debates about the Immaculate Conception, but concern about Mariolatry was much in the air before its official inception, much as discussions about evolution preceded Darwin. Because Jameson had a deep interest in the Madonna, it is likely that she would have been aware of the public debates about the Immaculate Conception, and thus her writings on the Madonna should be seen as participating in those ongoing debates.

Kimberly VanEsvald Adams notes that Feuerbach's notion of the feminized Savior makes way for Jameson to honor the "*Madonna* as divinized woman" and thus use the Virgin as a symbol for women's rights (42). As Adams asserts, George Eliot, Margaret Fuller, and Jameson position Mary at the core of their rationale for seeing women as part of the Christian godhead and as a causal link to arguments for giving women political power. Yet, says Adams, although the Madonna is an important symbol in the work of these women, given the material reality of women's lives in eighteenth- and nineteenth-century England and America, the Virgin Mary was an "as-yet unrealized ideal for women and thus also serves as the basis of a feminist social critique" (43).

In the case of Eve, Jameson's representation is strikingly similar to those of the utopian feminists, described in previous chapters. Like Charlotte Brontë, Jameson deplores "MILTON'S EVE" because she represents a "masculine standard of perfection in woman," for the great author focuses only on Eve's "graceful figure," "'coy submission,'" and "unreasoning willfulness" (*Commonplace* 115). Complaining about Milton's tired cliché that the snake practiced flattery on Eve, Jameson protests the assumption that the mother of all living was vain. According to Jameson, Milton's description belies the biblical depiction, which she says is "ampler, grander, nobler far":

> As the Eve of Paradise should be majestically sinless, so after the Fall she should not cower and wail like a disappointed girl. Her infinite fault, her infinite woe, her infinite penitence, should have a touch of grandeur. She has paid the inevitable price for that mighty knowledge of good and evil she so coveted; that terrible predestined experience—she has found it, or it has found her;—and she wears her crown of grief as erst her crown of innocence. (348)

Here Jameson shows high esteem for the first Eve because she "paid the price" of pursuing her desire for knowledge. Like Brontë's "mighty" mother, this Eve is not a mincing "girl." Rather, she is a majestic, worthy actor in the primeval drama about the inception of humanity. Jameson's Eve bravely embraces "mighty knowledge" so that her progeny may enter into the presence of the divine (348). Like any tragic hero, she pays the highest price. In fact, in this excerpt, like Sharples, Jameson admires Eve because she "reverses the accepted conditions and characteristics of sex" in her "desire of . . . Knowledge of good, bought dear by knowing ill" (*History of Our Lord* 1:106). Jameson's interpretation shames male commentators for their rejection of the idea that women could heroically encounter the tragic conditions in which God had put her. Implying that masculine scorn for Eve simplistically saw the Fall as about Adam being caught in a schoolboy lie, Jameson points up the cosmic import of Eve's tragic choice and, unlike her mealy-mouthed spouse, Eve's refusal to think only of her reputation.

Jameson's potent vision of Eve also suggests that Milton's version is inferior to Elizabeth Barrett's depiction. As Jameson contends, Barrett's *Drama of Exile* rightly figures a "noble picture" of Eve as "the Mother of our redemption not less than the Mother of suffering humanity" (*Commonplace* 347–49). In *The History of Our Lord* (1864), Jameson sounds like Joanna Southcott, who viewed Eve as equaling or even surpassing Christ's salvation of humankind. Elevating Eve above Adam's creation, Jameson reviles stereotypes that picture her as taken from Adam's rib. Instead, Jameson states that the rib motif "signifie[s] that, while the Second Adam hung on the Cross, His side was pierced, and the sacraments flowed therefrom," thus explicitly aligning Eve (and woman) with Christ's miraculous sacrifice and self-resurrection (1:93).

Jameson reasons, too, that Eve must be seen as a holy entity in Christian works of art, for it was she from whom Christ "deriv[ed] His human nature," and thus it is "*her* seed that was to bruise the serpent's head" (93). In this analogue, Eve symbolizes Jesus's own blood, the graphic process through which he saves humanity and becomes fully divine. Of course this view of female blood contrasts starkly with the horror of Mary's sanguinary processes seen in male debates about the Immaculate Conception. Further, by focusing on Eve's pivotal role in the triumph over Satan, Jameson mirrors Southcott's heretical view of Eve as equal to Jesus in her participation in the mysterious sacrifice for humanity's salvation. Like Southcott, Jameson suggests that those who do not recognize Eve as the rival of Satan and as a talismanic emblem of salvation must face not only feminist censure but the Savior's rebuke as well.

Like Southcott and the utopian feminists, Jameson also depicts Adam as at best self-righteous, and at worst effete. In her recuperation of Eve as a divinity in human form, Jameson slyly suggests, without naming names, that "[m]any" have written of Eve's moral edge over Adam; the coyly unidentified authors to whom she refers—might she be alluding subversively to the early nineteenth-century radical feminists—claimed, for example, that the foremother was made of "nobler materials" than those from which man came, that Eve was created from flesh and blood, whereas Adam was made from the dust. Furthermore, Jameson argues that while Eve was created in the Garden of Eden, Adam was engendered outside that paradisial place (*History of Our Lord* 1:94–95).

In feminist splendor on a par with Sharples and Wright, Jameson exults that Eve was "as much the work of the hand of God, whether taken metaphorically or actually, as that of Adam himself," and that Adam had nothing to do with his companion's creation. Jameson argues that Adam's presence is not "implied" in the narrative about Eve's creation because the Bible shows that God "'brought her' unto him" (95). It is important to Jameson, then, that Eve maintain an independent, separate identity from Adam in the creation story. Thus she derides the inaccuracy of the line "'He for God only, she for God in him'" as a "Mahometan doctrine." She suggests instead that, by virtue of the material reality of her creation and eternal essence, Eve was made by God and thus had equal access to that divine being (98, 102).

Urging her reader not to blame Eve alone for the Fall, in *History of Our Lord,* Jameson brazenly examines artistic depictions of the scene in the Garden of Eden to see if they lay the blame for the Fall on Eve. In doing so, she derides the tradition that Eve alone was responsible, mocking the early Church Fathers and monks who showed their "sour grapes" against the original female parent. Male clerics, she insists, suggest that the snake/Satan was merely a redundant entity in Eden because Eve was the "enemy of souls" (99). In contrast, Jameson sees Eve as a potent, profoundly important figure in the biblical story and claims that Michelangelo rightly made her birth the crux of the Sistine Chapel (93). Thus, her extensive remarks on Eve imply that Adam was a bit player in the Eden drama and that Eve had the most important role, for she wrestled with God for the very knowledge of which divinity consists. Milton, the Church Fathers, and monks may have tried to erase her magnificent achievement, but Jameson, along with Brontë and early nineteenth-century utopian feminists, fiercely condemns this insult. Preempting second-wave feminism, Jameson recognizes that male-driven religious and aesthetic constructions of Eve have everything to do with how her symbolic daughters are interpellated politically and personally, and she deftly deconstructs the foremother's reification.

Before I examine her views of the Madonna, it is important to note that Jameson does not consider Mary as the sole goddess in the Catholic Church. In *Sacred and Legendary Art,* she recognizes the metaphorical power of the "Virgin Patronesses," including St. Catherine, St. Barbara, and St. Ursula. She writes, for example, that these saints "were absolutely, in all but the name, Divinities" (276). Astutely asserting that these saints attained symbolic power, Jameson notes that even though the Church thought of the saint's power as merely "delegated," the layperson viewed them as strong "intercessors." As Jameson theorizes, when an ordinary member of the Catholic faith prayed to St. Catherine for special favor, it was with the absolute belief that she had the inherent power to bestow blessings (277). Jameson adds that the lower classes gained power over the Pope himself because they, not the Papal Father, endowed these saints with divinity (277). Jameson's historicization of female divinity implies that the engendering of God underwrites women's access to ideal modes of action, including responses to modern questions about female rights and powers. Her approach also exists in a subliminal site between the literal belief in a primal God above and outside human understanding and the necessity for the ongoing human construction of god as symbol, which would result in a more expansive and benign world here and now.

When considering her most famous work, *Legends of the Madonna,* as a Protestant, Jameson has to preempt charges that she views the Madonna through the lens of Catholic "superstition." She circumvents this challenge by explaining that she is interested not in worshipping the Catholic

Madonna but rather in analyzing Mary as an aesthetic figure in Western art.[8] Noting that the Madonna is a dominant motif in Renaissance and Medieval art, Jameson asserts and masks ideological points (xvii). Although she separates herself from Catholics who confuse the "creature with the Creator," Jameson argues that the Virgin fulfills a profound psychological need.

Mariolatry, she says, results from "deep sympathy—deeper far than mere theological doctrine could reach" (xix). Belittling the surly Christian God, Jameson hints that she prefers Mary's "ethics of human love," which is kinder and gentler than the "'strong hand and the might that makes the right,'" a slanted reference to the temperamental tactics of the Old Testament God (xvii–xix, xx). Like Sharples and other utopian radicals, Jameson argues, too, that Mary and the pagan goddesses signal "the coming moral regeneration, and complete and harmonious development of the whole human race, by the establishment, on a higher basis, of what has been called the 'feminine element' in society" (xix). In fact, this astonishing statement could have been taken directly from Sharples.

As in her discussion of Eve, Jameson skillfully obviates charges of paganism by referring to unnamed thinkers (perhaps the utopian feminists or historians such as Milman) who assert that most cultures Mary conquered already had a "dominant idea of a mother-Goddess" and distill those pagan beliefs in a Mighty Mother into the icon of the Virgin (xix). Jameson does not view the primal versions of the goddess as impure but as presaging future manifestations of a Mother in Heaven. For example, she claims that pagan goddesses were "the voice of a mighty prophecy, sounded through all the generations of men, even from the beginning of time" (xix). Untroubled by mixing polytheistic and Christian ideals of the Mighty Mother, Jameson implies that Mary's morality relates to these pagan foremothers.

In her own litany of the goddesses, Eve and Mary carry equal weight with their pagan alter egos: "Eve of the Mosaic history, the Astarte of the Assyrians—'The mooned Ashtaroth, queen and mother both,'—the Isis nursing Horus of the Egyptians, the Demeter and the Aphrodite of the Greeks, the Scythian Freya," were, Jameson concludes, "considered by some writers" as the "foreshadowing" of the Virgin Mary (xix). Jameson notes too that one of the pagan symbols associated with Mary was the "crescent moon beneath her feet," which suggested the "idea of her perpetual chastity" (xlvii). Jameson's egalitarian allusions to Mary's sister goddesses forgo challenges to Mary's exceptionalism and suggest that, like the Bible, pagan myths function as another witness of female divinity.

By historicizing how the Madonna became amalgamated with other feminine icons, Jameson recognizes women's need for a divine feminine, whether there might be an essential eternal difference between the sexes or not. Reviling the use of "certain phrases and epithets, as more applicable to one sex than to the other," Jameson deplores how said stereotypes create "unchristian confusion" about behavior (*Commonplace* 91). But although she argues that men and women should be held to the same religious standard for perfection, Jameson defers to difference feminism, because, one would imagine, Christianity was so top-heavy with masculinity. The gendering of divine perfection as male is not enough, according to Jameson, for it elides the most basic creative (reproductive) relationship, that of the father and mother. Like Bishop Ullathorne, Jameson reasons that a divine image of the mother is crucial, and she recognizes that men and women need divine models. She also accepts the idea of gender construction, remarking, for instance, that although the "model-man," the Savior, typified the qualities of both sexes, "the idea that there are essentially masculine and feminine virtues intruded itself on the higher Christian conception," causing the Church to respond to the need for a female divine (*Commonplace* 91; *Legends* xxii, xxi).

She quotes from H. Nelson Coleridge to explain the Christian longing for female and male models of divinity:

> So long as the ancient mythology had any separate establishment in the empire, the spiritual worship which our religion demands ... was preserved in its purity by means of the salutary contrast; but no sooner had the Church become completely triumphant and exclusive ... than the old ... appetite revived in all its original force, and after a short but famous struggle with the Iconoclasts, an image worship was established, and consecrated by bulls and canons, which ... differed in no respect but the names of its objects from that which had existed for so many [page break] Ages as the chief characteristic of the religious faith of the Gentiles. (*Commonplace* 163–64)

Analyzing this convoluted quotation, Jameson explains that before Christianity became predominant, it was separate from pagan religions and thus did not practice pagan goddess worship. Once Christianity became dominant, an "appetite" within Christian members caused the Church to include the worship of Mary, resulting in the *Bull Ineffabilis*. Jameson's use of this quotation suggests her direct knowledge of the 1854 endorsement of the Immaculate Conception. It also captures the idea that both pagans and Christians responded profoundly to the concept of a female divine.

Jameson suggests that pagans worshipped "*beauty, immortality,* and *power*" in their goddesses, while the Christian mythos reverenced "*purity, self-denial,* and *charity*" (163–64). In either case, she recognizes a human need for a symbolic divine Mother. In light of Coleridge's statement that at some point in history, new ideas about gender shaped the construction of Mary, we might also infer that Jameson is comfortable with the concept that "God" is always being metaphorically and historically reproduced and that it is important in *this* life to have access to rhetorical, symbolic renditions of women's divine potentiality. Thus she believes that mankind must recreate its god(s) in response to deep human needs, including the desires of women. Like the utopian feminists, then, Jameson contends that such recreation is necessary to making mortal existence more paradisial now.

Reviewing the history of early Church controversies over Mary's ontology, and showing that she had done her theological homework, Jameson explains the difference between the Nestorians and Monophysites, a debate that utterly affected Mariolatry. The Nestorians believed that the divine and mortal natures of Christ were kept separate and that Mary was merely the mother of Christ's human nature, with God the parent of his divine nature. In contrast, the Monophysites argued that Mary was the literal Mother of Christ because "in Christ the divine and human were blended in one incarnate nature." As Jameson is not hesitant to mention, when the Monophysites won the argument, "the representation of that beautiful group, since popularly known as the 'Madonna and Child,' became the expression of the orthodox faith" (xxii).

Thus Jameson highlights the fact that after this historic debate, every rendition of the Madonna and Child is a testament to the belief that Mary was included in Christ's divinity and Incarnation *because* she was his mother (*Legends* xxii). Jameson explains the Monophysite logic: after the fifth century it was necessary to believe in Mary as the Mother of divinity; ergo Mary also had to be included in that divine essence, for she was "'raised bodily into immortality, and placed beside her Son.'" Hence Jameson recognizes and takes pleasure in the fact that "The relative position of the Mother and Son being spiritual and indestructible was continued in heaven; and thus step by step the woman was transmuted into the divinity" (xliii). Although a Protestant, in this statement Jameson is quietly exultant about the moment of Mary's exaltation to divinity. Her ambiguous reference to "the woman" being transformed into "divinity" also carries subliminal aspirations about the power and potentiality of mortal women.

How well Jameson covers over subversive purposes can be seen in a review of *Legends* in *Blackwood's Edinburgh Magazine*. The disgruntled reviewer reviles the "evils of Popery" and Catholic excesses brought about "through orientalism and heathenism." The writer is particularly offended by the way devotion to Mary supplants worship of Christ, because the idolatry of "'The Queen of Heaven'" restores the "heathen title of 'Mother of the Gods'" (Eagles 35, 31, 30). Nevertheless, he accepts the gender ideology portrayed in worship of the Virgin:

> a thinking mind will not doubt that this feminine element, in cases where real essential Christianity had a looser hold of the people, tended greatly to ameliorate the manners of wild and boisterous periods in man's history, and to bring the civilisation of gentleness over barbarism. It tended greatly to raise woman; and it was better, by a romantic worship, that she should be lifted above an equality with man, than be degraded infinitely below him. . . . The feminine element, then, by the permission of Providence, had its good tendencies, notwithstanding its idolatry. Nor was this good confined to a few spots: it spread far and wide; nor is it yet lost in places where we might least expect to find it." (Rev. "*Legends of the Madonna*" 31)

Thus, although the writer deplores the "evil" popish plot of "setting up the mother as Divinity above the Redeemer-Son," he believes that in *The Legends of the Madonna,* Jameson was "not discussing religion" (35). Jameson's care in presenting her work as merely an evaluation of aesthetic depictions of the Virgin seems, then, to have mollified her audience regarding the possibility of her heretical or feminist intent. Certainly, in comparison to the vitriolic arguments between men about the Immaculate Conception, Jameson's rhetoric is mild and strategically intended to remain uncontroversial. Yet, coupled with commentary from the rest of her oeuvre, Jameson invokes earlier, more radical feminist interpretations of the female divine.

It is appropriate to end this chapter by examining Jameson's idea of the horizon of woman's divinity, which appears in her description of her favorite portrait of the Madonna. "I have seen my own ideal once," she says, "*there,* where Raphael—inspired if ever painter was inspired—projected on the space before him that wonderful creation which we style the *Madonna di San Sisto.*" She continues:

> there she stands—the transfigured woman, at once completely human and completely divine, an abstraction of power, purity, and love, poised on the empurpled air, and requiring no other support; looking out, with her melancholy, loving mouth, her slightly dilated, sibylline eyes, quite through the universe, to the end and consummation of all things;—sad as if she beheld afar off the visionary sword that was to reach her heart through HIM, now

resting as enthroned on that heart; yet already exalted through the homage of the redeemed generations who were to salute her as Blessed." (Jameson, *Legends* xliv)

In this description, the Virgin is no simpering subordinate but an "abstraction of power" representing love, which is, again, perhaps Jameson's way of questioning depictions of a harsh God the Father. In *Legends*, Jameson points out that the Nicephorus Callixtus's history of the Church adds "gifts of the poetess and prophetess" to Mary's other spiritual qualities (xliii). In her interpretation of Raphael's painting, Jameson focuses on Mary's prescient, prophetic eyes and their vision of the "consummation of all things." And, in fact, as Jameson implies, Mary might be a poetess in her ability to imagine new metaphors for godhood. Jameson is enraptured by Raphael's ability to capture Mary in the moment of transfiguration, in which she is both divine and human, powerful in her amorphous subjectivity. That Mary needs no "support" to maintain her elevated position suggests that she requires no propping up by male Gods or Church Fathers. Her divinity comes from her own goodness and from the spontaneous upwelling of love and devotion from her followers. She neither asks for adoration nor seduces men with her charms. Becoming God, she fulfills the mystic ideal of woman transfiguring herself through stages into divine potentiality.

4

Invoking "all the godheads"

ELIZABETH BARRETT BROWNING'S POLYTHEISTIC AESTHETIC

> [Miss E. B. Barrett] writes . . . like an inspired priestess . . . whose individuality is cast upward in the divine afflatus.
> —R. H. Horne, ed., *A New Spirit of the Age* 140

> I was in great danger of becoming the founder of a religion of my own.
> —Elizabeth Barrett Browning, "Juvenile Autobiography" 15

> Poetry is where God is.
> —Elizabeth Barrett Browning, "The Book of the Poets" 92; qtd. in Olivia Taylor 160

OLIVIA TAYLOR notes that Elizabeth Barrett Browning's statement that "Christ's religion is essentially poetry—poetry glorified" demonstrates her "conception of poetry as messianic" and the belief that the reform of society occurs through poetry (*Letters of EBB to MRM* 1:335; O. Taylor 160). Indeed, Barrett avowed that "the religious all-clasping spirit" must be "in degree and measure, the grand necessity of every true poet's soul" (*Essays on the Greek Christian Poets* 22). Although she must certainly be viewed as deeply committed to Christianity, Barrett also required the metaphorical flexibility of polytheism, for she was, in fact, drawn to "all the godheads" (*Aurora Leigh* 1:924).[1] In particular, Greek mythology resonated with her because it offered a numinous sense that gods and goddesses were still vitally present in nature. As Barrett understood, unlike the Christian mythology, whose monolithic male God ejected humankind from Eden for a mere misdemeanor, classical mythology made a plethora of gods available to mortals whatever their moral condition.[2]

In this chapter, I shall examine the polytheism in Barrett's masterpiece, *Aurora Leigh*. Noting that this epic combines disturbing images of the gods of Greece, Swedenborgian notions that the spiritual and material worlds are inseparable, and primal descriptions of god as Father *and* Mother with depictions of the Christian Father God,[3] I shall show that Barrett interrogates gender norms regarding the nature of god and human identity, similar in kind to Julian of Norwich's discursive practice. Likewise, I will show that Barrett's dynamic revision of deity displays traces of the titanic rhetoric and secular messianic yearnings of earlier radical feminists. Although her aspiration to be a poet-prophet was always troubled by Victorian ideas about the impropriety of women speaking in public, let alone speaking like prophets about the nature of God and the ethical duties of humankind, Barrett's adept masking of her ambitious intentions reflects some understanding of how her plain-speaking grandmothers were treated by the press. I suggest, too, that Barrett uses obscure rhetoric to create a palimpsest through which the savvy reader may access her more radical theological musings. Hence *Aurora Leigh* may be considered a protofeminist testament masquerading behind what appears to be, in the end, a conventional love story.

In a review of *Aurora Leigh,* the *Athenaeum* acerbically noted that it was Barrett's "contribution to the chorus of protest and mutual exhortation, which Woman is now raising, in hope of gaining the due place and sympathy which, it is held, have been denied to her since the days when Man was created, the first of the pair in Eden" (Chorley 1425). Women's rights advocates, did, indeed, view *Aurora Leigh* as a feminist classic. Susan B. Anthony took the text with her wherever she spoke on women's rights and, at the dawn of the twentieth century, donated her copy to the Congressional Library (Chaney 798). She wrote in the flyleaf: "This book was carried in my satchel for years and read and reread—. . . I have always cherished it above all other books—I now present it to the Congressional Library, Washington, D.C., with the hope that women may more and more be like 'Aurora Leigh'" (qtd. in Dalley 539). Feminists, including Frances Power Cobbe, Barbara Bodichon, Millicent Garrett Fawcett, and Bessie Raynor Parkes explicitly refer to *Aurora Leigh* as having influenced their progressive politics (Dalley 525). And, I suggest, Barrett's aesthetic and ethical principles were in keeping with those of the radical feminist socialist and millenarian grandmothers who preceded her.[4]

Writing to John Kenyon about her poem "The Dead Pan," Barrett asked rhetorically, "What pagan poet ever thought of casting his gods out of his poetry?" (qtd. in Hewlett 103) This query illustrates the premier Victorian woman poet's deep investment in the spiritual importance of poetry and her concern that as Victorian literature became increasingly secular, it elided the Christian God. To Barrett, if God were to have any meaning in modern life, He had to be palpably present in the culture's poetry in the same way that the gods and goddesses of ancient Greece were felt to be ever-present in nature and art.

Delineating the traces of mother-god-want in Barrett Browning's work, I suggest that she felt constrained by conventional descriptions of God because they captured neither the unlimited energy, variety, and vastness of the cosmos, nor the woman's part in its creation. An autodidact like her husband, Barrett had free rein in her father's library, which was filled with texts from the classical canon (David 101). Barrett, also one of the few Victorian women writers who was a scholar of the Bible, delved into Christian metaphysics and had a passion for Greek, which she mastered in part so that she could read the Greek fathers (Mermin 18).

In order to understand the polytheistic strain in *Aurora Leigh*, it is helpful to examine Schiller's "Gods of Greece," which Barrett's cousin John Kenyon had translated. So intrigued by the verse, which laments the modern period's loss of the classical gods when Christian monotheism emerged, Barrett asked Kenyon if she could keep his translation longer than originally intended (Hewlett 95). Beginning with an apostrophe to the gods, the poem venerates the early Greeks for whom "life's blood flowed throughout creation." Schiller's persona invokes an age in which the Greeks "Wrapped Truth" with "luminous imagination" whence "all things" "felt the hallowed spirit." To Schiller, "Heroes, Gods, and Mortals / United in the bond of love," as mortals became peers with the gods. In contrast, the German writer viewed moderns as able to find only "traces" of divinity, for the "godhead" is "from the picture banished." As in Swinburne's later "Hymn to Proserpine," Schiller found that where Greek culture was joyful, Christianity valued self-denial and shame. Schiller bemoaned the loss and beseeched the classical world to return. In a telling line, the poet mourns that "ye Gods" must "pass away" in order to consolidate the power of Christianity (the "One"), which makes men unaware of the goddess's presence (Selene) and "Unconscious" of "senses" that "year[n]" for "her all-inspiring flame" ("Gods of Greece").

The poems Barrett wrote in her childhood reveal a rambunctious attraction to the plenitude of a world rife with gods and goddesses, and she dares to participate with them in the high and holy task of creation. In her girlhood, Barrett had built "altar fires in the garden to Athena with matches stolen from the housemaid's cupboard" (Hewlett 26). Also from a young age, Barrett summoned Greek goddesses in her playful birthday poems for family members. In one felicitation for her sister Henrietta's birthday, Barrett pens the initial lines: "I sent a message to the Muse, / Last night, to leave Castalian dews, / And speed here, if twere in her power, / This morning at the breakfast hour— / But, above all, to keep in time, / As Reason would not wait for rhyme! / When lo (I never heard a better) / 'Stead of the Goddess, comes a letter— / A curious *MS,* to be writ / By hand divine—and this is it!!" (*Browning Correspondence* 189) With youthful brio, Barrett, the self-conscious child prodigy, all but equates her artistic powers with the puissant goddess she apostrophizes—and thus creates. Making a humorous but telling bait and switch, she wittily implies that her own writing is capable of replacing the frisson attendant upon the appearance of a goddess.

The precocious Barrett wrote a precursor to her full-blown fictional *Kunstlerroman* in the autobiography she penned at the age of fourteen. Titled "Glimpses into My Own Life and Literary Character," Barrett's memoir exhibits exuberance about reading Greek in contrast to poring over shame-based Christian texts. Her budding aspiration to be a poet-prophet is also apparent. She wrote that she had read many novels as well as the *Iliad* and other Greek literature by the time she was eleven. She remembers reading Locke when she was twelve and recalls that she felt that "I was in great danger of becoming the founder of a religion of my own. [page break] I revolted at the idea of an established religion—my faith was sincere but my religion was founded solely on the imagination" (EBB, "Juvenile Autobiography" 15–16). Barrett came by this religious bullishness rightly. In her prayer book, her father changed "Church of England" to "Church *in* England" and deleted the word "Established" from the phrase "with notes by a member of the Established Church" (Hewlett 6).

Just after writing that she came close to establishing her own church, the young author commented that this "time was the happiest of my life," a statement suggesting the freedom she felt when she toyed with the idea of creating a new religion ("Juvenile Autobiography" 16).[5] In light of this declaration, it should be noted that, like Florence Nightingale, Barrett often excused herself from going to church. We would expect that Barrett's health stopped her from attending, but her diary from 1831 to 1832 indicates that more often than not she avoided the chore of church attendance because the sermons were vapid and the gospel was not "consistently preached there" (*Diary* 124). Barrett's diary entries on Sundays also intimate that her study of classical writers was more inspiring matter than what she found at Christian worship.⁶

If, then, one cannot read Barrett's oeuvre without recognizing its deep engagement with spirituality, it is also imperative to understand that, like Brontë and Jameson, hers was an interrogatory, expansive spirituality constantly in danger of being repressed because of strong obligations to and anxieties about the religion of her fathers. "Glimpses," in fact, features a teenager who, when she forgets to pray one day, upbraids herself for the "fatal power of my imagination," which she contends leads her away from Christian devotion. Henceforth, she vowed to support the "cause of the Church of England" ("Juvenile Autobiography" 20).

By the time she turned fourteen, Barrett appeared to others to have gained control of her heretical leanings. However, she notes that "to myself it is well known that the same violent inclinations are in my inmost heart and that altho habitual restraint has become almost a part of myself yet were I once to loose the rigid rein I might again be hurled" far from "everything human everything reasonable!" (22, 23) Nonetheless, Barrett avowed that she reviled "feminine softness" and felt "an almost proud consciousness of independence which prompts me to defend my opinions" (35). In her own attempt to revive Ophelia, the adolescent writer already appears to understand that she must become inured to the "rigid rein" and that straining against the bit of Victorian proprieties was anathema for girls.

Yet, poignantly, she had a strong loyalty to what she felt to be her true robust self and already knew about masking such unfeminine propensities. Oscillating between being the conformist and the rebel, Barrett recognized the need to conceal her imaginative life in order to fulfill obligations to the Christian religion and her family. As we have seen in previous chapters, Anna Jameson experienced a similar form of repression. Likewise, as an adolescent and young adult, Charlotte Brontë often went into trances, and it is more than likely that she did so, in part, to escape the drudgery of female self-sacrifice demanded by her religion. This need to create a double life as an outlet for desirable but unapproved behaviors is reminiscent of Frances Wright's vehement aversion to Christian "priestcraft" that terrified women into leading straitened, listless lives devoted to selflessness and religious inanity ("Lecture I: On the Nature of Knowledge" 38–39).

As the iconic adult poet, Barrett Browning figured herself as both obedient and staunchly independent, making for some peculiar apologias. Coyly playing with her reader, she accepted that she was worthy of being a preacher/sage but figured herself as above such self-aggrandizement. For example, in a letter on 8 January 1844, she proclaimed that she was no "Pope Joan the second," for she has "no manner of pretension to any such dignity" ("The Religious Opinions" 25). As one version of the apocryphal story goes, Pope Joan was a well-educated woman who, at a young age, disguised herself as a man so as to enter and move up through the Catholic echelons of power. Alleged to have become pope in the ninth century, Joan was outed during a ritual procession in Rome when the popess was smitten by childbirth pangs and gave birth in that very public venue. At this point, of course, her gender became obvious as itself a crime (think, again, of Milman's comments about the primitive nature of women's breasts and organs of fertility that make them unsuitable for the roles of prophet or deity).

Barrett's demurral about being a Pope Joan tells us much about the convoluted strategies Victorian women writers utilized in order to retain integrity in their writing in the face of outright misogyny. Journalist R. B. Peake's piece in *Bentley's Miscellany* imagined a scurrilous bit of Joan's monologue that illustrates, through allusion to the fall, why men should be wary of headstrong women: "Why was not I the first created woman?" his imagined Popess protests. "I would have met the subtle plotting serpent, and by my arts annihilated the shallow fiend!'" (150). Any woman seeking such public spiritual power was abhorrent not only to Peake.

With gross crassness and a strong whiff of threatening menace, *All the Year Round* used the Pope Joan story as a prime example of provocative, unfeminine behavior. In "A Few More Odd Women," the writer warned that "Women there have been, and probably still are, odd in so far as they renounce their own sex, and follow avocations fitted only for men" (222). The piece includes Joan of Arc in the category of "odd" or "queer" women and malevolently concludes, "Some odd women have been so atrocious, that the sooner we get rid of them the better" (223). Such rhetoric is reminiscent of the journalistic assaults made on Buchan, Southcott, Lee, and socialist feminists. This rhetoric also broadcasts the kinds of attacks writers like Barrett could expect if they appeared to demand the religious or political mantle of authority meant only for men, or if they viewed inflammatory, heretical women in a positive light. No wonder the far-from-obtuse Barrett Browning asserted that she was no Pope Joan.

Regardless of her protestations, Barrett was, like Aurora Leigh, something of a popess. In the same letter in which she denied being a Pope Joan, she asserted that humans should be prophets and that Christians must "think and feel for ourselves in matters of religion," for "every man or woman of us all is bound to receive into practice the truth he or she consciously discerns, and *as* he or she consciously discerns it" (*The Religious Opinions*

25). Believing that every person imagines deity differently, Barrett suggested that spiritual knowledge must be processed through individual metaphors. Asserting that she was not inclined to put any denomination above another but instead desired to "reverence *the Churches,*" she was against "*sectarianism* in any sort or sense" (Letter to Merry 8 Jan 1844; EBB "Edgar Allan Poe," 11–12).

Thus, Barrett forthrightly stated that the "sectarianism of the National Churches, to which I do not belong, and of the Dissenting bodies [she was a Congregationalist], to which I do—stand together before me on a pretty just level of detestation" (*The Religious Opinions* 27; EBB, "Edgar Allan Poe" 11–12). Rejecting dogmatic religion, she explained that since "the Christianity of the world is apt to wander from Christ and the hope of Him," then "Truth (as far as each thinker can apprehend) apprehended—and Love, comprehending—make my idea—my hope of a Church" (11–12). Sounding like a prophet of relativism, the catholic Barrett also argued that just as there are many churches claiming to be of Christ, the "aspects of truth to the human mind are many indeed" (Letter to Merry 8 Jan 1844: 26).

Aurora Leigh should also be read in light of the writer's dramatic, gender-bending representations of the Christian Fathers (and Mothers). In *Essays on the Greek Christian Poets and the English Poets,* Barrett asks for an epiphany as she "look[s] back fathoms down the great Past" in order to hear "even" women's voices "rise up like a smoke" so that they can be heard in modern times (11–12). *Essays on the Greek Christian Poets* illustrates Barrett's protofeminist polytheism in its argument that the Greek Christian poets who came after the classical period were not the artists the classical Greek poets were. Barrett employs the image of a goddess to describe the distinction: "Not only was there a lack in the instrument,—there was also a deficiency in the players. Thrown aside, after the old flute-story, by a goddess, it was taken up by a mortal hand—by the hand of men gifted and noble in their generation, but belonging to it intellectually, even by their gifts and their nobleness" (15). In an age that viewed women writers as mimics of male genius, it is no small beer that in this trope for transcendence and art, the goddess is the great artist, and mortal men the clumsy imitators, and Barrett certainly knew she was upsetting staid gender binaries in this metaphorical flourish.

Also important to the themes of *Aurora Leigh,* Barrett Browning vigorously challenges the idea that any body of male writers or "Fathers" could have full access to truth and beauty, for she questions how great philosophical ideas could be comprehended if women were elided from the process of knowledge gathering. Unctuously acerbic, her assessment is detached and brutal—even condescending. Breathtakingly cocky, the young female poet and scholar limns the failings of the canonical forefathers whom she refuses to worship. One passage from Barrett's disquisition deserves to be read in full, for it typifies attitudes Aurora Leigh displays toward the male poetic pedigree:

> Still one passing remark may be admissible, since the fact *is* so remarkable—how any body of Christian men can profess to derive their opinions [page break] from the "opinions of the Fathers," when *all* bodies might do so equally. These fatherly opinions are, in truth, multiform, and multitudinous as the fatherly "sublime gray hairs." . . . What then should be done with our "Fathers"? Leave them to perish by the time—Ganges, as old men innocent and decrepit, and worthy of no use or honor? Surely not. We may learn of them, if God will let us, *love,* and love is much—we may learn devotedness of them and warm our hearts by theirs; and this, although we rather distrust them as commentators, and utterly refuse them the reverence of our souls, in the capacity of theological oracles." (*Essays on the Greek Christian Poets* 18–19)

In this raucous deconstruction of "Fathers" worthy of Irigaray, Barrett portrays Aurora's back-story. Suggesting that women writers do not have to abide by the words of rather silly old men, Barrett knows that in this presumptuous analysis she has undercut the male poetic canon and its assumed brilliance, privileged status, and aesthetic superiority. The rhetoric is also so well designed that she implicitly attacks patriarchy itself without appearing spiteful or extreme. Rather, such intentions seem to be just a throwaway that no one should credit. But, in fact, this remarkable excerpt takes the Fathers to task for their employment of the "god-trick," that is, the claim that males have a monolithic, objective, disinterested view from outside. Almost satirical, Barrett's tone out-patronizes patriarchy in its vivid superciliousness toward the supposed "sublime gray hairs." Furthermore, by not erasing the Fathers *tout court,* Barrett undermines the "decrepit" old patriarchs and their ostensible "theological oracles" even more than if she had rejected them wholesale. Yet given the arrogant put-down, Barrett also exhibits a measure of love for these doddering grandfathers who have facilitated her rise to achievements higher than they ever could have realized.

But it is the rebel grandmothers to whom we must turn now. If Barrett rewrites *Paradise Lost* by putting Aurora in the role of Eve, as Sarah Annes Brown suggests, Aurora, like her author, is no cringing violet (723). Indeed,

I suggest that Barrett Browning's mother-god-want is most fully articulated in her epic, in which Christian patriarchs such as Romney Leigh and God the Father are balanced by a basso ostinato of goddess imagery. As Ranen Omer contends, the poet's "struggle to legitimize a radical mythos of creative freedom through assimilating it to Christian tradition" ruptures the serenity for which *Aurora Leigh* strives (98). Aptly named after the Greek goddess of the morning, Aurora weaves together the obstreperously different Judeo-Christian and classical Greek myth traditions. In creating her own Homeric epic, Barrett suggests that a fictional female writer singing her tapestry of grace and love in the fallen nineteenth century *is* the prophecy needed in the modern age, prophecy that comes from a double-breasted being with a double vision who is both mortal and potential goddess.

Blackwood's Edinburgh Magazine complained that Aurora Leigh was "not a genuine woman," that she was too independent and that she "resemble[d] too closely some of the female portraits of George Sand" ("MRS. BARRETT BROWNING-AURORA LEIGH" 32, 33). Barrett, of course, greatly admired Sand, referring to her as a "priestess" after seeing the French novelist reigning over her French salon (Letter #106, 26 February 1852, BL Add. 42231). Barrett Browning shrugged off the press complaints about her epic. She wrote to Anna Jameson that when male writers were panned by the critics, they became whimpering "headless prophet[s]," whereas "*We*" women "die hard, you know" (Letter #261). Nonetheless, *Aurora Leigh* must not have had the radical impact Barrett Browning thought it would, for she admitted being shocked that it received a positive reception in general. She expected instead to be "put in the stocks and pelted with the eggs of the last twenty years 'singing birds,' as a disorderly woman and freethinking poet! . . . Think of quite decent women taking the part of the book in a sort of *effervescence* which I hear of with astonishment" (Letter #465).

The rhetoric here is stunning. Certainly Barrett knew that atheism was one of the meanings of "freethinking" and that "disorderly," "freethinking" radical women had been metaphorically "put in the stocks" for treading outside the path of conventional womanhood in her own century. Yet she flirted with being called an "infidel" and seemed disappointed that the public and press were not more scandalized by her female epic. Like her younger poetic self of the "Autobiography" in this admission Barrett Browning vacillates between being appropriately feminine and expressing willful desire to stand out, to be a woman like no other. But neither could Barrett afford to have the majority of her readers see through the palimpsest of *Aurora Leigh* to its polytheistic strivings.[7] Imagining a divine large enough to comprehend all kinds of love and all varieties of life, this modern epic implies that a monolithic male God simply could not fully encompass all creation and its meaning.

In fact, if, as is conventional in the epic, *Aurora Leigh* begins with an invocation to the God that is most influential in the text, that divinity must be judged as polytheistic. While Olivia Taylor suggests that *Aurora Leigh* foreshadows Julia Kristeva's critical theories about the "gestation and birth of a child," I assert that a mythical eternal mother initiates and acts as the metaphysical foundation of the poem (Taylor 155). In the opening lines, Aurora invokes and then merges mother-want and mother-god-want when she announces, "I have not so far left the coasts of life / To travel inland, that I cannot hear / That murmur of the outer Infinite / Which unweaned babies smile at in their sleep / When wondered at for smiling; not so far, / But still I catch my mother at her post" (1:10–15). Certainly, Aurora is describing infantine memories of her earthly mother who has passed away, but the reference to the "Infinite" depicts a maternal essence whispering to the child of its immortal origins, suggesting that the mother is at the heart of the eternal.

In fact, the cosmology represented in *Aurora Leigh* consists of a triune divinity as pictured in Aurora's primal memories of childhood, from which the "Infinite" speaks to her. Her mother is the chief deity, her father is the second (she remembers his "slow hand, when she [her mother] had left us both"), and the third is Assunta, the nurse whose name, of course, refers to the Virgin Mary ascended into heaven (1:20–21). In creating this trope, Barrett Browning reiterates an image she had used in one of the first poems she ever wrote. Although ostensibly about the male Christian God, this early verse ends by depicting Him as a mother, for He cannot be seen on earth, neither "above the pines" nor in the gold in mines, whereas one can always imagine the presence of a mortal mother. Thus, the young Elizabeth feels "His embrace" as though "my tender mother laid / On my shut lids, her kisses' pressure, / Half waking me at night, and said, / 'Who kissed you through the dark, dear / guesser?'" ("A child's thought of God").

Pam Morris argues that the mother is the one specific material entity that unites all human beings as a foundation for moral and social behavior, because every person psychically and physically has experienced being birthed (190). Hence, the "archaic memory of maternal love" becomes a veiled but "imaginative symbolization" that socializes citizens to love and feel loyalty to the community as a whole (190, 191). *Aurora Leigh* illustrates this understanding right from its beginning. In the epic invocation, Barrett implicitly insists that an abstract, distant male God cannot provide the emotional, psychic bond upon which to build a culture. The most sensually and spiritually effulgent god that she and the "unweaned bab[y]" of the initial lines can imagine is the very tangible mother whose life-giving breasts embody love.[8] This divine female's all-nourishing breasts will be re-presented explicitly and subliminally throughout the rest of the text as a reminder of the maternal foundation of the universe.

Thus the "mother-want about the world" that Aurora describes has cosmic and microcosmic repercussions, for the invocation registers both a material reminder of Aurora's deceased mother and the "Infinite" divine for which the earthly mother is a metonym (1:40). That she speaks of mother-god-want at the beginning of the epic intimates that this is one of the conundrums which the text will address and which will accompany all of Aurora's personal and professional desires. As in all of Barrett's work, the nature of God is at the core of life's mystery, and I should point out here that Barrett Browning idealizes the Christian Father in Heaven as an individualized deity who takes personal interest in Aurora's life.[9]

In contrast, she uses images of classical male and female gods to imagine Aurora's complicated understanding of her identity as poet-prophet through whom the divine speaks.[10] Barrett's depictions of mother-god-want, the double-breasted age, and classical gods with motherly instincts register indistinct images linked to the material reality of an absent earthly mother. Through this evanescent imagery, Barrett suggests that the foundations of the universe are feminine. From the beginning, this epic and its prophet-poet subliminally promise to restore that missing element and suckle the reader with intimations of that knowledge.

Because the orphan Aurora is full of mother-want—"father-want" is never really mentioned after her father dies—she has to be nurtured by "all the gods." As Aurora recalls, her father believed that "unmothered babes" need "mother nature" more than others, and thus "Pan's white goats, with udders warm and full / Of mystic contemplations" feed the "Poor milkless lips of orphans" (1:112–16). In the same way that Pan's goats succor her metaphorically, Aurora feeds on the painting of her mother, which portrays the bodily and abstract incarnations of the maternal, including the gorged breast. The painting's power lies in its divine inclusion of variety and unity, what Coleridge called "discordia concours":

> I mixed, confused, unconsciously,
> Whatever I last read or heard or dreamed,
> Abhorrent, admirable, beautiful,
> Pathetical, or ghastly, or grotesque,
> With still that face . . . which did not therefore change,

> But kept the mystic level of all forms
> Hates, fears, and admirations, was by turns
> Ghost, fiend, and angel, fairy, witch, and sprite,
> A dauntless Muse who eyes a dreadful Fate,
> A loving Psyche who loses sight of Love,
> A still Medusa with mild milky brows
> All curdled and all clothed upon with snakes
> Whose slime falls fast as sweat will; or anon
> Our Lady of the Passion, stabbed with swords
> Where the Babe sucked, or Lamia in her first
> Moonlighted pallor, ere she shrunk and blinked
> And shuddering wriggled down to the unclean;
> Or my own mother, leaving her last smile
> In her last kiss upon the baby-mouth
> My father pushed down on the bed for that,—
> Or my dead mother, without smile or kiss,
> Buried at Florence (1:147–68).[11]

Numerous are the interpretations of this famous description. Patricia Murphy examines Mariolatry coupled with the "sinister potentiality of maternity" featured in these famous lines (22). Joyce Zonana suggests that Aurora's description of her mother is representative of the patriarchal West's "traditional, highly bifurcated images," while Kathleen Renk sees the portrait as a summary of the stereotypes of women in art and literature (Zonana 248; Renk 41). Barbara Charlesworth Gelpi observes that the ambivalent images of "angel," "witch," "Medusa," and "Lamia" illustrate that by choosing to be a poet, the protagonist may reject the mother's role, but her maternal instincts will ultimately "betray" her art (38).

I suggest, however, that this famous depiction also returns our attention to the beginning of the epic when Aurora equates the "Infinite" with a divine and earthly mother's succoring at the breast, for even the Medusa in the portrait has "mild milky brows." If the universe that succors Aurora is effulgently feminine and polytheistic, Barrett suggests that divinity is manifold and continually mingled with the mortal. The divine, then, is at once Medusa, Lamia, Psyche, Our Lady of Passion generously full with milk, an earthly Father and Pan's goats, all of which are mystically expressed (like milk) through and in all things. Her depiction also resists patriarchal attempts to transmogrify the meaning of the feminine.

This description of Aurora's mortal/Infinite mother illustrates Barrett's belief in the very presence of the "godhoods" in the material world and the permeable boundary between the holy and the profane. The imagery also illustrates Barrett's Swedenborgian sense that earthly existence is literally accompanied by divine intimations all around, although we need the poet-prophet to remind us of the unseen (see line 1:858–942). Barrett had written to her sister Henrietta that she was "a Swedenborgian you know, and believe[s] in 'spheres,' 'atmospheres' and 'influences'" (*Letters to Sister* 12 October 1857, 283). Taken by Swedenborg's idea that souls that had passed on were actively present in the world, Barrett conceives her own conglomeration of millenarianism and spiritualism. A true believer in millennial spiritualism, she writes that "manifestations are deepening and widening . . . day by day, . . . We read of a prophecy concerning 'angels ascending and descending upon the son of man.' What if this spiritual influx and afflux is beginning? It seems to me probable—but we have to wait quietly and see" (*Letters to Sister* 26 July 1853, 190). In light of this belief in millenarianism, Barrett was pleased that ex-patriots in Florence spread rumors that "spirits" had transmitted *Aurora Leigh* to her through automatic writing (*Letters to Sister* 10 January 1857, 265).

In keeping with her attraction to the Swedenborgian immanence of the eternal, Barrett notes, "No writer can render human nature fully, who does not render the inner and spiritual life as well as the conventional and material exterior of life" ("Charles Dickens" 12). Aurora makes this clear in her statement that philosophers are wrong who think of the world "too insularly," as though "No spiritual counterpart completed it / Consummating its meaning, rounding all / To justice and perfection, line by line / Form by form, nothing single nor alone" (8:617–21). *Aurora Leigh* desires to make the "spiritual counterpart" present to weary, alienated Victorians, so many of whom, having experienced a crisis of faith, could barely imagine God, let alone a universe pulsating with the vitality of godheads. Further, like medieval female mystics, Barrett suggests that humans are engaged in becoming divine just as the divine is ever engaged in infusing the mortal. For example, when Aurora describes participating in the female accomplishment of painting, she chortles, "I drew . . . costumes" of "nereids" who wear "smirks of simmering godship" (1:420–22). In this image, Aurora's polytheistic mother-god-want implies that "godship" comes about through a "simmering" or apprenticeship, meaning that all nature may evolve toward the divine. And it should be noted that Aurora is the artist and agent who simmers these aesthetic gods.

As noted previously, Barrett believed that if the gods were *in* nature and mortals, their presence should be felt viscerally. The brilliant section that depicts the soul as a "palimpsest" supports this commingling of the divine and earthly: man, Aurora writes, is "born in ignorance," his "spirit-insight dulled / And crossed by his sensations." But at times in the midst of mundane life, he is "quicken[ed]" with fleeting "oracles of vital Deity." Thus, she proclaims that the soul is a "palimpsest, a prophet's holograph / Defiled, erased and covered by a monk's,— / The apocalypse, by a Longus! poring on / Which obscene text, we may discern perhaps / Some fair, fine trace of what was written once, / Some upstroke of an alpha and omega / Expressing the old scripture (815–32).

As Barrett's alter ego asserts here, the material self is shot through with divine inklings, and the very intermingling of the celestial and the obscene seems to be the necessary dynamic that creates the divine soul during its apprenticeship on earth. Thus, contrary to Milman's views of women and divinity, in *Aurora Leigh* it is possible to see an obscene siren such as Lady Waldemar as a potential palimpsest through which the goddess expresses her dynamic, loving womanhood, pompous breasts and all. Even if Aurora sees Waldemar as her sinister enemy, according to her own idealistic philosophy, the naughty Lady may simply need more simmering before attaining a higher spiritual level.

Concomitant to troping the mortal soul as a palimpsest, Aurora ponders how the finite enwraps the Infinite: "What, if even God / Were chiefly God by living out Himself / To an individualism of the Infinite, / Eterne, intense profuse—still throwing up / The golden spray of multitudinous worlds / In measure to the proclive weight and rush / Of His inner nature,—the spontaneous love / Still proof and outflow of spontaneous life?" (3:750–57) This is one of Barrett's most articulate inscriptions of the male Christian God and His desire. Putting pressure on language to make the inherent "nature" of this usually individualized monolithic God more extensive, Barrett suggests that He naturally seeks "spontaneous" generation of "multitudinous" forms of life, including "godheads."

Hence, it is appropriate that Aurora notes that when she is filled with the divine afflatus, it is as though Zeus has "set me in the Olympian roar and round / Of luminous faces for a cup-bearer, / To keep the mouths of all the godheads moist / For everlasting laughters,—I myself / Half drunk across the beaker with their eyes!" (1:922–26). Comprehending, describing, and existing in a world that encompasses all the godheads *is* Barrett's answer to mother-god-want. Indeed, describing Marian's understanding of God, Aurora limns the deity's "grand blind Love" as coming from "a skyey father and mother both in one" (3:898–99). Even the Christian God's proclivities are, then, amorphous and divisible, multitudinous and gender bending.[12]

As noted earlier, Barrett is cognizant that God is a metaphor and that humans create what God might be: thus, not only are humans Gods in process, but they also create that entity. Insisting on the multeity of divinity, Barrett both deconstructs and clings to the trope of the Christian God as a numinous manifestation of the Real. As Barrett's alter ego preaches, nature cannot exist without the spiritual, just as the spiritual requires the sensuous. Thus mortals must "firmly" grasp the "natural" in order to "pierce through, / With eyes immortal, to the antetype." This antetype is usually thought of as the "ideal," but Aurora argues that it should be "called the real, / And certain to be called so presently / When things shall have their names" (7:779–85). God, she exults, is just as real as humans and should be wrestled to the earth by mortals every day. The reality of God cannot be known, she argues, until humanity learns to name things by their real names. The lesson is clear: the poet's prophetic metaphors open our vision to the divine enveloped within the mundane. It is as though the "skyey father and mother both in one" is incapable of articulating its reality except through the poet-prophet, who is invested with both the divine and the mortal, the male and the female, the natural and the man-made.

Barrett's tendency to image God as gender bending carries over into her descriptions of the male and female characters in the poem. Barrett's portrayals underscore her sense that the universe is mutable and multitudinous rather than stable and unified, and the protrayals are redolent of Julian of Norwich's accounts of a multi-gendered god. At one point, Aurora describes Romney as a "male Iphigenia" bound by the inability to think differently about gender, Aurora's career as a poet, and Victorian conventions about marriage. In the same vein, at the end of the poem Aurora figures her beloved as the Angel in the House (2:779; 9:369). The heroine also repeatedly refers to herself as a man, in one case boldly saying to Romney, "You face, to-day, / A man who wants instruction, mark me, not / A woman who wants protection" (2:1061–63; see also 7:213). Similarly, when attempting to repress her love for Romney, Aurora commands herself to "Let him pass. I'm not too much / A woman, not to be a man for once / And bury all my Dead like Alaric" (7:984–86). The text suggests, too, that the male god Phoebus Apollo is the soul within Aurora's soul, and, upending gendered stereotypes, Romney avers at the end of the poem that he is the earth that depends upon the nourishment of Aurora's sun (5:414; 9:907–912).

Deconstructing gender categories, Aurora also takes on the tiresome stereotype that women are changeable, asserting boldly that men are the true chameleons: "But a man— / Note men!—they are but women after all, /

As women are but Auroras!—there are men / Born tender, apt to pale at a trodden worm" (7:1016–19). Stepping from behind a protective mask, Aurora directly chastises men for their centuries-old misogynistic depictions of women as unpredictable and unstable. In a time when men could get away with making all manner of outrageous public statements about women and gender roles, Barrett Browning's Aurora boldly exclaims that she will define what men are, and, seemingly unafraid of the very real consequences, she demands that men listen—"Note men!" Thus, Aurora repeatedly figures herself as a kind of Pope Joan (or Joanna Southcott) at the head of her own church. Like a seer, she leads her followers to remember the Infinite Mother behind and in all things. At the same time, she limns herself as having the soul of a male god while appealing directly to both men and women to hear her revelations about the gender of deity and the deconstruction of gender. Asserting that gender constantly changes, Barrett implies that polytheism duplicates the polyvalent qualities of humans who should not be labeled under the two puny categories of "male" and "female."[13]

But what are we, then, to make of Aurora's exclamation at the heart of the epic that the Victorian age no longer needs "half-gods, Panomphaean Joves, / Fauns, Naiads, Tritons, Oreads and the rest," that is to say, the idea that the gods were in the reeds, rivers, and all living things (5:112–13)? One expects at this point that Barrett will draw the protective mask over her heretical theology and point to the monotheistic, monological Christian God as the answer to the modern crisis of faith. Instead, she guides the reader's attention back to Mother Nature, or mother-god-want. She explains:

> See the earth,
> The body of our body, the green earth,
> Indubitably human like this flesh
> And these articulated veins through which
> Our heart drives blood. There's not a flower of spring
> That dies ere June, but vaunts itself allied
> By issue and symbol, by significance
> And correspondence, to that spirit-world
> Outside the limits of our space and time,
> Whereto we are bound." (116–25)

Here Barrett figures *Nature* as the liminal entry point between the divine and material, the abstract and particular, the human and divine, the male and female. This Romantic image of Mother Nature also figures the earth as the embodied form of a spirit world that just seems to be only a binary opposite to man's material condition. This understanding of nature accompanies Aurora's theory of poetry set forth in the middle of Book V, just a few lines after the paean to nature. In this instance, Aurora compresses her theory in the credo that "poets should / Exert a double vision; should have eyes / To see near things as comprehensively / As if afar they took their point of sight, / And distant things as intimately deep / As if they touched them" (183–88). Here again, Barrett concludes that a complex, multiform universe could be imagined only by a titanic, protean, desiring entity that yearns toward complexity, spontaneity, and double vision.

Aurora's double vision culminates in what I believe is the most astonishing image in the text: the "full-veined, heaving, double-breasted Age: / That, when the next shall come, the men of that / May touch the impress with reverent hand, and say / 'Behold,—behold the paps we all have sucked! / This bosom seems to beat still, or at least / It sets ours beating: this is living art, / Which thus presents and thus records true life'" (216–22). Marjorie Stone's suggestion that this image retains its shock value even for modern readers is apt, especially since, as Stone shows, at the beginning of the description the reader believes that the passage describes a male breast (751–52). Indeed, the image of the cross-dressing breast is shocking when we realize that the veins that pulsate and the "paps" being sucked are female, even though patriarchy is expert at concealing its milkless breasts. If this epic poem is full of double meanings, its protagonist contends that only a female poet with double vision can make sense of the age's confusing, explosive creativity. If the modern poet-prophet must have the "great gift" of having a "twofold life," s/he must carry the "staggering" weight of being merely mortal at the same time that s/he must "stand up straight as demi-gods" who carry the "intolerable strain and stress / Of the universal" (5:380–86).

In a bizarre image that leads up to the climactic metaphor of the double-breasted age, Barrett essentially suggests that Eve must be recuperated before any New Jerusalem can be established. The trope is startlingly reminiscent of Southcott's restoration of Eve. Contemplating the influence of her own oeuvre, Aurora analogizes lifeless poetry with the earth "shut up / By Adam" as a "mere dumb corpse" in a tomb. In millenarian imagery, Barrett envisions Christ as coming "down" to revive the dead earth by first of all "straighten[ing] out / The leathery tongue turned back into the throat" of the dead corpse. Barrett figures the dead tongue as part of Mother Earth's body. Resurrected, "she"—Mother Earth—"lives, remembers, palpitates / In every limb, aspires in every breath, / Embraces infinite relations" (103–12). In these extremely obscure lines, Barrett reconstitutes the Fall metaphorically as a masculine obliteration of Eve's body and tongue as well as of poetry itself. In this revision of the Genesis text, like Joanna Southcott and Eliza Sharples, the female poet-prophet generates a Revelation of her own, in which the Second Coming restores the Word, the female tongue (and the female "Earth" and "Age") to their original divine essence. I would argue, then, that in the famous "paps" imagery that follows this restoration of Eve, female poetry, and Mother Nature's dead tongue, Barrett consolidates the radical image of the feminization of the age with the coming of a female messiah/Eve foretold in the early decades of the nineteenth century.

If, in her artistic credo, Aurora asserts that the poet must look backward as well as forward, Aurora's "full-veined" age looks back to and feeds from the breasts of a previous generation. Indeed, the Amazon-like Victorian age with its bursting, effulgent paps had its grandmothers who imaged a masterful Eve and a potent female Messiah who would initiate the secular and spiritual millennium to which Barrett Browning looks forward. As with Southcott and Sharples, Barrett so closely aligns her female image of the age and its revolutions with the prophet who initiates and voices visions that it is impossible to separate them. Indeed, the poet-preacher-prophets Southcott, Sharples, and Barrett are immediately and always incorporated in the epic female mythoi they create. In other words, these female prophets virtually become the symbolic goddesses they recreate in the form of Eve, Isis, and the double-breasted age, respectively.

But we must wonder where mother-god-want disappears when Aurora links the poet directly with a Heavenly Father. In an ecstatic prayer, Aurora cries, "O my God, my God, / O supreme Artist, who as sole return / For all the cosmic wonder of Thy work, / Demandest of us just a word . . . a name, / 'My Father!'" (434–38). In terms of the multivalent credo Barrett Browning articulates throughout the epic, this heavenly "Father" must link back to the "Infinite" "paps" that begin the poem and that attain their climactic meaning in the section on the "double-breasted" age. This extraordinary depiction of the age might also connect with the female savior figure imagined by millenarians and radical socialist feminists who preceded or were contemporaneous with Barrett Browning. Mary Carpenter contends that Aurora Leigh seems to have vestiges of the "woman clothed with the sun," which would also bear connections with the millenarian Southcott, who claimed to be that feminine incarnation of God ("Romola" 116). When Aurora reiterates her belief that divinity demands to be named, she suggests her own power over the divine, because as poet she is the master of naming, just as she has given life to the female tongue that had been buried by Adam. In addition, the necessity of naming returns the reader to the metaphorical nature of God: the Creator must be named but cannot name itself, and even the naming cannot capture the effulgence of God.

Barrett uses polytheistic imagery to design the relationship between the metaphorical divinity and the metaphor-creating poet. In a violent depiction, she limns the prophetess at Delphi receiving the divine word: "the god comes down as fierce / As twenty bloodhounds, shakes you, strangles you, / Until the oracular shriek shall ooze in froth!" (5:943–45) As is seen throughout this text, if the Word is what God brings, only the poet gives it birth and articulation. It should be noted that there is a messianic cast to the process described, for God allows the self-sacrificing poet to be mangled and torn so that humankind will have access to the Word. Since this God is figured as male and the poet as female, there is an evocation of rape leading to a forced orgasmic "oracular shriek." Because she is using the tropes of Greek mythology, Barrett is all but forced to see this merging of the divine and mortal as a confluence of the human female/Leda and the male God/swan. Language—and gender ideology—is, at this moment, uncontrollably violent. But Barrett takes heart that the female poet's double vision and double breasts invoke a double sacrifice producing more meaning and power than are available from patriarchal Christianity's rigid notions. And in terms of Barrett's powerful aesthetic and potent sense of self, this description is an *image* that the gender-bending poet may transform in future incarnations.

The lower-class Marian, of course, is subject to a kind of extended gang rape throughout the text, a subliminal representation of the effects of patriarchy on women. Like the utopian feminists who decried the socioeconomic indignities of marriage just as they condemned the destructive inequities of the class system, Barrett Browning intimates that religion is beneficial only if it actually makes a difference in the material lives of human beings. In regard to the material conditions of England as the first modern capitalist society, just as Aurora Leigh articulates and navigates the crisis of faith, the problem of the Real, and the Woman Question, Barrett Browning's epic also seeks to answer the Condition of England question. In *Essays on the Greek Christian Poets,* Barrett argues that God can be found everywhere: "In the loudest hum of your ma- [page break] chinery, in the dunnest volume of your steam, in the foulest street of your city" (206–7).

Thus Barrett suggests that the problem of life on "the foulest street" can be solved by marrying the lower and upper classes—not by conjoining Romney and Marian, but by uniting Marian (a "figurative Madonna") and Aurora as sisters (LaMonaca 148). As the protagonist exhorts Marian, "I being born / What men call noble, and you, issued from / The noble people,—though the tyrannous sword / Which pierced Christ's heart, has cleft the world in twain / 'Twixt class and class, opposing rich to poor, / Shall *we* keep parted? Not so. Let us lean / And strain together rather, each to each, / Compress the red lips of this gaping wound / As far as two souls can,—ay, lean and league, / I from my superabundance,—from your want / You, joining in a protest 'gainst the wrong / On both sides" (4:120–31).

In this naïve, middle-class Victorian approach, Aurora seeks an individualized Romantic response to class inequality rather than a systemic alteration of class structure. Nevertheless, the metaphor carries a shocking alternative. Perhaps Barrett thought that the imagery of gender bending via homoeroticism was an exact analogy of the democratization of the classes. In other words, the "strain[ing] together" of two women from vastly different ranks literally sutures the "red lips" of the "gaping wound" of class warfare as though their own lips—in Irigaray's double sense—were compressed together in erotic unity. As with Aurora's self-sacrificing submission to rape in order to attain control of the Word, Barrett suggests that in order to effect class harmony, Aurora's flights into the abstract Ideal must accompany entry into the obscene hell of Victorian poverty in order for her spirituality to have real consequences. Trudging into the backstreets of the slum Marion inhabits, Aurora exults that she is a savior to the melodramatically downtrodden Marion, just as Barrett's double-breasted Amazon revels in being part of and succoring the debased humanity inhabiting gritty, capitalized culture.

In this scenario Barrett sounds much like the socialist utopians in her insistence that female saviors must accompany God into the "hell" of the gritty streets inhabited by so many Victorians. Barrett's graphic consideration of the homoerotic as part of this suturing is in keeping with her polymorphous descriptions of gender and the godheads, for she recognizes that sexuality might be as infinitely variable as the individual characteristics available to each human being. In the spirit of making genealogical connections between feminists, Christine Chaney argues that *Aurora Leigh* "achieves both cross-generic and crossgenerational connections by providing a hybrid textual link" between "the polemical strategies of Wollstonecraft's self-narration and the gendered subjectivity of Woolf's fiction" (793–94). In the homoerotic imagery of this particular scene, Barrett also boldly engages in cross-sexuality.

This insistence on crossing the actual threshold of Victorian slums and violating the boundaries of aesthetic decorum also underwrites Robert Owen's English brand of socialism. More often than one would expect, Owen's straining after the numinous is startlingly similar to Aurora's yearning toward Marion. The Owenite journals *The Crisis* and *The New Moral World* boldly asserted that religion has no legitimacy unless it encourages its devotees to immerse themselves in the material needs of the age. For example, in 1834 in an article titled "Sunday Evening," Owen could have been preaching from the pulpit when he proclaimed, "The second coming of Christ" announces the truth that there can be no "'peace on earth and goodwill to man,'" if one does not "'love his neighbour as himself'" (3). In the same sermon, Owen earnestly implores his audience to live up to the Christian ideal by imagining if not experiencing the material conditions of their poor neighbors. He asks, for example, "Will the followers of the 'Benevolent Jesus of Nazareth' stand still, and adhere to olden times, when it was stated that men, for a season, owing to their ignorance or partial blindness, were compelled to see as through a glass, darkly?" Like a prophet, he solicits his listeners to succor those who "are daily dying of famine around us." Pleading with his listeners to help these brothers and sisters so that there "shall be no wailing or repining in our streets," Owen calls for an end to "ignorance," "poverty," and "crime" ("Sunday Evening" 3).

Using biblical poetics to make political points, the radical Owen, like Barrett Browning, deployed a discourse that pulses with moral affect, making the classes understand the material effects of the Industrial Revolution on the individual body and body politic. Like all writers of the time who saw something sinister in rising capitalism, including Dickens, Mayhew, Carlyle, and the radical socialist feminists, Owen illustrated how capitalism's elision of Christian love resulted in the loss of the real self, making for a society of soulless souls. Thus, both the poet-prophet Aurora and the political prophet Owen utilized Christian imagery for much the same purpose. Both insisted that Christians should live up to the theology they honor with their lips but too often reject in their daily actions. They wanted nothing less than that Christians truly live according to the Christian beatitudes about succoring the poor and needy. Hence, Barrett shared with early nineteenth-century feminist utopians the belief that poetic language resurrects Christianity's own radical commitment to the poor and necessarily makes its metaphysics palpable through the actual political work of creating a paradise on earth for all humanity.

Barrett Browning might be expected, then, to applaud the socialist agenda. In 1837 in youthful bravado she declared that while her father and brothers went "the full length of radicalism," she went "so much beyond them into republican depths" (*Letters to MRM* 1:25). Whether Barrett knew of individual early nineteenth-century feminist socialists and millenarians is unclear, although it only makes sense that if she had read of their attempts to speak as empowered prophets about gender-bending god(s), she would have been most interested. In any case, she certainly had kept up to date on

Fourierism, socialism, and class agitation: witness her letters and the internal evidence of *Aurora Leigh*. Given her own progressive politics—she was democratic, anti-slavery, pro–Reform Bill, and pro-Risorgimento—Barrett was well versed in general about the utopian politics of the age (see Lewis on Barrett's politics).[14]

Her aesthetic also would seem to support Owenite principles, for she writes that "*wherever there is room for* HUMAN FEELING *to act, there is room for* POETICAL FEELING *to act*. We cant separate our humanity from our poetry—nor, when they are together, can we say or at least prove, that humanity looking downward has a fairer aspect than humanity looking towards God. I am afraid that the matter with some of us, may be resolved into our not considering religion a subject of *feeling*, of real warm emotion & feeling—but of creed & form & necessity. If we feel, it is wrong to show that we feel!—& this, only in religion!" (142). As Barrett keenly understands, it was offensive to the English to emote publically about religion. Thus, whatever route the utopian radicals took in their hortatory engagements with Christianity—either decrying it as superstition or demanding that it live up to its ideal of loving one's neighbor—they could not help transgressing the taboo about not speaking with "real warm emotion" about religion. One would imagine that if Barrett had read some of the above-quoted excerpts from Owen, she would have recognized the deep feeling he seems to have had about religion fulfilling its obligation to transcend mere cant.

Nevertheless, given Barrett's middle-class status, it should be no surprise that *Aurora Leigh* derides Romney's Fourierist phalansteries, because, as Aurora explains, Fourier ostensibly eschewed the arts as a force for healing the class divide. "Your Fouriers failed," she avows, "Because not poets enough to understand" that "life develops from within" (2:483–85). Indeed, she ridicules Lady Waldemar's reading of the socialists "Fourier," "Proudhon, Considerant, and Louis Blanc, / With various others of his socialists" (3:584–86). More importantly, the epic ends with Romney admitting to his beloved that the socialists he believed in were at best ineffectual and at worst detrimental to the interests of the poor.

I suggest that this confession is a necessary part of his declaration of love—and submission—to Aurora. In other words, because he has so thoroughly subordinated the feminine in his politics, at this crucial point, when the epic becomes a domestic novel, he must acknowledge her poetics as superior to masculinist socialist rhetoric. Thus, not only is Romney debilitated by his blindness; he almost grovels when confessing that "Fourier's void," "Comte absurd, and Cabet, puerile" (9:868–69). When Romney rejects the political system to which he has given his life, it is a more emasculating prophylaxis than the blindness that has been engineered for him in the denouement.[15]

One has to wonder how Barrett Browning's epic would have changed had her Romney been reading Sharples, Wright, or even Southcott. In any case, Romney's capitulation is part and parcel of Barrett's aesthetic argument. She needs to show that resolving the degrading effects of poverty through a poetry that would inspire its readers to actually save the lower classes one Marian at a time is far more effective and emotionally and spiritually authentic than the Fourierism she depicts as the enervating antagonist of her poetry and art. In a letter to Isa Blagden, written in 1850, Barrett declared, "If Fourierism could be realised (which it surely cannot) out of a dream, the destinies of our race would shrivel up under the unnatural heat, and human nature would, in my mind, be desecrated and dishonored. . . . Genius is always individual" (qtd. in Dalley 529). In another epistle, she reviled socialism because it supposedly imposed conformity and thus undermined the genius as *rara avis*. "I love liberty so intensely," Barrett exclaimed in 1850, "that I hate Socialism." She adds that socialism is "the most desecrating & dishonoring to Humanity, of all creeds," and melodramatically claims that she would rather live "under the absolutism of Nicolas of Russia, than in a Fourier-machine, with my individuality sucked out of me by a social airpump" (*Letters to MRM* 3:302). Seeing herself as filled with the divine afflatus, Barrett intimates that her cultural role would be literally deflated by a politics that ostensibly sucked away the essence of artistic genius.

Lana L. Dalley observes that Barrett's "rejection of socialism is couched in the vocabulary of liberal economic theory, particularly in its emphasis on the individual and the contention that there can be no 'progress without struggle'" (529). Likewise, Linda Lewis remarks that Barrett's was a "hypothetical Christian ideal in which the rich will be inspired by love to part with their world's goods to feed the poor" (130). But Aurora and Barrett's condemnation of Fourierism also signifies that class struggle must be filtered first through the aesthetic of the individual genius before it can be considered in systemic sociopolitical terms. It is not just that the socialists are not poets; Barrett's conviction that poetry is where God is compels her belief that the poet must have the first and last Word about love, class issues, and the relations between the genders. Thus Barrett's alter ego is insulted that Romney would consult political writers about the Condition of England before consulting her own poetic, godlike intellect. Likewise, she cannot imagine a hybrid form of writing that might be political and aesthetic except the writing composed by legitimate, recognized poets like herself. Barrett's faith in the fluid, amorphous, and permeable thus collapses at the moment that she declares the monolithic superiority of her vocation and her voice.

In fact, binary logic takes over when Aurora claims that her genius cancels out other, would-be hierophantic tongues, and Barrett Browning protests too much regarding Aurora's efforts to establish poetry as more powerful and essential to political reform than the rhetoric of political reform itself. After all, like Barrett, the radical utopians knew they needed a new language that would help them establish their claims and have the kind of influence that changes class attitudes. But although she mixes genres in *Aurora Leigh,* Barrett has little taste for such hybridity in radical socialists, whom she sees more as artistic than as political enemies. Although she uses what were considered vulgar tropes in her narrative (*Blackwood's Edinburgh Magazine* suggests that her images are "hideous," "revolting," and "calculated to disgust"), Barrett could not accept the new language developed by socialists such as Owen who created hybrid imagery and themes in conjugations similar to her own ("MRS. BARRETT BROWNING-AURORA LEIGH" 33–34).

Hence, although at the end of the epic, Romney encourages Aurora to put her "woman's lip" to the "clarion" and "blow all class-walls level as Jericho's / past Jordan" so as to bring about the "new oeconomies" and "new societies" that God requires to "make all new," the millennial rhetoric hinges upon Aurora's individual(ist) voice (9:929–33, 947–48). In the final lines, the poet-prophet-goddess Aurora conceptually builds the millennial New Jerusalem as she names and sees the jewels that are its foundations: "jasper," "chalcedony," "amethyst," and "sapphire" (962–64; Rev. 21:19–20). Like Southcott and Sharples, who rebuked male political systems in favor of female rule, Aurora co-opts from Romney the male right to be a seer because his political systems have been feeble and inadequate. She also seems to bury the radical tongues of the grandmothers in order to give precedence to her own voice, in an age that too often demeaned the female writer.

But it would be too harsh to end with such a critique. I suggest, instead, that the reader must confront *Aurora Leigh* with a kind of double vision. We can see, for example, that Aurora and Barrett spoke like the radical women who had informed secular and spiritual millenarian aspirations with visions of an omnipotent Eve and a commanding, unconditionally loving female savior. But Barrett was also righting and rewriting history in her condemnation of masculine socialist schemes for changing the world. It is as though she were demanding that the fathers of socialism give credence to female tongues instead of deriding them as Romney had inadvertently done. Ironically, the virtual erasure of earlier radical feminist voices from the historical record—she did not seem to have heard of them—underwrites Barrett's fierce dedication to the recuperation of female tongues. Seeing herself as the lone female poet who could compete with political and poetic Christian and socialist (fore)fathers, Barrett did not see the shoulders upon which she stood—those of the radical female political figures who preceded her and helped to make her protofeminist rhetoric possible.

This insight must be tempered by the recognition that few twenty-first-century feminists have heard of or acknowledged these same grandmothers, who are still there to be recuperated. In terms of Victorian protofeminists, it may be that Barrett's poetic ambitions and the profoundly misogynist milieu within which she lived dictated that she see Aurora's poetry as originary and unique rather than following upon an earlier, if muffled, radical female politics. Of necessity, then, eliding the feminist radical history that comes before Aurora's invention of a New Jerusalem, Barrett's inimitable epic, nevertheless, retains its polytheistic, millenial inclinations. With its scandalous, stark imagery of Eve and Mother Nature's tongue (Word) buried by the old Adam and the female paps that remind the reader of the universe's founding feminine principle, *Aurora Leigh* masks *and* circulates the voices of its radical grandmothers.

5

Eve, the Female Messiah, and the Virgin in Florence Nightingale's Personal and Public Papers

> Dreamed in the very face of God . . .
>
> —Florence Nightingale, Nightingale Papers XII, 17 Janvier 1850, *NP* 45846
>
> Nightingale subverts a fundamental Western myth—that of God's incarnation as man—by suggesting God's alternative incarnation as woman.
>
> —Ruth Y. Jenkins, "Rewriting Female Subjectivity" 24

IN 1833 the Owenite journal *The Crisis* published a letter from a feminist socialist who invoked Cassandra in her call for women's rights. Using the pseudonym "Concordia," the writer took Owen to task for presuming that he could institute laws in favor of equality without consulting women in the process. She explained that men would not succeed in legislating the rights of females, because woman "has always been forgotten when the work of legislation has been performing." Thus, fair legislation could not be enacted "until woman shall be permitted to have a voice in all enactments that concern her; until, in short, she shall be permitted to *legislate for herself*" (Concordia 254). Prior to Harriet Taylor's and John Stuart Mill's famous arguments for women's rights, Concordia reasoned that women had been oppressed for so long that they did not know their own feelings. As a result, before any laws could be considered, woman would need to become acculturated to examining her desires and discovering where the "false arrangements of society have grievously led her" (255). Despite presenting a powerful argument, Concordia feared that her words would be ignored, and she herself viewed as a "mere Cassandra" (254).[1]

Almost three decades later, a more famous Cassandra[2] wrote similarly about women's oppression when Florence Nightingale inscribed her feminist masterpiece, "Cassandra," which insists that political reforms must take account of the social construction of women.[3] Noting that "the next Christ will perhaps be a female Christ," Nightingale was not sanguine about the prospect because there is no "woman who looks like a female Christ," nor is there a female John the Baptist "to go before her and prepare the hearts and minds for her" ("Cassandra," in *Suggestions* 408). In this remarkable political analysis, Nightingale complains that it was impossible to produce a female savior because women were educated to ignore their god-given talents and instead urged to become social butterflies.

Nightingale also implied that even if there were a female messiah ready to come forth, patriarchal Victorian society scarcely took women's spiritual, intellectual, or political thoughts seriously. Hence, Nightingale suggested that although a female messiah might have been in their midst, Victorians would not have known her if they saw her or heard her speak. As with Concordia–Cassandra, who argued that progressive legislation must consider the effects on women because women are constructed differently and thus have different realities than men, Nightingale suggested that a culture's beliefs about deity affect women's intellectual, political, and spiritual potential.

Seeking genealogical connections between modern feminists and their forebears, Elaine Showalter has claimed, of course, that Nightingale's "Cassandra" provides the missing link between the feminist works of Mary Wollstonecraft and Virginia Woolf ("Florence Nightingale's Feminist Complaint" 396). I suggest, however, that Nightingale's rhetoric harks back more to late eighteenth- and early nineteenth-century female millenarians and socialist feminists like Concordia than to the more famous Wollstonecraft, who, in her Deist leanings, never recuperated Eve or imagined a female messiah as a means of invoking the rights of women. And, although Wollstonecraft certainly supported the French Revolution and reviled the English class system, unlike the millenarians and socialist feminists, she did not link progressive reforms with a material or symbolic religious utopia.

As I shall argue in this chapter, while Nightingale may not seem a protofeminist, in many ways her theological interrogation of gender and class politics often reverberates with barely masked radical intensity worthy of

Southcott and Sharples. In addition, there are strong historical and rhetorical commonalities between the female millenarians, feminist socialists, and Nightingale, and I conclude that Nightingale most likely knew of these grandmothers' radical incarnations of Eve and the female savior. Further, I will show that although Nightingale deeply venerated the Christian Father in Heaven, her construction of deity is hardly conventional, for she also believed in pagan, non-Christian mysticism and exhibited a poststructural willingness to play with the concept of the divine. Determined to be a prophet and theologian in her own right, Nightingale recalled the visions and politics of her radical grandmothers, ultimately imagining powerful emanations of Eve, the female messiah, and the Virgin Mary that hint at her own aspirations to be these divine entities.

Nightingale's contribution to nineteenth-century revisions of deity is always underwritten by her belief that women's voices were not included in the historical record of theological debate. It is no surprise that she vigorously attempted to rectify this lack. A letter to her father in 1846 illustrates her anguish about the absence of female voices in Church history. "Why," she wonders, "cannot a woman follow abstractions like a man? has she less imagination, less intellect . . . less religion than a man? I think not. . . . She has never, with the exception perhaps of Deborah, the Virgin, & the Mère Angélique, been deemed a fitting vessel for the Spirit of God—she has never received the spark of inspiration" (*Ever Yours* 30). Distressed that the Virgin Mary's words were the only ones spoken by a woman who had become universal, she derides the way Victorian middle- and upper-class women were educated to focus their conversations narrowly on their own mundane lives rather than on anything approaching theoretical rumination. In 1846 Nightingale passionately insisted as well that her culture should view woman as a "worthy House for the Spirit of Truth," and women's voices as "worthy" to "proclaim the service of the Kingdom of God" (30).

Deeming herself a credible recipient of divine inspiration, Nightingale had trancelike epiphanies or "call[s]" on a regular basis throughout her life, beginning "as early as her sixth year" (Cook 1:15).[4] Interactions with her Voice were concerned with understanding the nature of perfection and deity, establishing nursing as a respectable career for women and making governments provide for the health of their citizens. Putting herself forward as a sage, Nightingale had no qualms about her gender when working on an essay titled "What is the Character of God?" Its thesis was that according to God's plan, "every one of us is on the way to progress towards perfection, i.e. happiness" (17 August 1871, *NP* 45783: f.258; qtd. in *Ever Yours* 274). Nightingale also shed false feminine modesty in a letter to Julius Mohl in

1873 in which she asserted that "nothing solaces me so much as to write upon the Laws of the Moral World; especially as exemplifying, if possible, the character of a Perfect God, in bringing us to perfection thro' them in eternity" (351). The insistent moral import of her writing and her sense that women should be the instruments for and voices of God's work of perfecting human beings suggests that Nightingale did have ambitions to be a prophet.

Finding that her own generation might not attach significance to her theological discourse, perhaps she hoped that her written disquisitions on God would be discovered and revered after her death, as we know that those of her feminist "Cassandra" have been. But what kind of religion did Nightingale profess and prophesy? Mary Keele points out that Nightingale's was a syncretic, open-minded approach to spirituality that was uncommon for her time and may have been partially due to her father's Unitarian background, although her conventional mother ultimately decided to raise her daughters in the Church of England (*FN in Rome* xvi). Nightingale's deep interest in every kind of spiritual mysticism led her to many of the world's religions. "[Y]ou must go to Mahometanism, to Buddhism, to the East, to the Sufis & Fakirs, to Pantheism," for the "right growth of mysticism," she asserted in March 1853 (Calabria and Macrae, eds., *Suggestions for Thought,* xiii). Like Barrett Browning, she also disavowed sectarianism, remarking that God's truth should not "be narrowed and confined to one book, or one nation" (Cook 1:72). Nightingale's letter to Miss Blanche Smith in 1847 illustrates her more-than-broad Church view that the Mideast was a place "where one can be Christian in the morning and Pagan in the afternoon" (*FN in Rome* 134).

Catholic in her religious studies, she read a range of authors, including Plato, the Gnostics, Spinoza, Darwin, Confucius, John S. Mill, Augustine, Erasmus, Catherine of Sienna, and Islamic and Egyptian religions tomes. Nightingale also viewed Osiris as a sacred being, and, of early Egyptian religion, she exulted in her diary in 1850 that in the temples of Ramses II she "felt more *at home,* perhaps, than in any place of worship" (qtd. in Calabria, *FN in Egypt* 23). Indeed, in 1850 she wrote that her trip to Egypt was a "spiritual and intellectual whirlwind" (20 July 1850, *NP* 45846). It is fascinating, then, to learn that Nightingale read Brontë's *Shirley* during the trip to Egypt, for while imbibing Brontë's depiction of a titanic Eve, Nightingale herself was absorbed in intense repartee with God about her own spiritual and intellectual life as a woman (10 Fevrier 1850 *NP* 45846). As I will show presently, like Brontë she also recuperated Eve.

Central to Nightingale's theology was the unorthodox belief that mortal life was a process of attaining perfection and becoming god. Nightingale's journals indicate that during her visit to Egypt, she read and repeatedly referred to Hermes Trismegistus. In Nightingale's words, Hermes Trismegistus theorized that the soul "went through several mystic regions before it began again the course of its transformations—those transformations, which only meant the trials, the stages which the divine emanation has to go through before arriving at perfection" (qtd. in Calabria, *FN in Egypt* 29). In the diary kept during her time in Egypt, Nightingale often tersely lists her daily doings. For example, she writes on "Janvier 21, 1850," "Wrote Hermes Trismegistus letter." One wonders if she mistakenly penned "wrote" instead of "read" in a remarkable Freudian slip of the tongue (*NP* 45846). On the other hand, if she intended the word "wrote," we are caught between two extraordinary interpretations of her word choice: she was either writing *to* the long-dead pagan mystic or writing *for* him—with either feat being tantalizing. Neither interpretation is beyond Nightingale's confident sense of herself as a recipient and voice for sacred mysteries (*NP* 45846).

It is worth citing extensively from a letter Nightingale wrote on New Year's Eve 1847 to show how confidently interrogatory her spirituality was and to understand how insignificant the Christian sects were in her theology:

> Are you afraid that I am becoming a Roman Catholic? I might . . . , if there had been anything in me for Roman Catholicism to lay hold of, but I was not a Protestant before. Protestantism is confining Inspiration to one period, one nation, and one place, . . . and within that period, that nation, and that place of inspiration, allowing you all possible freedom of interpretation and thought. Catholicism allows Inspiration to all times, all nations, and all places . . . , but limits the inspiration of God to herself as its only channel. Can either of these be true? Can the "word" be pinned down to either one period or one church? . . . When the day shall come when our (now so poor, so weak) ideas require *no* form, then people will cease to use the word "My *church*" when they mean "My *religion*," and will not confuse, as now, "My *theology*" with "My *faith*," . . . As the language is to the mind, expressing it, and, by re-action influencing it, so is theology to faith, but God forbid, that we should really degrade faith to be nothing more than language! (*FN in Rome* 155)

Many elements of Nightingale's syncretic theology appear here, including her almost postmodern understanding of the cultural construction of religion and God, although she is unwilling to describe faith as consisting merely of "language." Unwilling to label herself Protestant or Catholic, Nightingale seeks the freedom to intellectually explore and passionately respond to the "inspiration of God" through every channel available. Ironically, too, this passage suggests Nightingale's understanding that by inhabiting such a freethinking position, she is able to attain an even more profoundly felt belief. In this mode of philosophical play, Nightingale recognizes that if God created human beings, they return the favor by continually (re)creating God. Concomitantly, she gives women power to revise theological territory. As Nightingale so presciently remarked, "People must *make* a God till they can *find* one. It has always happened that some have made such a God as could be imagined by them, and others have taken Him from them" (Calabria and Macrae, eds., *Suggestions* 103).

That Nightingale inscribed the following words in her journal further intimates her nuanced appreciation of the human construction of God: "'The problem is to enlarge & raise the notion of God, which for so many ages religious dogmas'" were "'furiously raging to shut up in the narrow limits of symbolism'" (*NP* 45841 f4). Similarly, on New Year's Eve of 1847, she wrote to her father, "All churches are, of course, only more or less unsuccessful attempts to represent the unseen to the mind, to give form to 'things hoped for,' intangible" (qtd. in *FN in Rome* 155). These statements express Nightingale's insight that discourse about God always relies on metaphorical language, although, to her, it is never mere language. Nightingale seems more hopeful than tragic in her comprehension of deity's fictionality and humankind's construction of God. In fact, she seems to believe that being expansive in one's creation of God generates a more generous, sublime soul; likewise, the deity *she* constructs is spacious enough to measure the ambit of every entity in the cosmos.

In addition, Nightingale's God is subject to interrogatory discourse beyond a professional inner circle of narrow-minded Church Fathers, for she insists that divinity be not only available to women's appeals but also subject to their analysis. Nightingale's intimate friend and suitor manqué Benjamin Jowett (who referred to her as "Goddess Athene") remarked Nightingale's obsessive desire to know God coupled with her refusal to define Him concretely (332). "During the ten years & more that I have known you," he complains, "you have repeated to me the expression 'character of God' about 1,100 times, but I cannot say that I have any clear [idea] of what you mean, if you mean anything more than divine perfection" (qtd. in *Ever Yours* 209). Clearly, Nightingale took as much pleasure in monastic devotion to questions about God as she did in the work of nursing, and her refusal to label the divine suggests her attraction to a fluid understanding of subjectivity prototypical of third-wave feminist thinking. It also implies her desire to be schooled in a wide range of theological discourses and her intellectual capacity for remaining in a state of deferral about truth, a state that allowed for Nightingale's almost sensuous delight in protracted spiritual ecstasy.

Nightingale's descriptions of spiritual ecstasy imply that she often apprehended more than a Voice. In a handful of instances she describes seeing God's face, although she coyly masks the experience. In 1879, Nightingale sketched an anomalous interaction with deity in rhetoric that is spontaneous, mystical, and self-consciously artistic. On a tedious draft outline titled "System of Nursing" that hardly captures the reader's attention, at the bottom of the page an interruption appears, as though *in medias res*, with no indication of when it was written or how it relates to the outline at the top of the page. The inscription reads: "Love sprang up under her steps But now she '*knows*' and '*sees*' that "'sight of sights,' the 'unveiled majesty of God She has entered in" (*NP* 45750 f.163). In both instances, the writing is almost certainly in Nightingale's hand, although the passage at the bottom of the page is not as neatly set to paper, as though it were inscribed while she was trying to remember a sudden thought before it faded completely. The matter at the end of the page is reminiscent of Brontë's trances in content as well as lack of punctuation in the impulsiveness of the script. It is as if Nightingale had been working on a mundane project and was suddenly transported by an epiphany. Yet the quoted passages in her transcription of the vision reveal that she may have been comparing her vision with other renditions of the ultimate mystical experience. Re-presenting the ecstatic moment in self-reflexive language registering her lack of inhibitions, Nightingale is absolutely in control of the scene of divine *jouissance*.

This transcription is reminiscent of a scene in "Cassandra" describing the visionary protagonist. She "had seen the face of God," wrote Nightingale, and "that face was Love—love like the human, only deeper, deeper—tenderer, lovelier, stronger. She could not recall what she had seen or how she had known it; but the conviction remained that she had seen his face, & that it was infinitely beautiful" (*NP* 45844 f.7). This provocative passage allows the reader to experience the effects of Nightingale's decision to change "Cassandra" from a first-person autobiography to a third-person fictional narrative (see Showalter, "Florence Nightingale's"). The narrator's hazy identity and the "she" who is having the experience magnify and shroud the epiphanic episode. While the confusion about what is actually seen muddies the identity of the narrator, deity, and recipient of the vision, the ambiguity distances the would-be reader from the mystical revelation and creates a desire for the full disclosure *of* God.

In "Cassandra" the primal voice in the mangled manuscript cries out for the author's face to be revealed from behind the feeble mask of the fictional Nofriari. Re-presented as a fictional narrative based on Nightingale's experiences, the passage defies generic labels—it is both fiction and mystic revelation, much like Brontë's sutured fair copy of Shirley's vision of Eve. Nightingale makes the female writer, rather than God, the powerful creator of the sacred scene, although her fictional alter ego, Nofriari, swoons like a neurasthenic Victorian heroine. Thus, in contrast to Showalter, I suggest that even if the revised "Cassandra" is disjointed and self-conflicted, it still illustrates Nightingale's self-conscious control of the rapturous scene, which is in keeping with her belief that women could create their own God, their own religion, and their own perfection.

In fact, although Nightingale transcribed a dialogue with deity in April 1888 that includes her plea, "O God I throw the whole charge of my life upon Thee. Will Thou accept it?" and God answers, "Yes: but then you must be as if you were not," Nightingale at times prescribes rather than prophecies God's actions as though exasperated with an impractical or inefficient deity (*NP* 45844 f.35). What, for example, is the use of a God one cannot talk to, she wonders. Hence, in Nightingale's religion the boundaries between the self and the divine are thin, for it is in the egalitarian relation with deity as much as the identity of deity that human perfection occurs. Reminiscent of the Beguine nuns, Nightingale avows that God "communicates with us by His nature actually becoming ours," with the agent of the "becoming" being both human and divine (*NP* 45840 f.60).

In another instance, Nightingale amended the Lord's Prayer to make it an intimate site of communion between equals. Implying that this famous prayer had become banal, she prophetically[5] reinterprets its meaning, averring that "the soul ^ herself ["herself" is above the caret] should be heaven: that Our Father which is in heaven should dwell in her" (*NP* 45841 f.12). In this mystical description, Nightingale insists that religion and spirituality are within the tabernacle of the self and that the soul creates the conditions for deity to be present to and in the self. But in this metaphor, the female soul is procreative, giving space to a rather passive male God. Acting as the fructifying agent, the female soul generates the desire for divinity in a constantly dynamic, relational, soul-making process. In contrast to the biblical Lord's Prayer, then, in Nightingale's version, the female soul becomes the lord and shepherd guiding God to perfect humanity.

This Romantic view of God as in the human breast or as metaphorically part of a generative human process occurs often in Nightingale's thinking. In a dense mystical description, for example, she writes that "God is a spirit— / He creates other spirits— / These spirits create their own casing— / When He throws off the germ, the germ creates its own body, its own material always the same" (*NP* 45845 f.47). In what is essentially a theological mini-discourse, Nightingale accepts the heretical notion that Southcott and Sharples also supported—that is, that human beings participate with God in the salvation of the soul. And, like Southcott, Nightingale's rhetoric makes it difficult to distinguish between the creator and the created.

Just whose "material" is referred to, and what exactly is the relation between the "spirit," "casing," and "germ"? Who, one ultimately wonders, is creating whom in this description of divine creation, for at certain points that which has been created takes over the procreative process. This intimate, self-confident merging of self with God also appears in Nightingale's ecstatic exclamation, "What if He should be in us after all, *& working in us this way? Just this very way of crying out after Him*" (*NP* 45845 f.154). Likewise, when Nightingale writes, "Where shall I find God?" she answers, "In myself. That is the true Mystical Doctrine" (qtd. in Cook 2:233).

Illustrating the Hermetic canon, these statements erase the notion of God as distant, hierarchical, and masculine and focus on the self as in the process of becoming deity. Characterized by rhetorical informality, spontaneity, immediacy, and blissful rapture, Nightingale's dialogues with God suggest her egalitarian approach to the divine. Discarding rote, Nightingale's transcriptions of her prayers use "OG" for the phrase "Oh, God," in a foretelling of modern emoticons and abbreviations like "OMG." Illustrating her sense of what Michael Kalton refers to as "horizontal transcendence" *with* God,[6] Nightingale uses casual rhetoric not to imply her shallow spirituality but rather her long-term familiarity with an entity she spoke to as a peer (187–200).

To call them prayers, even, is erroneous because they achieve a more mutual and intimate immersion in the other than prayer might. Hence, ignoring conventional grammatical practices, Nightingale creates a secret shorthand, illustrating that in her engagements with deity she has become so adept at horizontal transcendence that she—at least temporarily—can achieve the "I AM" of God. If we return to William de Thierry's theology that underwrites much of Beguine mysticism, the God who exclaims "I am who I am" in Ex. 3:14 must be linked with the New Testament statement by Christ, "I am in the Father and the Father is in Me" (John 10:18; qtd. in Brunn and Epiney-Burgard xxvi). In this interpretation, Christianity's aim is for the self to be with/in God and to have God in the self as it moves "*to become what God is*" (Brunn and Epiney-Burgard xxvi).

The form Nightingale's writing takes is as indicative of her yearning to break hierarchical boundaries as is the substance. Consider a memorandum in 1850, which reads, "God called me in the morn & asked me 'Would

I do good for Him, for Him alone without the reputation'" (*NP* 45846). Although there is a sense of profound intimacy in this description, one cannot help feeling that her God is just a phone call away. Similarly, in October 1892, in a shorthand account of her interactions with the divine, Nightingale invited the deity in almost as though He was as close as next door. "Come in, Lord Jesus, Holy Spirit, come into my heart now. drive [*sic*] out self—monstrous self," she writes (*NP* 45844 f.86). On 26 May 1892 comes another visitation:

> You are keeping the Lord waiting—the indwelling God [indwelling love, gentleness, faith, meekness, temperance] that your light may give light to all that are in the house
> Oh come to Jesus now
> Jesus is *here*
> O Father of an Infinite majesty waiting for me. (*NP* 45844 f.79)

Like Sharples, Nightingale insisted that God must be democratized, that, in other words, women, should be able to dialogue—and be taken seriously as theologians—about the deity's ontological meaning. And, like Sharples, Nightingale insisted that God's meaning must have practical effects in the daily lives of the sick and needy. The voluminous inscriptions of Nightingale's prayers indicate her demand that spirituality be linked with making material existence better for the lowly of the world. For instance, when working in India in 1877, she wrote, "OG [Oh God] who makest the stars, the sun, the moon to obey Thee, who makest the beautiful sunrises, can nothing be done for these poor people in the Indian Famine?" (*NP* 45847). In this orison, Nightingale automatically links the transcendent cosmos with the microcosmic site/sight of the forgotten of the world, enjoining God to live up to her activist understanding of Christianity. Likewise, she wrote in her diary in December of 1877, "If it be possible, take this cup from me" (overseeing irrigation projects in India), not because she does not want to work for Indian subalterns but because she felt how impossible it is to achieve success as a private citizen (*NP* 45847). God, she insists, should be actively involved when she edits her practical book for nurses. "O Lord tell me what to say," she pleads, "in this revision of Nursing & Training of Nurses. Tell me, inspire me, direct, control, suggest this day All I should think or do & say" (*NP* 45844). Thus it is no surprise that Nightingale gives short shrift to the earthly titles of men. In feminist revisionism worthy of Sharples, she asserts that a girl who saved two babies from being run over by a train "was a greater preacher of the ways of God than all the Fathers of the Church who ever were born to write" (*NP* 45843 f.262).

In keeping with her political agenda, Nightingale emphasized that God "is always descending into hell" and that "we should always be ready to descend into hell with him" (*NP* 45845 f.6). In the same passage, she refers to prostitutes and convicts as "pioneers," who also repeatedly descend into sites of ultimate suffering (*NP* 45845 f.6). In a sense, then, Nightingale saw no difference between God, the fallen woman, and herself, for all are engaged in the task of savioring, or, as Grace Jantzen explains, being "divine" for others (Jantzen 17; see also E. Johnson 68, 69). In Nightingale's theology, the little girl who saves babies and the prostitute who daily traverses a nightmarish world are equal in their enactment of godness for others. Nightingale boldly wrote, too, that such self-sacrifice should not be seen as subservient, and that she does not believe that God desires docile obedience from believers. "The word '*worship*,'" she exclaims, "seems hardly to express what God wants of us. He does not want to be praised, to be adored, to have his glory sung. . . . What he desires seems to be . . . that we should be one with Him, not prostrate before Him" (qtd. in Calabria, *FN in Egypt* 24). Here, again, Nightingale views God as an equal.

I suggest, too, that Nightingale's catholicity and self-reflexive rhetoric allow an amorphous understanding of divinity that would include dissolution of gender. The ability to remain fluid in her thinking allows Nightingale to create extraordinary metaphors about spiritual progress that elide gender stereotypes. In a description of John S. Mill after his death, Nightingale ascribes to him a godliness that obviates gender binaries. Writing to Edwin Chadwick in 1873, she exclaimed:

> The loss we have in John Stuart Mill is irreparable—I think there must have been a Goddess called "Till Passion of Reason" in olden times: & *he* was that Goddess returned in the flesh to life. And he would not at all have considered the gender humiliating. For he was like neither man nor woman—but he was Wisdom "thrilling" with emotion to his fingers "ends" (which last was truly said of him)—impassioned Reason—or reasonable Passion—in the sense which one supposes the Greeks had in their mind when they made Wisdom a Woman. Or shall we call him Sancta Sophia? (*Ever Yours* 343)

In this passage, Nightingale's is almost a mystical voice revealing the very mystery and ambiguity of gender and divinity. As with Barrett Browning's gender bending, God/Goddess/Sancta Sophia can be simultaneously or interchangeably a man and a woman. This understanding of the rhetorical nature of belief never binds the nebulous profundity of spiritual creation and existence. Thus, in Nightingale's revelatory trope, Mill is spiritually and intellectually a "Goddess" because he himself had articulated and attempted to live beyond the human binaries and because in the cosmos Nightingale and Mill attempted to construct gender is fluid and without oppressive stereotypes. Indeed, as one delves more deeply into Nightingale's theology, it becomes increasingly apparent that although, as Showalter rightly suggests, Nightingale viewed herself as serving a masculine God, she also understood deity in more flexible terms (Showalter, "Florence Nightingale's" 402).

Nightingale's annotations of her Bible reveal that she was genuinely disturbed by the almost monolithic masculinity narrated there. Revising the sacred text to make it more inclusive, Nightingale changed "men" to "we" or adds the word "daughters" to references to "sons." In her iteration of the Lord's Prayer, she added the phrase "daughters with a loving father. . . . Thou art Love, and she that dwelleth in Love, dwelleth in Thee, and Thou in her," rather than using the masculine pronouns. Intriguingly, referring to St. Paul as "Paula/Paul," Nightingale playfully extended the role of apostle to women with the addition of just one letter of the alphabet. In another instance, Nightingale sounds like a modern Julian of Norwich when referring to God as "Father to me Thou art and Mother too and Sister dear" (*FN's Spiritual Journey* 70, 283; see also *NP* 45843 f.66).

In a comment illustrating Kristevan semiotics avant la lettre, Nightingale cites an Italian writer who noted that "all scripture but speaks to us of God as a mother makes soft inarticulate sounds to her babe, the babe that could not otherwise understand her words" (Note, *NP* 45843 f.292; qtd. in *FN's Spiritual Journey* 71). Nightingale's attention to the maternal as a necessary aspect of deity, alongside her insistence that women are worthy hierophants, makes for a strong connection with Mothers Ann Lee and Luckie Buchan. In fact, in Genesis, Nightingale glosses "the Almighty God" as "El Shaddai," explaining, "Shaddai derived from 'Mamma'—the Breast and signifies that we are as dependent upon God for every blessing as the infant on its mother's breast" (*FN's Spiritual Journey* 105).

As with Sharples's merging of Isis and Eve, Nightingale's mixture of pagan goddesses with Christian mythoi rejects the ideology that women are inferior. Like Anna Jameson, Nightingale delivered her thealogy, if you will, under the cover of art criticism. Her description of the "colossal head of Juno" at the Ludovisi Gallery is a case in point. Bracingly, Nightingale included the reflection that this is the "only Goddess I ever saw—all other Goddesses have been to me but beautiful women—nothing the least divine, like Jupiter Capitolinus and the Apollo, so that I always thought *we* should be *men* in the next stage—as there could not be made an ideal of a woman—but now I have seen a Goddess" (1 February 1848; qtd. in *FN in Rome* 219–21). Referring to her belief in Hermetic mysteries, Nightingale implied that human beings evolve into divinities in later phases of eternal existence. She contended, as well, that seeing Juno gives her an actual model for what females might become, so that women no longer need be confined to a male type of godhood for "the next stage."

Nightingale's interpretation of Eve is not as contrary to mainstream Christianity as is Brontë's, but there is an unconventional element that is reminiscent of Southcott, Sharples, and Wright. Indeed, like these earlier writers, Nightingale stated that the Fall did not result in the damnation of mortal men and women. Rather, she saw the first couple's "expulsion from Paradise" as initiating salvation (*NP* 45843 f.267). Like Southcott and Jameson, Nightingale perceived Eve as the transcendent heroine in the story of the Fall, and Adam as spiritually and physically effete. This is apparent in a letter to her sister on 17 January 1848, in which Nightingale describes Michelangelo's *Creation of Adam and Eve*. Observing the "extraordinar[y]" "difference between the characters of man and woman" in the painting, she writes that Adam is not depicted as "speaking purely from *heart* to *heart*" with God. She notes, too, that there is "nothing of the *inward* consciousness of the Divine Presence" in the depiction of Adam. Instead, the Creator reveals himself to Adam by an "outward manifestation" (*FN in Rome* 171).

In contrast, Nightingale asserts that "any body looking at the Creation of *Woman,* will see the difference." She describes "the lovely new born woman" Eve as kneeling "before her Creator, who, in his unspeakable Goodness, has stripped himself of all his Power and Majesty, and stands before her in the semblance of a man, her father, and her friend, and yet, such is the sublime idea of M. Angelo, that there is nothing lost of dignity in the figure." Noting that "Adam continues sleeping" when God appears, Nightingale derides his profound insensibility: "No woman would have done this, she would have been warned (by her quicker perception) of the presence of a supernatural being. Eve, kneeling in perfect love and devotion, receives with entire submission, the commands of her Creator, which come straight from His *spirit* to hers, without any material manifestation of Power. She is lovely beyond description" (171).

The Christian creation story signs Adam as having a more sacred relation with God than does Eve. But as illustrated in her prayers, Nightingale sees women as capable of a spiritually refined and intimate communication with deity that is more difficult for men to achieve. Teasing out what it means when, despite her subordinate position, Eve is sentient while Adam lies inert and unconscious, Nightingale's account of Michelangelo's "Creation" interprets God as trusting the "sublime" Eve so much that He strips himself of his outer divine accoutrements to present himself in His noumenal godliness. But not only is Eve capable of standing in the presence of deity without being obliterated; in this interpretation, godliness *consists of being equal* with the human, implying that God can be man (or woman, in this case), and woman can be God. Further, in Nightingale's view, Michelangelo limns a spiritually receptive Eve whose converse with God requires no speech. Meanwhile, Adam's weakness (sleeping) makes him a hanger-on in the myth created just for him, for he is all but literally dead to the spiritual and physical world God has created for him. Nightingale almost seems to see Adam as so self-involved that he exists in absolute inanition, while Eve, utterly open to all creation and the Creator, is effulgent in her *jouissance*. Thus, her strong agency and meticulous susceptibility to the spiritual allow her to steal Adam's, and even God's, starring roles.

Nightingale's Eve is an effulgent precursor for the female messiah she envisions. As noted in the introduction to this study, the idea of a female messiah had an earlier iteration among the English Civil War sects, when women rebelled against the father's law practiced in the religious, political, and domestic spheres by imagining a "spiritual democracy" and a female messiah (B. Taylor, "Woman-Power" 122). The notion of a female savior may go as far back as the fourteenth and fifteenth centuries, when lower-class radicals read the works of Hermes Trismegistus and spoke of a Christ-like goddess; the concept erupted again at the end of the eighteenth century in response to the French Revolution, which, apocalyptic in its magnitude, increased prophetic discourse during the last two decades of the eighteenth century (B. Newman; Harrison, *Second Coming* 5, 30).[7] Linda Lewis muses that the female messiah, imagined by the millenarians and depicted in Shelley's "Revolt of Islam" and Nightingale's "Cassandra," might have represented the merging of the woman as wisdom motif (Athena and Sophia) with the motif of Christ as the Word or Wisdom (173–74). Nightingale's allusion to a female deity underscores her concerns about the oppression of women and links her with her radical grandmothers, Southcott and Sharples, who equate Eve with deity and foretell a coming divine female.

Seemingly unacquainted with earlier historical iterations of the female savior, Showalter suggests that Nightingale originated this concept. Rather than creating a new concept, most likely Nightingale came across the radical concept and used it for her own protofeminist purposes. With extensive knowledge of so-called heretical religions and an obvious interest in the gendering of God, Nightingale could have read about the female savior in press accounts about post–French Revolution radical groups and the millenarians Ann Lee and Southcott. Certainly Nightingale might have learned about the Owenites and St. Simonians in British or French journals.[8]

Her correspondence with Jowett indicates her awareness of the millenarians and other fringe Christian groups that believed in continuing revelation. In 1865, Jowett explicitly refers to millenarians when he writes to her about their goal to improve the world: "the stream of improvement is so narrow in the whole of the world . . . that instead of casting your eyes far & wide" it is better to look "forward to some ideal future. . . . I suppose we should . . . get the habit of looking onwards to the future & not backwards to the past. *This would be a new kind of Millenarianism* founded on fact & not on the interpretation of prophecy" (41; emphasis added). Likewise, the content of a letter Jowett wrote to Nightingale in March 1865 hints that he was responding negatively to her possible attraction to Mormonism, a religion that posited the existence of a Heavenly Mother and the idea that humans could become gods (Jowett 46; "Heavenly Mother" *Mormon Encyclopedia*). In any case, these letters signal that Nightingale examined many religions and forms of spirituality in her quest for spiritual perfection.

Internal evidence in a fragment of "Cassandra" shows that Nightingale knew of the Fourierists: "You are a This is not Fourierism in everything but his matrimonial scheme. [new paragraph] 'No, I am not. I think The Fourierists" (*NP* 45839 f.168). This all-but-deleted passage implies that Nightingale was working out her own feminist political utopia vis-à-vis those offered by the radical generation that came before her. We know that the Fourierists and St. Simonians foretold a coming female messiah and that St. Simonian emissaries made contacts with English radicals, trade-unionists, and cultural savants in the first half of the century (Malmgreen 10, 6). In fact, the young John Stuart Mill was favorable toward the Saint-Simonians and may have written an open letter in *Le Globe* to that effect in 1832 (Moses 241). Mill explicitly named the St. Simonians as an inspiration for his feminist agenda, noting that he "honoured them most for what they have been most cried down for" (qtd. in Malmgreen 10). Nightingale knew Mill well enough to share with him the manuscript in which "Cassandra" appears. Although I am not aware of letters between them that explicitly refer to a female deity, it would seem likely that Mill would have commented upon Nightingale's allusion to the female messiah. It is perhaps not a coincidence, then, when the nephew of the radical James Elishma Smith wrote that his uncle admired Nightingale's "inspiration that glows, the vestal fire that ever burns," because he had such "a strong faith in a female Messiah" (274).

Jowett's comment about "Millenarians" appears to be part of a conversation with Nightingale that may include her own revisionary rhetoric about this movement and that points toward Nightingale's habit of reinvigorating clichéd terms. Indeed, when Nightingale refers to the female savior in "Cassandra," it is congruent with her ongoing dialogue with and practical adaptation of many forms of political and religious thought. In this case, it is probable that she appropriated and redefined the concept of the female messiah that had circulated in print media by or about such radical groups. Nightingale was adept at taking well-known spiritual concepts and making them new again, as prophets are supposed to do for their particular age. She performed such a revision, for example, when she said of evolution, "The real demoralizing theory is not that we once were apes but that we are no more than apes now in capabilities for 'high emprize'" (*NP* 45843 f.177).

Similarly, Nightingale adapts the image of the Holy Family to argue that every family is a holy family, and each child a holy child. Indeed, à la Jameson and Sharples, she asserts that daughters should be allowed to develop their sacred intellectual talents as God intended. Asserting that the family unit acculturates girls to waste time on the frivolous, Nightingale explains that in this way daughters are "slowly put to death at home" (*NP* 45843 f.10, f.18). In a draft of "What is the type of a family in God's mind," she imagines a "'holy' family" that would replace the modern family, which she regards as in a "*State of War*" (*NP* 45843 f.1, f.4). In Nightingale's theology, the child should develop her god-given talent and use it both publicly and privately for the good of humanity. She reasons that parents who require their child's absolute devotion to the domestic sphere negate that child's spiritual responsibility to live a life devoted to God (*NP* 45843 f.20). Nightingale does not see a woman's commitment to God's work as a sacrifice, because the "holy family" must seek "the development of each Individuality according to its type, so that each individual may be working out" a "part of the great whole which is working with God by God" (*NP* 45843 f.22). As she sees it, then, dedication to God is also the ultimate form of individualism.

Thus, like *The Isis*, Nightingale combines the spiritual with the political to make a practical, moral argument. In other words, as Ruth Jenkins suggests, Nightingale views women who make unconventional choices based on their talents as holy martyrs fighting patriarchal dominance ("Rewriting Female Subjectivity" 17). Indeed, in a feminist tour de force, Nightingale bluntly queries what purpose keeping women buried in the domestic sphere can serve: "What is this but throwing the gifts of God aside as worthless, and substituting for them those of the world?'" (qtd. in Jenkins, "Rewriting

Female Subjectivity" 18) Reared in a family that repressed her outsized intellect, organizational skills, and Herculean dynamism, Nightingale suggests that family life is too constricted to create the immortal deities God intends human beings to become. Since Nightingale envisions a holy family that would allow single women to use their abilities to do good in the domestic *and* public spheres, her desires intersect with political efforts to find what religion can do to help women achieve their potential (Calabria and Macrae, eds., *Suggestions* 256). In fact, there is a startling similarity between Karl Marx's view of the "holy family" and Nightingale's, for he writes that "once the earthly family is discovered to be the secret of the holy family, the former must then itself be criticized in theory and revolutionalized in practice" ("Theses" 70).

As with the "holy family," Nightingale revises the concept of the female Christ. Consider the famous section from "Cassandra" where Nightingale's alter ego, Nofriari, remarks, "Christ, if He had been a woman, might have been nothing but a great complainer." The passage goes on to say that "the next Christ will perhaps be a female Christ. But do we see one woman who looks like a female Christ? Or even like 'the messenger before' her 'face,' to go before her and prepare the hearts and minds for her?" ("Cassandra," in *Suggestions* 408).[9] Implying a reference to previous uses of the phrase "female Christ," the word "perhaps," coupled with her other references to Fourierism, strongly suggests Nightingale's awareness rather than creation of the concept of the female savior. Interpreted in this way, like Concordia–Cassandra, Nightingale shows that she had something to add to the previous generation's radical politics. As Nightingale argues, even if a female savior did appear—as early nineteenth-century socialists and millenarians prophesied she would—she still would be saddled with the culture's misogyny. Nightingale understands, then, that if Christ had come as a woman, even He could not have been recognized as God in his first incarnation, for spiritual illumination absolutely depends upon the culture's construction of gender.

Nightingale's representation of the female savior thus mirrors and revamps radical feminist discourse, in particular Sharples's statement that Christ would return as a secular "second Messiah of republicanism and happiness" ("Second Person of the Trinity" 614). Like Sharples and Southcott, Nightingale contends that Christ's self-sacrifice had to be duplicated by earthly (female) saviors for any sort of true salvation to be achieved. Likewise, Nightingale, Southcott, and Sharples see humankind—women, in particular—as the key to spiritual and material redemption. In other words, Christ could not save human beings without the help of human saviors and without salvation, including the improvement of mankind's material conditions. Cognizant of the political ruptures in the modern state, Nightingale rejected the idea that "the time is past for *individual* saviours" and preached that "even when Europe has burst her chains" the "world cannot be saved, except through saviours" (Calabria and Macrae, eds., *Suggestions* 201). Referring to Europe's class hierarchies, which radicals from the French Revolution forward attempted to destroy, Nightingale's Realpolitik contended that no such reform would occur with just a storming of the barricades.

Her famous statement that "the next Christ will perhaps be a female Christ" should be seen, then, in light of her other references to the term "savior," for they illustrate her belief in horizontal transcendence (408, 201). As Barbara Montgomery Dossey argues, Nightingale's was a "mysticism that focused on creating a better life for mankind here on earth through social action" (325). In fact, in a time of Victorian laissez-faire attitudes, Nightingale insisted on the government's spiritual obligation to ensure the safety, sanitation, and health of its citizenry. She boldly asserted, "The objects of the statesman, the lawyer, the doctor, the merchant, the shopkeeper, the day labourer" are as "sacred as those of the priest" (*NP* 45841 f.31). Likewise, she contends, "We can only know God's nature & man's nature by improving our social arrangements" (*NP* 45843 f.189). Hence, although not as republican as Sharples's belief that the Second Coming would establish political equality, Nightingale's view of the savior's role in society is political, for she essentially demands that the modern welfare state be established forthwith and that the "statesman," the "lawyer," and the "doctor" be saviors in deed and word.

Textual evidence indicates that Nightingale palpably felt the desire to be more than just a metaphorical savior. Explicit about her aspirations in her diary in 1837, she transcribes the words of a Heavenly voice that reminded her: "It is 15 years to-day since I called thee to the perfection of my service" (*NP* 45844 f.6). Audaciously connecting her own ostensible martyrdom with Christ's, Nightingale also writes on 28 July 1865, "on the Cross I shall see his face / Am I being offered to him?" (*NP* 45844 f.7) A little after this, she inscribes the words, "And is it not worth all to see his face? And may I think that I am another Himself, another like that? . . . oh too blessed to think that He should look upon me as another like that" (*NP* 45844 f.7).

In this euphoric passage, Nightingale vacillates between envisioning herself as being "like" the Savior and *being* the Savior—"another Himself"—with the border between the two entities being extremely tenuous. The paucity of punctuation and lack of capitalization erase the boundaries between the self and God, making it difficult to tell where God begins and Nightingale ends. It appears that the two have had a long relationship, and there is no need to establish a hierarchy or separation between ostensibly different divine and human identities. In fact, in these entries, Nightingale's radical horizontal transcendence results in her sense of simultaneously being both divine and mortal. Hence, despite often seeming rigidly self-righteous, Nightingale also feels the instability of her spiritual selfhood as it imagines or rehearses godhood.

Noting that she had once ended a letter to a cousin as your "poor Cassandra," Nightingale's biographer Edward Cook asserts that "Cassandra" is autobiographical (Cook 1:116; qtd. in Showalter, "Florence Nightingale's Feminist Complaint" 410). In fact, in a deleted section of "Cassandra" that describes the protagonist's spiritual crisis, Nightingale imagines herself to be a female savior. It is important to point out that Nofriari's martyrdom reads exactly like Nightingale's diary accounts of her own heroic self-sacrifice for God: "I remember the day. It was like a day of Crucifixion to me. It was like death. As each confession came out I feared I should not have strength to make the next confession and drive the next nail. But I did. I went through the whole. And when it came to piercing the side, I did it too" (*NP* 45839 f.242). "Cassandra" also limns this spiritual ambition in the section after Nofriari—Nightingale's doppelganger—proposes that the next savior will be a female. At this point, her brother, the narrator of "Cassandra," comments: "'Now I don't wonder,' . . . 'at your being unhappy'" if "'you have that . . . ambition to be a Christ or a John the Baptist'" (*NP* 45839 f.284). Though Nofriari dies without achieving her ambitions, Nightingale lived a long life devoted to savioring.

But if associating herself with a female savior was an inordinate "ambition," Nightingale also appropriated the role of the Virgin, whom she seemed to view as the supernal deity. In fact, Nightingale considered converting to Catholicism, in part because of the freedom it allowed its adherents to venerate the Mother of Christ. Nightingale felt a profound connection to the Madonna, and this iconic figure appears often in her unpublished writings. In a letter to Jowett in 1867, Nightingale equated herself with the Virgin Mary when she contemplated the famous interchange between Mary and God at the Annunciation:

> "Behold the handmaid of the Lord: be it unto me according as Thou will. 1. What a wonderful favour to be chosen before as many thousands to be the handmaid of the Lord. 2. What return does God expect from me—with what purity of heart & intention should I make an offering of myself to Him—And when that offering is made, what a life ought I to lead? 3. I give myself up entirely to Him that He may do with me whatever it pleases

Him—and I earnestly desire that He will never think of sparing me and let no occasion pass of mortifying my pride & trying my temper. 4. God forbid that I should glory save in the Cross of our Lord Jesus Christ." (*NP* 45783 ff.112–13; qtd. in Dossey 334)[10]

Indeed, the passage is another example of Nightingale's hasty discursive practice that results in the reader's inability to infer who is speaking and who is acting upon or with whom he is acting. With no names to indicate the speaker, it is increasingly problematic to discern between Mary as purported speaker and Nightingale, the Virgin manquée. Moving immediately from Mary's statement to the Angel in the Bible to inserting herself in the place of Mary, in this impulsive rhetoric Nightingale fulfills her belief that humans are in the process of becoming gods, or that God is in the human self, or that mortals continually recreate the concept of God. The outcome is an uncanny blend of humility, submission, and self-glorification as Nightingale, for an ecstatic moment, becomes the Virgin. Transitioning between self-abnegation and interrogation of the concept of divinity, and imagining herself as deity, Nightingale creates a spiritual mode that underwrites her activist Christianity. Given the amorphous nature of her rhetoric, one might conjecture that Nightingale discovered a mode of being that fluctuated between godhood and the corporeal. In these sites, she perhaps achieves what Ann Taves refers to as "discontinuities of consciousness, memory, and identity" when Nightingale's normal sense of self as "embodied agen[t]" could be said to have virtually disappeared (9).

In keeping with her dislike of sectarianism, unlike Henry Hart Milman, who deplored the early Church's intermixture of pagan elements with the Virgin Mary, Nightingale was unperturbed by this prospect. In *Suggestions for Thought,* she accepted that though pagan religions had died off, "traces" of the old religions remained. She did not take issue with the fact that the Catholic worship of a divine female probably originated in the veneration of the goddess Diana (244). She remarked, too, that, as a symbol of wisdom, the Virgin was analogous to the pagan divinities Athena and Minerva. Like the radical Sharples, then, Nightingale conceived of pagan deities as symbolically equivalent to Mary, and she viewed both as responsive to a profound human need. Thus she asks rhetorically, "Is the worship of the goddess of wisdom by the ancients more unreasonable than the worship of the God of the nineteenth century?" (190) This query is in keeping with Nightingale's remark that there was more truth in the pagan religion of "thankfulness to the River Gods, the fountain nymphs, spreading plenty wherever they reach go" than in the harsh "Calvinist God" (*NP* 45843 f.67).

Nightingale's belief that the Virgin was an outgrowth of the pagan goddesses expands this entity beyond the strict confines of the Christian Mary in the same way that Sharples reconfigures deity. Respecting the indeterminate nature of the mystical and the divine, Nightingale's theological understanding of the Madonna is more fragmented than her disquisitions on the triune God. Obsessive about inscribing her every idea, Nightingale often wrote on any slip of paper at hand (including used envelopes). The archive at the British Library is full of these scraps as well as voluminous drafts of essays, books, letters, memos, and reports. An example of the disconnected nature of her thought about the Madonna is graphically apparent in her statement, "The great legend of the Virgin Mother—its true meaning is this . . ." (*NP* 45843 f.307). Shockingly, Nightingale fails to complete the epiphany at hand. We do not know if at this point she had a revelation that was beyond the ability of words to describe, or if she felt incapable of recording the experience because of the onset of writer's block, or if she was interrupted, a not unreasonable speculation since she kept to such a hectic schedule. Or if, god literally forbid, she was afraid to posit god's supernal essence as female.

Such engagements with the Virgin suggest that Nightingale realized she was composing a new theoretical discourse about the female divine, as though she were in the beginning stages of imagining this entity. We can piece together from her other writings what the spiritually unconventional and interrogatory Nightingale found so compelling about the Madonna. In one example, she inscribes the words, "all history, all society shews it us that there is a profound truth in the *idea* of the 'Virgin Mother'—" (*NP* 45843 f.66). Providing more substance than her incomplete transcription of Mary's meaning supplied, this dramatic proclamation runs short, again, on the actual "idea" of the Madonna, as though she is the ineluctable essence to be found behind the Veil of Isis.

In her cryptically abbreviated diary from 1850 during her time in Egypt, in jumbled notes that appear to be the beginnings of a philosophical paper regarding Catholicism, Nightingale refers to its "dishonest compromise." With no hypotactic connections between her thoughts, Nightingale outlines a sketchy list: "a dead church & no creed the throne of the Fisherman, built by the Carpenter's son household thought—& dearest of sympathies—love of the Virgin" (*NP* 45846 f.66). Despite the discordant tone, limited punctuation, and lack of cohesive connectives, it appears that Nightingale assumes the superiority of the "dearest" Virgin as the climactic element of her spontaneous litany. Curiously, the throne built by Christ is for the Madonna rather than God the Father, who is completely absent. One might conclude that in this minimalist theological disquisition, Nightingale affirms that modeling

Christ was just practice for becoming the most sublime instance of deity, the Mother in Heaven.

Another example of this fragmentary mode compares the Virgin with God, with Mary being deemed as a higher form of divinity. In fact, Nightingale implies that the Judeo-Christian metaphor of the jealous Father pales in comparison with the merciful, more human(e) Mary. Thus Nightingale does not blame Catholics for praying to the Virgin. "Is there not more truth of feeling," she asks, "in the devout Roman Catholic woman who tells you that she cannot doubt the existence of the Virgin, because she feels the proofs of her goodness '*there, so near me*' (tho' for God she puts Virgin) than in the expressions *we* use of 'God' being a 'jealous God,' an 'angry' God, & of praise to God," because "he does not desire the [page break] 'death' of a sinner" (*NP* 45843 f.65–66). In the margin, Nightingale lines out her completion of the statement thusly: "because we see truth in the idea of the Virgin Mother's goodness" (*NP* 45843 f.67). Manifesting no anxiety about the Catholic woman replacing God with the Virgin in her devotions, Nightingale logically concludes that metaphorically the Virgin is more godlike than the harsh, biblical God who appears wrathful toward His children too much of the time. Known for compassionate nursing, Nightingale seems incapable of venerating a surly, willful being who psychologically manipulates and irrationally disciplines those he ostensibly loves.

In these musings on the Madonna's appeal, particularly to women, Nightingale also defends her (Catholic) sisters against the condescension to which they are susceptible, because they worship this ostensible stand-in for God. In 1873, she wrote in a manuscript that was never published, "say not that a large section of us does still believe in the Virgin. It is the 'feeble multitude' and the 'helpless' sex either in man or woman, whose 'zeal fains intensity,'" toward the Virgin Mary (*NP* 45482 f.110). In this instance, Nightingale rejects the male dread of the emasculating Madonna. She puts the ostensibly feminine qualities of ineffectuality under question with her air quotation marks around "feeble" and "helpless," stereotypical feminine markers even today. Nightingale also demands that the stereotype describing deity as masculine be interrogated and resisted, since any kind of gender stereotyping detoured god from working with the unique "Individuality" of each mortal being (*NP* 45843 f.22).

Thus the pushy crusader cannot resist making a jab at masculine Godhood on Christmas day 1888, no less. She writes, "I don't like the X Commandment—it is all 'you shall *not*, you shall *not*, . . . Negation never gave love. . . . And I don't like the perpetual telling us of the perfection of having *no* other will but God's. It ought to be a *strong* will, to *second* His. That is the real end & aim & perfection" (*NP* 45844 f.37). Enlarging the male Christian God's character, Nightingale demands that He move beyond His own monolithic will to include the "*strong*" willfulness of his children, including his female daughters, like herself, Cassandra, Eve, the female savior, and the Virgin.

To conclude, then, Nightingale, like Sharples, worked for material redemption that depended on transformation of sociopolitical systems in order to bring about earthly horizontal transcendence. Indeed, in their efforts to imagine horizontal transcendence by democratizing God, Nightingale, Southcott, and Sharples went a long way toward reconstructing earthly forms of hierarchical power, for all three deconstruct traditional Christian dogma, particularly about Eve, the Virgin Mary, and the gender of the Savior. Nightingale recuperates Eve and imagines herself to be the female savior and the Virgin Mary; Sharples figures herself as the pagan goddess Isis and a reconstructed Eve; and Southcott claims to be the Virgin and the woman clothed with the sun as well as a second godlike Eve. Likewise, each disturbs the binary featuring man as prophet and deity. Thus, to figure Nightingale, the more mainstream of the three female prophets, as the link to the secular feminist Mary Wollstonecraft does justice neither to Nightingale's overdetermined commitments to feminist spirituality and the political and social rebirth of the world, nor to her feminist forebears who were perhaps more radical than Wollstonecraft in using spirituality to feminize God and politically transform the world.

6

Ariadne and the Madonna

THE HERMENEUTICS OF THE GODDESS IN GEORGE ELIOT'S *ROMOLA*

> Every God, even including the God of the Word, relies on a mother Goddess.
> —Julia Kristeva, *The Portable Kristeva*, edited by Kelly Oliver 322

> She [George Eliot] is the first great *godless* writer of fiction that has appeared in England.
> —W. H. Mallock, "Impressions of Theophrastus Such" 562

IN THE FINAL CHAPTER of this study, I turn to the 1860s and George Eliot's early novel *Romola*, which revolves around the eponymous heroine who is constantly referred to as "Madonna." Eliot, who was called "Madonna" by G. H. Lewes, and "Our Lady" by her friends, also felt a deep admiration for Raphael's *Sistine Madonna*, the painting Anna Jameson praised so highly. However, unlike Barrett Browning, Brontë, Nightingale, and Jameson, who can be said to have been believers, Eliot was an agnostic. Thus her reverence for the Madonna is a conundrum for modern readers. I suggest that Eliot's attraction to the Virgin can be explained in part by closely reading the goddess imagery in *Romola*, for in this novel Eliot merges the Virgin with the pagan goddess Ariadne in order to imagine an ethical system complex enough to confront the trauma of modern life. I suggest, too, that by combining classical and Christian female gods, *Romola* follows a pattern set by freethinker Eliza Sharples, who figured the Virgin/Isis as the horizon for female perfection, thus making Utopia available through the political acts of educated, loving women in the public sphere. I will show that the setting of quattrocento Florence for *Romola* is crucial to creating a dynamic horizon of opportunity for the heroine. That dynamic includes the unique combination of Catholic worship of the Virgin, zealous Renaissance study of the pagan mysteries and antiquities, and a republican form of government underwritten by Christian belief.

Eliot first saw "this sublimest picture," Raphael's *Sistine Madonna,* in Dresden in 1858. Her journal describes sitting "down on the sofa opposite the picture for an instant, but a sort of awe, as if I were suddenly in the presence of some glorious being, made my heart swell too much for me to remain comfortably, and we hurried out of the room" (Haight, *George Eliot* 264). We might expect such a response from Florence Nightingale, who was an adept of mystic states, but not from the agnostic Eliot. It appears, however, that she was genuinely overcome by mystical ecstasy of some sort when gazing upon what she perceived as the originary site of love and feeling. Indeed, the experience sounds like a Pauline road to Damascus moment, when the renegade is struck down physically and psychically by a numinous encounter with a "glorious being." Eliot did not convert overnight to any religion as Saul did. Rather, she represents a unique modern sensibility, which allowed her to experience a mystical encounter while retaining the belief that no single god was complex enough to explain or comprehend modern existence. As Peter C. Hodgson writes, hers was an "agnostic, apophatic faith, which kept the reality of God in suspense even as it affirmed the reality of duty and love" (2).

Eliot's translation of Ludwig Feuerbach's *Essence of Christianity* aids the reader in understanding the fear and rapture she experienced upon seeing Raphael's famous painting. Like Sharples and Eliot, the German intellectual interpreted God as a projection of the highest ideals of human behavior; in other words, the sacred was in man and in the world, not outside in some separate heavenly sphere (see Susan E. Hill). Following upon this logic, Feuerbach contends that "to think is to be God" (*Essence of Christianity* 40). Eliot concurred with Feuerbach's relativist approach, writing, "The contemplation of whatever is great is itself religion," and "The idea of God is the idea of a goodness entirely human" (*GEL* 4:104; 1:98). Rejecting abstract dogma, Eliot believed that only "truth of feeling" could create love and generosity between human beings, and then only gradually (Hodgson 19; *GEL* 1:162). As she wrote on 11 December 1880, "the reason why societies change slowly is, because individual men and women cannot have their natures changed by doctrine and can only be wrought on by little and little" (*GEL* 7:346).

Feuerbach's *Essence of Christianity* underwrote Eliot's belief in the religion of feeling. Asserting that feeling is what "makes God a man" and "man a God," the German author described the purest human emotions as "religious." He suggested, as well, that the human "yearning after God is the yearning" for what God essentially is—"unlimited," "undisturbed," "uninterrupted, pure feeling, feeling for which there exists no limits, no opposite" (281, 283). Feuerbach points out, though, that the supreme mystery, Christ's passion, is a misnomer because only humans can suffer, and thus they are, in effect, superior to God (333). Viewing love as the premier emotion, he concludes that *caritas* is "essentially feminine" and that any belief in divine love must acknowledge that the highest form of godhood was feminine (70, 72). In keeping with his adulation of women, Feuerbach decries the irrationality of a heavenly Trinity that includes the Father and Son but not the Mother (72). For Eliot, the *Sistine Madonna* seems to have captured this notion of supernal, motherly love, although when faced with the majesty of the painting, she could not manage this religion of feminine feeling that overwhelmed her.

Eliot's encounter with the *Sistine Madonna* might also remind us of the medieval Beguine Beatrijs of Nazareth. Naming the seven stages through which mortals pass to merge with God's love, Beatrijs depicted the third phase as one in which the self recognizes its inability to love perfectly. Hence the mystic experiences "*Excess*," "*torment*," and "*violence*" because, although she feels an upwelling of love for God/Love, she simultaneously suffers because she cannot enact perfect caritas (Petroff 58–59). Perhaps Eliot felt a form of "unlimited," "uninterrupted feeling" when she saw the *Sistine Madonna* and thus experienced a glimpse of godhood or perfect love in herself. Feeling the excess and violence necessary to produce perfect love, and cognizant that Victorian society expected such love from all women, the tormented Eliot ran from the room. Or, more precisely, in coming face to face with the image of the Madonna, perhaps Eliot *felt* the violence at the heart of her own demand that supernal love required "resignation to individual nothingness," and at that point she was ineluctably shaken to the core (see *GEL* 2:49). Held captive in that epiphanic moment by the prospect of divine, interminable, unlimited love and its extraordinary, even nauseating, expectations, Eliot may have rushed away to the serene attractions and relative stability of atheism.

Nevertheless, in her writing, Eliot courageously returned to what the Madonna figure represented as a model for human behavior, despite the terrifying cost to the self. Finding in Christianity the altruism necessary to withstand existential angst, Eliot acerbically commented to her friend Barbara Bodichon, "The highest 'calling and election' is to *do without opium and live through all our pain with conscious, clear-eyed endurance*" (*GEL* 3:366). She wrote this gloomy statement the day after Christmas in 1860, one of the holiest times of year for Christians, when Eliot was about to begin her research for *Romola*. Perhaps more telling regarding Eliot's analysis of gender, hermeneutics, and the solution to ethical impasse was her comment that she began writing *Romola* as a "young woman,—I finished it an old woman" (qtd. in Haight 362). If Eliot focused explicitly on the Madonna, in *Romola* she also referred positively to the "great goddesses." She may have been inspired by Margaret Fuller, who argued that in ancient times women were valued because mythologies featured "'great goddesses'" like the Egyptian Isis, whose wisdom was unrivaled (*Woman in the Nineteenth Century*). Eliot would certainly have been aware of Fuller's admiration for pagan goddesses, since she had reviewed Fuller's work. Further, given Wollstonecraft's and Fuller's scandalous reputations, choosing to review Fuller's *Woman in the Nineteenth Century* and Wollstonecraft's *Vindication of the Rights of Woman* (1855) was a bold move for Eliot, who lived openly with a married man. But perhaps there was something equally scandalous in Eliot's revival of the notion of the great goddess.

It is helpful to review the trajectory of Eliot's theological heuristics as a context for understanding the complex, seemingly contradictory ethical system she develops in *Romola*. As a young woman, like many evangelicals Eliot was deeply immersed in the prophetic Book of Revelation and its depiction of the millennium. Like the feminist utopians and millenarians, many evangelicals believed that the extraordinary historical events beginning with the French Revolution pointed to the Second Coming. In a letter to Maria Lewis in 1838, the young Mary Ann Evans wondered whether her friend was "fond of the study of unfulfilled prophecy" (*GEL* 1:11–12). Deriding the "vagaries of the Irvingites and the blasphemies of Joanna Southcote," Evans admitted that "prayerful consideration of the mighty revolutions ere long to take place in our world would by God's blessings serve to make us less grovelling, more devoted and energetic in the service of God" (11–12). Avidly watching the signs of the times like Southcott, Evans contemplated writing a history of divination, an "Ecclesiastical Chart" that would correlate God's prophecies with contemporary sociopolitical occurrences. She gave up the project only when she learned that other scholars had already published such charts (Krueger 239–40; see also Carpenter, *George Eliot* 3–29).

Gordon Haight argues that as she aged, Eliot became increasingly conservative in terms of gender and class politics, but it would be simplistic not to acknowledge that her political conservatism, like that of Ruskin and

Carlyle, had a hefty strain of the radical in it. The radical strain in Eliot was a result of her early friendship with Charles and Caroline Bray, whom she met when she and her father moved to Coventry in 1841. Attracted to radical ideas and scholarly discussion, the Brays held a salon known as the Rosehill Circle, which included many of the intellectual elite of the day. Through the Brays, Eliot made social and intellectual connections with Robert Owen, Saint-Simon, Harriet Martineau, and Herbert Spencer.[1] Illustrating her meticulous awareness of political events, Eliot noted in her journal on 18 July 1869 that she and a group of friends, including feminist Barbara Bodichon, participated in "Some conversation about Saint-Simonism, àpropos of the meeting on Woman's Suffrage the day before, M. Ariès Dufour, being uneasy because Mill did not in his speech recognize what women owed to Saint Simonism" (Eliot, *Journals* 136; see also *GEL* 1:xliv).

Bray analyzed the French Revolution and socialism in *The Philosophy of Necessity* (1841), and statements in this text are mirrored in some of Eliot's rhetoric. Condemning capitalism for making society more selfish, Bray agreed with the "advocates of 'The New Moral World,'" a radical journal of the early part of the century. As Bray acknowledged, Engels and his ilk held that while "the law of universal brotherhood is inoperative" in a capitalist system, socialism advocated that citizens "would be as one family, each bringing what he possessed to the common stock for the general good" (393, 394). Bray also stated that socialism was possibly the last and highest form society would take in its movement toward "perfectibility" (412). However, he did not become a socialist because he did not consider the working classes evolved enough yet to follow its precepts (411). Nor did he believe that governmental entities had achieved the stability and power necessary to effect universal benefits for the working classes. For Bray, the only solution was to help society change gradually. As he remarked, "all great revolutions, to be permanent and efficacious, must be the produce of time; they cannot be brought about suddenly," for the "mind requires to undergo a similarly gradual process in any great alteration of feeling and opinion" (404, 405).

Like her friend Bray, Eliot was also a gradualist who reasoned that the English masses were not quite ready for the progressive measures they demanded. But this did not cancel the author's erstwhile belief in reform. In 1848, in a long letter to John Sibree, Jr., son of an Independent minister, Eliot comically referred to the "Millennium" that would come upon the heels of the recent revolution in France (*GEL* 1:252). She begins the letter by complimenting Sibree on being "sansculottish and rash" and explicitly worries that the Victorian period was what Saint-Simon referred to as a critical age, that is, one that could not produce change, in contrast with organic ages that were capable of revolutionary action. Seriocomically Eliot also writes of wanting to see "such a scene as that of the men of the barricade bowing to the image of Christ 'who first taught fraternity to men'" (253).

In a shift of tone, Eliot then brutally decries the French king who had been overthrown. "[P]reserve me," she exclaims, "from sentimentalizing over a pampered old man when the earth has its millions of unfed souls and bodies" (*GEL* 1:254). Following this denunciation, Eliot could not be clearer about where her sympathies lay regarding England's own historically deposed King: "I think the shades of the Stuarts would have some reason to complain if the Bourbons who are so little better than they, had been allowed to reign much longer" (254). But while she does not distinguish between the Bourbon and Stuart kings, Eliot notes a marked distinction between the contemporary English and French working classes. She asserts that, full of "selfish radicalism" and lacking intellect and the aspiration for justice, John Bull was "simply destructive." In contrast, she observes that in France, "the *mind* of the people is highly electrified" by ideas, and thus their desire for social reform is authentic. Viewing the British as "slow crawlers," Eliot argues that they were ready for only gradual reforms (254).

Eliot's writing illustrates her exposure to the shaping forces of millenarianism and socialism. We have seen how Feuerbach strongly influenced Eliot's thinking about what the concept of god encompassed. It is important to note her reactions to the writings of Auguste Comte as well. Remarking to Mrs. Richard Congreve that she was attracted to the "illumination" of positivism, Eliot added that she was "swimming in Comte" (along with "Euripides and Latin Christianity") (*GEL* 4:116, 333). Like Feuerbach, Comte secularized the Christian religion, asserting that mankind moved through three historical phases, from polytheism, to monotheism, and finally positivism, a "religion of Humanity" based on scientific knowledge and altruism.[2] Comte's theorizing, like Feuerbach's, is much in keeping with the secularization of religion and altruism. In fact, Comte was the first and most venerated disciple of the radical socialist reformer Henri de Saint-Simon, after whom the Saint-Simonians were named.[3]

As with Feuerbach, Comte viewed women as the eidolon of the age and asserted that they would make a secular millennium possible. Comte probably acquired the view of woman as savior of the new age from the Saint-Simonians, although, ironically, he had originally broken from the Saint-Simonians *because* of their religiosity and their belief in a coming female divine.[4] Nevertheless, Comte would end up asserting that the Catholic Church made a brilliant choice when, during the transition from polytheism to monotheism, it allowed its followers to continue their adoration of the Virgin. The originator of positivism saw the Virgin as a means of appealing to deep emotional needs and a step toward his own idea of humankind's highest aspirations. As Comte wrote, "It is from the feminine aspect only that human life, whether individually or collectively considered, can really be comprehended as a whole," because woman "is the purest and simplest impersonation of Humanity" who personifies "the principle of Love upon which the unity of our nature depends" (qtd. in Bullen 429, 433).[5]

Although Eliot may have been the "first godless writer," as asserted in an epigraph to this chapter, when examining Eliot's credo one should also consider Pamela Sue Anderson's concept of the goddess as a model for what can exist in terms of human behavior and social regeneration (118, 158, 241). Indeed, the myth system Eliot brings to fruition in *Romola* rests, in great part, on her personal, ecstatic, mystical experience; radical notions of deity; and strong belief in the power of caritas to gradually bring humanity to a state of perfection. Here, we must return to her encounter with Raphael's *Sistine Madonna*, a representation of woman as deity, as the source of unlimited feeling, unconditional love and symbol of the imagination's horizon of goodness. Eliot is, after all, remembered for maintaining the "essence of Christian self-sacrifice through the apotheosis of human feeling" (Gilbert and Gubar 468). And, like Comte and Feuerbach, Eliot believed that women enacted the most supernal forms of self-sacrificing love with more agility and sublimity than men.

Eliot's only novel set outside nineteenth-century England, *Romola* takes place in quattrocento Florence. Many Victorian critics panned the novel because Eliot's research in the Florentine archive drowns the narrative. Some contemporary critics also suggest that Eliot should have stayed with her tried-and-true method of concentrating on nineteenth-century England and its domestic life rather than focusing on the politics and philosophies of fifteenth-century Florence.[6] Nevertheless, recent scholarship shows that the setting is crucial to the novel's meaning. Karen Chase and Felicia Bonaparte contend that *Romola*'s mise-èn-scene allows Eliot to depict the powerful struggles between Christian and classical thought in Western civilization. Bonaparte argues that Tessa and Romola are the pagan fertility goddess and Virgin, respectively, illustrating how Western civilization has been caught between the appeal of joy (the classical motif) and the belief in suffering (the Christian motif) (243, 25). Chase, on the other hand, suggests that *Romola* marries the West's two cultural traditions of Christianity and classicism (320).

In some sense, then, as Chad May argues, the "conflation of Romola with the Virgin Mary is only possible because of the specific cultural conditions of fifteenth-century Italy" (May 19). In fact, the quattrocento setting allows the author to pass off a startling *donné* to the Victorian audience: the moral center of the novel is a woman who, reared as a classicist and an atheist, is not a believer in Christianity. Romola's pagan father raised his daughter to reject Christianity and, instead, to base her actions on "cultivated reason" (*Romola* 154). Indeed, Romola was allowed to be her father's amanuensis only because the son, Dino, had blasphemed his father's belief system when he became a Catholic monk. After meeting Savanarola, Romola comes to feel there "is some truth" in Christianity and in her brother Dino's visions, but she never fully commits to Christian dogma (178). Thus Romola does not truly convert to Christianity although she pays tribute to its sign system, including reverence for the crucifix and the Madonna. As Julian Corner suggests, Romola is fragmented by her immersion in pagan classicism and Savonarola's Christianity, never finding wholeness in either (Corner 71). Quite rightly, too, J. B. Bullen and Maria LaMonaca argue that despite the heavy-handed references to Romola as the Madonna, this motif must be seen as Eliot's secularized answer to a world without God (Bullen 434; LaMonaca 171–72).

If Eliot, then, was determined to "preserve the essence of Christian self-sacrifice through the apotheosis of human feeling," I suggest that in *Romola* she argues that the private arena of affections must find its context and meaning in a political republic founded on sacred altruism, a vision very much reminiscent of Sharples's religion of humanity (Gilbert and Gubar 468). In other words, Eliot chooses quattrocento Florence as the setting because it allows Romola more access to power than Dorothea of *Middlemarch*, who has few options as a Victorian woman. The unique combination of fierce republicanism, Catholic worship of the Madonna, and Renaissance fervor for the scholarly and mystical achievements of the pagans gives a much higher horizon of opportunity in which Romola may attain political, intellectual, and spiritual autonomy and power.

Scholarship on this novel has not focused on how the interconnections of republicanism, Madonna worship, and research on pagan antiquities and philosophies create a complex synthesis with which Romola achieves spiritual independence and political and intellectual self-rule. First, I would suggest that the setting allows Eliot to allude to the scholars who ecstatically responded to the trove of newly discovered, ancient, and often obscure philosophical texts that became available in the West during the Renaissance. As the narrator of *Romola* points out, the members of the Academy in Florence felt an urgency to divine the meaning of these texts that were replete with philosophical mysteries about the gods. *Romola* refers to the Platonism of Marsilio Ficino and the "heterodox theses" of Pico della Mirandola, illustrating that Eliot had read these philosophers' attempts to unify the wisdom traditions of the Cabala, Hermes Trismegistus, Orpheus, Plato, and Zoroaster as prophetic precursors of Christianity (339).

Ordered by Cosimo de'Medici to learn Greek so that he could translate classical texts, Ficino published his translation of the works of Plato in 1484 an important year in Eliot's novel. As a Renaissance interpreter, he was certainly not viewed as *merely* translating the classical texts, but as participating in the sacred hermetic act itself. As Michael J. B. Allen points out, Ficino boldly endeavored to fuse Christian theology with Platonism, and, in doing so, he "revived and refined the ancient notion of a secret, esoteric" tradition referred to as a *"prisca theologica"* that had ostensibly "prepared for Christianity" (xvi). Remember that Florence Nightingale, a cousin of Eliot's close friend Barbara Bodichon, was much enamored of Hermes Trismegistus and the idea that mortal life is a time to seek and obtain ultimate knowledge as one evolves toward godhood. In keeping with a secret wisdom tradition, Eliot includes a reference to "Shekinah" in one of the sermons by Savonarola. The Penguin edition of the novel defines this Hebrew term as the "visible manifestation of God" (611n1). Only to be found in the Holy of Holies, the Shekinah was a Judeo-Christian equivalent to the Veil of Isis or the Platonic *nous,* which few adherents were ever blessed with deciphering, let alone seeing.

Feminist scholars have taken issue with Romola being depicted as a translator. The landmark *Madwoman in the Attic* links the character Romola with Eliot's view of herself as an editor who merely translated works by men like Strauss, Comte, and Feuerbach (Gilbert and Gubar 450). Margaret Homans asserts that the heroine "submissively bear[s] the word of women's exclusion from and silencing within literature, which is the same as her being reduced to mere body or to the literal with respect to language" (201). However, in response to concerns about Romola's submissiveness, Homans admits that regardless of how we read the character Romola as a translator, Eliot herself seemed to kick against the pricks of literal translation (178–79). Remarking that the German language and Feuerbach could be "very longwinded," with one sentence being "a page and a half long!" Eliot hoped that her editing of *The Essence of Christianity* contributed to "the perfecting of a mental product" (*GEL* 2:147, 141). In this statement, Eliot, who is a master of subtle intimations, hints that she actually refines Feuerbach's stolid, unprocessed prose. Indeed, she comments, "With the ideas of Feuerbach I everywhere agree, but of course I should, of myself, alter the phraseology considerably" (153). Eliot understood that "phraseology" was not just the outer shell of ideas but organically part of a text's meaning. Thus, when she asks the rhetorical question, would it be appropriate to "weave" some of Feuerbach's sentences together to provide more stylistic panache and coherence? Eliot participates in the creation of meaning (147).

I suggest that in writing *Romola*, like Ficino, Eliot came to see herself as an interpretive seer of a wisdom tradition rather than as *just* a translator of works by men. Eliot's response to Richard Holman Hutton's review of *Romola* is illuminating. She wrote, "It is the habit of my imagination to strive after as full a vision of the medium in which a character moves as of the character itself" (*GEL* 4:97). Perhaps, too, she saw doing in-depth research for this novel as part of the visionary process of knowing another age and, like God, creating ex nihilo an authentic world and characters. Eliot's response to Hutton includes a statement that "great, great facts have struggled to find a voice through me, and have only been able to speak brokenly" (97). Here again, although she belabors her humility, as most women writers did in the Victorian period, Eliot sees herself as a prophet bringing truth to humanity. Based on the narrator's statement that Romola "had a constitutional disgust for the shallow excitability of women like Camilla, whose faculties seemed all wrought up into fantasies, leaving nothing for emotion and thought," Homans argues that Eliot loathes Camilla because she fashions herself as a prophetess (*Romola* 441; Homans 194). I would argue, however, that it is not the idea of *women* prophesying to which Eliot is averse. Rather, she takes issue with females of "shallow excitability" ("silly women") becoming prophetesses, for they doom women in general to never being taken seriously as prophets or savants.

In terms of the connection between republicanism and Christianity, scholars have noted that Florence was the first city in the West to experiment with and achieve a concentrated form of republican government, and so in choosing this milieu, Eliot consciously correlates fifteenth-century Florentine republicanism with the French Revolution and the reform movements leading to democracy occurring during the Victorian period (Wihl 248, 249). Suggesting that millenarians and many evangelicals interpreted the spectacular events of the French Revolution and the 1848 revolutions as fulfilling the signs of the coming millennium, Mary Wilson Carpenter argues that *Romola* subliminally reiterates these millenarian prophecies (Carpenter, *George Eliot* 3, 61). *Romola*, of course, features the charismatic reformer Girolamo Savonarola who receives apocalyptic revelations from God, who enjoins him to establish a true republic based on spiritual idealism. In response, Fra Girolamo "insisted on the duty of Christian men not . . . to spend their wealth in outward pomp even in the churches, when their fellow-citizens were suffering from want and sickness" (*Romola* 8).

Broadly millenarian in its aims, *Romola* seems to be Eliot's depiction of the conditions necessary for Utopia, for the new form of sanctified secular life Eliot depicts is always organically inherent in the defiant republicanism of the "sacred rebel," Savonarola (523). I would argue, then, that for all the criticism of *Romola*'s political back-story, Eliot repeatedly explains that the political context for the heroine's individual narrative is absolutely linked to her altruistic obligations. As the narrator asserts, the "fortunes of Tito and Romola were dependent on certain grand political and social conditions which made an epoch in the history of Italy," a time when "the Republic had recovered the use of its will again" (207, 208). Significantly, the text's credo is that "life cannot rise into religion" unless the self's feelings harmonize with the aspirations of a "grand and remote end" (500, 499). The narrative makes clear, too, that in order to achieve the "perfecting of the Christian life," it is absolutely necessary to establish "a good government" (485).

Republicanism is central to the novel, which begins with the citizens buzzing about the possibility of "'real reform,'" "'a new order of things,'" and the "desire for government on a broader basis" (23, 75, 86). In contrast to other readings of Romola's submission to Savonarola, I argue that the frate teaches Romola that her surrender to domestic duties has been parochial and narrow-minded. Instead, he requires her to enter the public sphere and seek "[c]hanges in the form of the State" so as to help establish a "'popular government, in which every man is to strive only for the general good'" (249, 343). Thus, when Madonna Romola flees her husband the first time, Fra Girolamo does *not* call her back to obey Tito, although that can be read as the surface intent. More important, Savonarola tells Romola that "'a Florentine woman, should live for Florence'" because the "'servants of God are struggling after a law of justice, peace, and charity, that the hundred thousand citizens among whom you were born may be governed righteously'" (357).

This wider view of Romola's duties makes her feel that she is being beckoned to "something unspeakably great," that as a Florentine citizen she should succor the poor whom she has rather brazenly ignored up to this point in her materially comfortable married life (361, 363). Ultimately, Romola believes in a "heroism struggling for sublime ends" and knows that "'good government is needful to the perfecting of Christian life.'" Hence, she realizes that the sacred cause Savonarola gives her includes "'guard[ing] the Republic'" from Tito's "'treachery'" (439, 485, 406). Hence, when Romola realizes that rebellion is as sacred as obedience, the revolt she enacts is in support of the republic and against the marriage tie (468).

In terms of goddess imagery, though it is de rigueur to point up the connection between Romola and the Virgin (LaMonaca 162–63, 171–89), the novel also compares the heroine to the goddesses Minerva, Aurora, and Ariadne. Gilbert and Gubar observe that Eliot's interest in the Virgin Mother and Saint Theresa should be viewed as the author's desire to construct a "symbol of uniquely female divinity" (468). Although this comment supports my approach, even more compelling is their argument that the connection Eliot makes between Romola and Ariadne ultimately fails because, as the representation of the "vagrant propensity of the female mind," Romola resists escape from the labyrinthine gender constructs she inhabits (53–54). Certainly the myth of Ariadne acts as a symbol in this text, but I interpret it as part of a more complex feminist statement by a female writer who did not really like women very much and who was herself drawn to the notion of being, like the Madonna, a woman unlike any other.

I suggest that in secularizing the Christian Madonna and sacralizing the pagan Ariadne, Eliot gave women an avenue to independence while also modeling a credo that withstands the onslaught of skepticism and selfishness figured in *Romola* and felt in Victorian England.[7] I focus, then, on how Eliot combined the qualities of paganism (Ariadne) and Christian morality (the Virgin Mary) as an ideal mode for facing modern skepticism and guiding personal and political reforms. This approach is similar to Sharples's view of the Virgin and Isis as the same symbolic goddess in different cultural venues, whom nineteenth-century woman should model in their pursuit of intellectual knowledge and republican utopia.

Tito, of course, compares Romola to Ariadne when he commissions Piero di' Cosimo to design a triptych for his fiancée as a wedding present featuring Tito as Bacchus crowning his Ariadne, Romola (185–87, 200, 327). In choosing this design, Tito does not attach importance to the wisdom of the goddess Ariadne. He is intent on the more commonplace depiction of his beloved as a sublunary goddess based on her beauty and sexual attraction. Melema is not attracted to the idea that Romola might be a seer like Ariadne (or her counterpart, Arachne) who gives Theseus a ball of thread so that he can escape the Minotaur's labyrinth. Ariadne's very name offers the potential for spinning meaning out of oneself, but Tito has no interest in how this myth associates Ariadne with navigating the hermeneutic process itself. Rather, his design for the triptych focuses on his love domesticating Romola as his household goddess.

While imagery of the Virgin highlights Romola's unselfish character, the novel's plot and theoretical underpinnings depend as much on the motif of Ariadne as weaver and interpreter. Indeed, Ariadne is essential to constructing an answer to the novel's bleak world-view because she represents the philosophical play necessary to imagine revolutionary reform. The novel begins by tasking the reader with the labyrinthine interpretive process, perhaps associated with Ficino's pursuit of the ancient mysteries that conceal and reveal god but also related to the mythical Cretan labyrinth associated with Ariadne. Immediately challenging the reader's hermeneutic abilities, the "Proem" introduces a Florentine student who "had been questioning the stars or the sages, or his own soul, for that hidden knowledge which would break through the barrier of man's brief life and show its dark path, that seemed to bend no whither, to be an arc in an immeasurable circle of light and glory" (3). Not finding the key to all mysteries, the student can only hope to obtain the knowledge that would assuage a life that seems to "bend no whither." The text, then, enjoins the reader to question her very soul but does not provide the "arc" to do so successfully. In fact, just a few pages later, the narrator describes Florence as being heir to a "strange web of belief and unbelief" that includes "strange prophecies" and "fetishistic dread," thus leaving the reader in a "web of inconsistencies" (3, 8, 558).

In the seemingly minor scene in the marketplace that follows the Proem, Florentine traders and shoppers argue with a character named Goro who claims to have seen in the sky a "'big bull with fiery horns coming down on the church to crush it'" (19). There is neighborly chaffing about whether Goro actually saw such a heavenly sign and, if so, what it means. This conversation leads to apprehensive banter about the meaning of the recent death of Lorenzo de'Medici, the autocratic ruler of the city. As the conversation continues fast and furiously, the narrator pictures Bratti, a quiet member of the crowd, as "mentally piecing together the flying fragments of information," signifying the difficulty not only of obtaining the facts but of deciphering their import as well (20). Finally, an unnamed member of the crowd asserts that whether a sign be a "'revelation,'" a "'portent,'" or merely "'the written word,'" it always carries indeterminate shadings, and only the "'illuminated'" can reveal the significance of said sign (22). At this point, the barber Nello wryly points out that even though Savonarola and Fra Menico are holy interpreters of signs, neither of them agrees with the other (22). Hence, this first scene indicates that from the hoi polloi to the elite, the quotidian banter of the crowd to the sacred portents of the frati, no one in Florence is capable of interpreting the simplest of signs. Likewise, the reader learns that she, too, must make her way through a labyrinth in this insistently complex text.

The epistemological maze is highlighted further when the heroine steps on the stage. Immediately, Romola misjudges the character of her new acquaintance and admirer Tito. In fact, the narrator reveals the almost solipsistic nature of relationships, for Romola's understanding of Melema is merely a "vision woven from within" (70). Even Dino's vision that so sensationally acts as a turning point for Romola is "woven" from the "threads" of his beliefs (324). Likewise, when Tito becomes entangled with Tessa, it is as though he has "spun a web about himself and Tessa" that cannot be broken (301). Similarly, when Romola becomes aware of Tito's true character, not only does she feel as though caught in a "tangled web"; she is also aware that no "radiant angel" will give her guidance (325). Thus, when the heroine contemplates fleeing Florence a second time, she feels "confusion," for "all effort" seemed a "mere dragging at tangled threads" (499). Even Savonarola reaches a point when his mendacity is "entwined" with all that is good in him, just as his self-justification is "inwoven" with dedication to noble ends (520). Unknotting vision from buffoonery, self-aggrandizement from self-renunciation, meaningful signs from insignificant solipsistic symbols is all but impossible in this text. Yet it still demands a disciplined, charitable response to the world.

The Ariadne motif points the reader toward the difficulty of interpretation and the desire to attach meaning to signs. The fictional Bardo is akin to Mirandola and Ficino, who obsessively seeks to find the text that is the original key to all mysteries. Romola comes by her role as weaver of meaning (Ariadne) partially through her father. Bardo asserts that through his scholarship he intended to "'gather, as into a firm web, all the threads that my research had laboriously disentangled,'" something the female mind, he argues, is incapable of doing (53). But if in plotting and theme *Romola* is about "philosophic uncertainty," this condition is particularly harrowing for the female protagonist who is constructed as the symbol (Ariadne) but not as the subject of interpretive strategies (Robinson 31). This conundrum is as important as the one Homans poses about Romola and Western aesthetics, that is, that women are traditionally seen as symbolic bearers but not creators of the word (Homans). If existential despair and feminist angst are at the heart of *Romola,* Eliot's novel contends with the view of woman as object of hermeneutic crisis.

Regardless of her father's assertion that women cannot navigate meaning, more than the pseudo-scholar Bardo, more than the ethicists Savonarola and Dino, and more than the casuist Tito, Romola signifies the psychic, intellectual aptitude to weave meaning and escape webs of despair. Thus, as with Sharples's vision, Romola becomes a Madonna typified by her wisdom as well as her self-sacrificing love. By the end of the novel, Romola is superior to Savonarola and other male philosophers when she becomes the Visible Madonna and the uncrowned Ariadne, that is, when she rejects the need for masculine approval. At the end of the novel, literally weaving her own meaning, Romola consciously decides to wear the "disguise" or clothing of a nun when she leaves Tito a second time. "Why," the free indirect discourse asks, "should she care about wearing one badge more than another, or about being called by her own name?" (498) Although Homans asserts that the nun's habit signifies Romola's self-renunciation, I argue that at this point, like Teufelsdrockh, the heroine symbolically weaves her own raiment, identity ("name"), and meaning as she prepares to defy other cultural authorities (Homans 206). To Romola the hermeneutics of naming leads to the existential query, "What force was there to create for her that supremely hallowed motive" for doing one's "duty" to one's society? She concludes that "some form of believing love" gives one the authority to pierce the hermeneutic chaos and design strategies for taking meaningful, ethical action in the world (498).

But because the "bonds of all strong affection" are "snapped" when she leaves Tito, Romola feels she is in a cul-de-sac of signification, and she wishes to die (498). Whether Eliot means that Romola considers suicide at the climax of her existential distress, the author prophetically claims in 1863, "'Drifting away' and the Village with the Plague belonged to my earliest vision of the story and were by deliberate forecast adopted as romantic and symbolical elements" (*GEL* 4:104). As Romola drifts out to sea, she, who has experienced "memories of a dead mother" before "was touching the hands of the beloved dead beside her" and psychically returns to the womb. In this scene, even the verb tense changes from the simple past tense to past progressive, thus mimicking the mystical timelessness of epiphany (62, 502). A number of critics argue that in this scene Romola overcomes her (and Eliot's) mother-want. As Corner suggests, Romola must re-experience her mother's death in order to survive because the heroine's inability to fully embrace a creed is due to the early loss of her mother, making it impossible to transition to other objects as sources of meaning (71–73).[8] Pam Morris argues that Eliot's ethics are tied to material specificities. That is, the Madonna figure is the one material entity that unites all human beings because their own natal experience creates a psychic, material attachment to the physical act of birthing and maternal love (190). This "archaic memory of maternal love" becomes a veiled but "imaginative symbolization" that socializes citizens to feel duty toward the community as a whole, says Morris (190, 191; see also Carpenter "Trouble" and Simpson "Mapping *Romola*").

Morris's argument links the political back to the domestic, and I would suggest that this approach aligns with Eliot's belief that if human suffering transforms the maternal into a site of love equal to the divine, it also makes the symbolic maternal a means to hermeneutic vision and sacred political rebellion. Indeed, in the chapter on drifting, when Romola imagines her death and summons the significance of her life up until that point, she rebirths herself into a future of sacred rebellion as the secular Madonna *and* goddess of hermeneutics. This combination of two forms of the symbolic feminine divine—the wise and the loving—finally gives her authority in the public and private spheres.

Romola illustrates that authority publicly when her drifting takes her to a small village infected with the plague. A frightened priest, who should be a visionary leader to the villagers, has hidden in the church to escape his duty to his flock and to the immigrant Jewish families who were the carriers of the plague. Romola finds water for one of the plague victims and saves a little boy, whose family has died, thus beginning the task of reweaving a social and political community that has unraveled. She finds the priest and calmly tells him, "'I am come over the sea to help those who are left alive—and you, too, will help them now'" (554). She adds, with "encouraging authority," that no longer will he fear his duties as pastor and citizen (554).[9] The new, quietly masterful human goddess does not leave the shattered town until she has guided the priest to return to his role as spiritual leader and resettled the community, leaving for Florence only after the villagers sow their crops and set up a system for obtaining water from the well, which are classic indications of the establishment of civilization (554–55).

The narrative that follows illustrates the centrality of hermeneutics in Romola's new life. The chapters that immediately precede the "Epilogue" depict a web of inconclusiveness that must be confronted. In these penultimate chapters, Romola deconstructs Savonarola's self-aggrandizement and annihilation, discrediting his egotism and demystifying his sublime, prophetic signage. Hence Romola must make sense of the (self)destruction of the man who first gave her a belief in something spiritually and politically larger than herself. The description of his downfall is devastating: Savonarola's desire for public acclaim, "want of constancy," and "retraction of prophetic claims" "warp" the "strictness of his veracity." But there is another layer of deceit, the "transpositions and additions" of a devious notary who transcribes the Frate's confession, further warping Fra Girolamo's already counterfeit words (565, 566, 567). The pressure on representation itself and the hermeneutic challenge to the reader are all but insurmountable. The reader must accept that the superlative, inspiring force for good up to this point in the novel, Savonarola, is a "mixture" of "falsity" and "special inspiration," a man whose "doubleness" and "twofold retractation" leave the making of meaning and sacred political revolution almost impossible (568, 569, 573).

The epilogue, then, must make sense of this linguistic doubleness and respond with a doubleness of its own. The ending has received extraordinary scrutiny from feminist critics, who make convincing arguments that Romola is male-identified (she is), and passively submissive (yes and no) to patriarchy (yes and no). I have been arguing that Romola achieves a kind of protofeminist stature, even though many feminist scholars have taken issue with Eliot's commitment to women's rights. Eliot was no feminist partisan in her remark in 1853 that suffrage "only makes creeping progress" and that this was probably best because "woman does not yet deserve a much better lot than man gives her" (*GEL* 2:86). But this statement also registers the same disgust Sharples and Wright felt about society's aim to keep women ignorant. As Eliot sardonically explains about ignorant women in her essay on Wollstonecraft and Fuller, "your unreasoning animal is the most unmanageable of creatures." She concludes that there are two possibilities for dealing with stupid women: "the old plan of corporal discipline" or a "thorough education of women which will make them rational beings in the highest sense of the word" ("Fuller and Wollstonecraft" 989). Eliot may have not cared much for her sex, but one cannot imagine her supporting the first option.

Critiquing *Romola*'s ending, Homans argues that in the final scene, Eliot privileges a patriarchal writer (Petrarch) whom Bardo earlier in the narrative had used to rationalize the subordination of women. According to this interpretation, Romola is still the "transmitter" who ensures the "textual transmission from one generation of men to the next" that she was at the beginning of the tale (Homans 197).[10] Lesa Scholl remarks, too, that the ending indicates that Romola has always been, and always will be, immersed in masculine ideologies, including those of Savonarola, Tito, and Bardo (17). Gilbert and Gubar comment, "Wearing the mantle of invisibility conferred by her omniscience and the veil of the Madonna conferred by her message of feminine renunciation, Eliot survives in a male-dominated society by defining herself as the Other" (476). This approach highlights Eliot as Romola's slyer alter ego, suggesting that "renunciation" is a savvy disguise for her inordinate self-regard. But in the most damning evaluation, Shola Elizabeth Simpson confronts the fact that when Romola teaches Lillo, she "perpetuat[es]" a "system in which boys learn while girls do not" (Simpson 64).

Although these are astute readings of *Romola*'s conclusion, I am more in agreement with Alison Booth's incisive observation that Romola has an astonishing amount of freedom when compared to most Victorian women. As "an aristocrat with a complete classical education," Romola obtains a "vocation of public service, travels unchaperoned, and becomes feme [*sic*] sole under law." In a novel with an open-ended closing, the epilogue, in which Eliot appears to prop up patriarchy, actually interrupts it, argues Booth. Indeed, Romola is conveniently gifted with the killing off of her real and symbolic fathers (112, 116, 117). Teaching Tito's son to give up his individual desires for happiness, Romola performs her "duty of rebellion" against gendered narratives she has been trained to fulfill (127). A rebel in disguise, Romola, as Booth perceptively points out, is much like Eliot's activist friend Barbara Bodichon and the independent Florence Nightingale. Finally, Booth notes that Eliot's depiction of Romola as a self-sacrificing Madonna is so brilliant that the Victorian audience never noticed the radical implications of the final image of an all-female group (118–19).

I would add, as well, that making sense of the "warped" "veracity" that precedes the ending, the epilogue doubles the powers of the self-made symbolic goddess and woman who has become Ariadne–Madonna. Consider Ninna, the so-called neglected girl in Romola's household. At the beginning of the epilogue, this prepubescent child is depicted as having "wisdom" as she "instruct[s]" her mother in the art of "weaving" flowers (576, 577). Amidst the ineffectual Tessa and Monna Brigida, representations of an earlier generation of silly women who would appear to be dying off, Ninna seems to symbolize a new cohort of girls, who, like Ariadne, will weave meaning in themselves and their work. Ninna would also seem to be a temporal rendition or earthly precursor, on the order of John the Baptist, to the sublime weaving of the priestess/goddess Romola, who is also engaged in the role of teaching. In a trance in which she weaves an invisible vision of meaning as she gazes intently into space, Romola makes her pupil Lillo wait upon her. Unlike his sister Ninna, Lillo (the future of masculinity in this society of women) appears to have greater access to reading than Ninna, but he has no interest in it. Instead, quite the reverse of the active, self-confident, independent Ninna, like a puppet—and like his dense mother, Tessa,—he passively waits for Romola to come out of her trance and reveal to him the meaning of his life.

Why does the narrator not afford Ninna the same attention? In a letter to John Blackwood dated 9 November 1867, Eliot blithely commented:

"I have been of late quite astonished by the strengthening testimonies that have happened to come to me, of people who care about every one of my books and continue to read them—especially young men, who are just the class I care most to influence" (*GEL* 4:397). In addition, in her journal on 9 March 1880, Edith Simcox noted that Eliot confessed that she was much more influenced by men than by women. Simcox transcribed Eliot's admission that "she had never all her life cared very much for women." Although she cared very much for the "womanly ideal, sympathized with women and liked for them to come to her in their troubles," she admitted that the "friendship and intimacy of men was more to her" (9 March 1880, Simcox *Autobiography;* qtd. in *GEL* 9:299). Simcox also described an awkward conversation between herself, Eliot, and Lewes in which Eliot and Simcox end up debating who is more generous to them personally, men or women. In Simcox's account, Eliot accuses Simcox of viewing men negatively. While Simcox admits that she feels women always treat her with more kindness, Eliot remarks that she feels cold-shouldered by them and is much more comfortable with men (9 November 1877, Simcox *Autobiography;* qtd. in *GEL* 9:199–200).

An ungenerous interpretation of Romola's apparent partiality toward Lillo might conclude that the novelist did not achieve the progressive thinking that she disdained silly women for opposing, perhaps because, disabled by patriarchal institutions Eliot tried so hard to deconstruct, too often she was still amenable only to excruciatingly gradual changes on behalf of women. In addition, for all Eliot's allegiance to feminine self-renunciation, one often senses that the lady doth protest too much, thus highlighting debased humility that, on a continuum, is ultimately closely connected with arrogance. It should be remembered that the novel ends depicting Romola as, like the Madonna, a woman physically and psychically alone among her sex. As Julia Kristeva astutely remarks in "Stabat Mater," the male-defined Virgin Mary is unique among women and mothers and, as such, is an "inaccessible goal" for all women (327). One might suspect that Eliot, who allowed herself to be called "Madonna," probably enjoyed viewing herself as like Mary or Romola who is "'not like the herd of thy sex'" (*Romola* 130).[11] It must be admitted that in the room where we last see Romola and her followers, they all occupy the same space, but Romola is physically separated from Ninna and the lesser devotees Tessa and Monna Brigida. Romola appears most comfortable with Lillo, but only because by teaching him she is able to pursue (and disguise) her primary goal, the quest for knowledge and wisdom.

Interpreting Eliot's motives for focusing on Lillo more generously, we might surmise that any feminist would find it tedious and ineffectual to train the feminine automatons Tessa and Monna Brigida, whose behaviors would hopefully die out with them. And possibly the self-assured, remote, wisely weaving Ninna is, like Sharples and more so than Eliot, psychically establishing herself as an independent woman. There is nothing as well to suggest that Romola has not spent time teaching Ninna, for Romola is the hierophant to the whole group. Indeed, Ninna's weaving and wisdom suggest that she has already learned from her mentor, and Ninna appears to be naturally more intellectually capable than her dull-witted brother. Likewise, to picture Ninna as "wise" does upend the patriarchal norm that was depicted in Savanarola's mentorship of Romola. Perhaps, given Ninna's self-containment and pursuit of Ariadne as model, Romola does not need to instruct her in the same way that Lillo needs to be trained to be a "'great man'" who has "'wide thoughts, and much feeling for the rest of the world as ourselves,'" and who must try to "'raise men to the highest deeds they are capable of'" (578). It is possible, then, that Romola is attentive to Lillo because men as well as women must change in order to establish an equal society. The crawl toward women's rights would not reach its conclusion unless men were included in the project. Feminists, after all, must train both sexes, and each must find the rhetoric and audience they are most skilled at using and influencing.

Eliot knew of what she spoke when it came to changing men's attitudes about women. This study has pointed out the fear that masculinist institutions had about female empowerment as embodied in feminist goddess symbols. Some reviews of *Romola* show just how much the male population needed to be educated. Taking advantage of the debates about the Woman Question and making light of what could in our century be called the "chick novel," the *Saturday Review* complained that the tiresome Romola was "too much of a goddess to make it fair play for such a weak mortal as Tito to have to love her" (*"Romola"* 125). In a similar vein, a curious review titled "Epigrams on 'Romola'" carped, "Women must love their sex's type to see / Embodied in such goddess-majesty; / But surely man can hardly relish so / In lapdog prettiness to sit below!" Other epigrams step up the noxious tone. For example, "Women invented lies: yet, here [in Romolo], forsooth, / The wife impugns the husband's want of truth." The last stanza is viscerally binary in its logic: "'Man is a meaner animal than woman, / With whom her higher self has nought in common.' / Such is the moral of your book, George Eliot / And it's high time that somebody should tell ye't ("Epigrams" 1871:32). But the heart of the epigrams gets at the false binary patriarchy constructs. Noting that *Romola* is "for women, not for men," the versifier plays his trump card, asserting that although "The thrice three [female]

Muses form a glorious ring," in the "centre sits Apollo—king!" ("Epigrams" 32)

This versifier did not have to say that in Victorian culture the male holds political power, and it is high time George Eliot, the female writer, figured that out. Just the fact that he felt the need to bring the male God forward to undercut the female muse (Eliot) suggests that Eliot had touched a patriarchal nerve with her depiction of woman as goddess. The *Westminster Review* was more sophisticated and less generous in its patronizing attitude toward Eliot. The review contends that "this long and elaborate disquisition on the relations between the sexes" is anachronistic in that it brings Victorian views on gender to a story about fifteenth-century Italy (*"ROMOLA"* 348). Grumbling that the novel is a badly disguised modern tale, the review points out to the female writer that concern about the relations between the sexes was not on the minds of quattrocento women and that those relations were not a universal (read: women's history is not of universal import) (348). It is with such stuff that Eliot contends in her sometimes belabored and unsatisfying efforts to imagine a symbolic goddess who would model charity to men, the pursuit of progressive politics, and the achievement of a higher hermeneutic potentiality for women.

In *The Religion of the New Age* (1850), Georg Friedrich Daumer proposed that women be worshipped as divine entities. Marx derided the author for not dealing with women's devastating material conditions (Marx and Engels, *On Religion* 94–96). Similarly, Kristeva calls for a *"herethics"* that obviates the need for goddesses ("Stabat Mater" 330). As Kelly Oliver, editor of *The Portable Kristeva*, notes of Kristeva's argument, the cult of the Madonna must be deconstructed because it does not allow real mothers to articulate the actual experience of maternity (297). However, Kristeva's herethics is complicated, allowing contradictions about the goddess to be simultaneously legitimate. She suggests that behind the Mariolotry, "one might also detect an ambivalent conspiracy, through excessive spiritualization, of the mother-goddess and the underlying matriarchy with which Greek culture and Jewish monotheism kept struggling" ("Stabat Mater" 310). Thus, while Kristeva seeks to move beyond the psychological "want" that produces the need for a goddess, she recognizes that the culture's overdetermined response to the Madonna indicates that the goddesses which ancient Greek and Jewish culture tried to stamp out have their symbolic revenge in the masked Virgin.

Concluding this study, I suggest that in *Romola*, Eliot performs her own ambivalent "herethics" by using the Madonna as a cover for Ariadne. Thus she is able to refer positively to the rebellious traces of the ancient goddess tradition that the masculinist thinkers Bardo, Dino, and Savonarola would deplore. Less disruptive than Brontë's titanic Eve, Eliot's Great Goddess is not omniscient or omnipotent, although one imagines that an omnipotent, masculine God is not really the kind of deity Eliot would be interested in honoring. Eliot deemed women's capacity for sublime—and unlimited—feeling for others as more godlike than the masculine divine traits of omniscience or omnipotence, which are rather cold, arrogant attributes after all. When Romola subliminally desires her own death, the narrator remarks that the "Great Mother has no milk to still" human pain, perhaps a nod to Feuerbach's idea that the gods are inferior to humankind when it comes to the capacity for suffering (502). In this allusion to the Magna Mater, Eliot also accepts that feeling and suffering are necessary to deepen human knowledge, hermeneutic insight, and charity so that humanity can move from solipsism toward the communal. In *Romola,* the Great Mother *desires* to offer the [breast] milk of kindness, a desire based upon unlimited feeling and familial unity.

That the narrator refers to the goddess at this moment (she appears and does not appear) points toward Eliot's agnosticism and her construction of the symbolic female divine as what can exist as an ideal for *human* behavior. In *Romola,* Eliot allows that although the "great nature-goddess" of the past was "not all-knowing," her "life and power were something deeper and more primordial than knowledge" (97). Like Brontë, Barrett Browning, Nightingale, Jameson, the millenarians and feminist socialists, Eliot imagined a symbolic goddess who combines classical, pagan, and Christian elements, as though no one entity were effulgent enough by itself to represent divine potentiality. In a novel in which no being is omniscient, where the highest entity is a mortal woman who combines the hermeneutic powers of one symbolic divine female and the sacred, political rebellion and charity of another, Eliot intimates that more profound even than the fiction of an "all-knowing" God was that of the titanic women who named and generated the divine, making the human concept of god and hermeneutics possible through their primordial yearning toward all living beings. As LaMonaca asserts, "Romola's transfiguration into the Virgin Mary suggests that true moral heroism depends upon [page break] *becoming God* ourselves, so that perfect benevolence becomes an inherently human (rather than divine) attribute" (184–85). Weaving a richly dense narrative, Eliot bears/bares the consequences of unlimited feeling and pulsating yearning to know and interpret the other, making hers an immaculate conception that rewrites the mystifying Word/word.

Afterword

IN 1995-96 when I went up for tenure and promotion, Brigham Young University fired me, ostensibly for preaching doctrine heretical to the Mormon faith. The letter that informed me of the termination of my appointment noted that I had "enervated the very moral fiber" of the university. My "apostasy" was based, mainly, on the charge that I had stated in a talk at a conference organized by Mormons that I found comfort in meditating about Father *and* Mother in Heaven. Although BYU's termination letter essentially depicted me as a heretic, it did not release me from teaching my last class in the summer of 1996; neither did my local ward (parish) leader begin excommunication proceedings. Having been hired to begin teaching in the fall of 1996 at a university in another state, I found that the ward I attended there saw me as a worthy, capable teacher of seven- and eight-year-olds, who were being prepared for a crucial Mormon rite, baptism into the church. Thus, in the aftermath of being fired from the flagship university of my church, I was left with the schizophrenic consciousness that mine was both a dangerous and an edifying voice, particularly in terms of teaching Mormon young people, considered the most precious segment of the faith.

One of the ironies of the whole episode was that I had learned of a Mother in Heaven from Mormonism, which professes belief in this deity. The very language I had used to articulate my thoughts about Mother and Father in Heaven came from my immersion in church rhetoric. Like Nightingale when she saw the bust of Juno, I experienced a kind of *jouissance* when realizing, as an adult, that my church provided a divine horizon or model for female spiritual perfection, and it was important to me to express my thoughts about this female deity in a meaningful way. Apparently, though, I had made a mistake in thinking that I could publicly comment on praying to both parental deities without some kind of punishment from the Mormon patriarchy. Indeed, after experiencing the wrath of the Mormon male hierarchy, I came to see how appropriate the term "enervate" was to my termination from Brigham Young, for one of the meanings of "enervate" is "to castrate" or "unman." In using the Mormon rhetoric of personal revelation to describe my experiences with a Mormon Mother and Father in Heaven, I, *as a woman,* had undermined the male leadership by taking away their absolute power to prophesy authoritatively on church doctrine and dogma. Quite simply, I had not masked my words with palimpsestic metaphors or feminine submission, and the Mormon patriarchs had not learned how to converse with its female members with anything but condescension. It is no surprise, then, that I was captivated by the stories and words of the grandmothers I write about here who conjured numerous ways to articulate their songs.

Notes

Chapter 1

1. See Steinmetz, "Images of 'Mother-Want.'"
2. While Geertz contends that religious language perpetuates "*pervasive, and long-lasting moods,*" those moods, as Braude suggests, underwrite society's constant reexamination of gender (Geertz 90; Braude xix).
3. *The Dictionary of the History of Ideas* asserts that the notion of a "Great Goddess" is "well attested in the Neolithic period, and finds subsequent expression in many of the famous goddesses of the ancient Near East" ("Goddess Worship" 2:333). Viewing much scholarship on goddess worship as ahistorical and simplistic, Katherine K. Young notes that that there is no evidence suggesting there was a time when matriarchy was prevalent. Nor does the fact that a culture acknowledges a goddess necessarily mean that women have political power in that culture (Young 105–79). Regarding debates about the existence of a primal matriarchy, see Gerda Lerner's *The Creation of Patriarchy;* Marija Gimbutas's *The Language of the Goddess;* Naomi R. Goldenberg's "The Return of the Goddess: Psychoanalytic Reflections on the Shift from Theology to Thealogy"; Kathryn Rountree's "Archaeologists and Goddess Feminists at Çatalhöyük: An Experiment in Multivocality"; and Mary R. Lefkowitz's "The New Cults of the Goddess."
4. See Felicitas Goodman's *Ecstasy, Ritual, and Alternate Reality,* which refers to a medical experiment conducted in 1972 describing physical responses to trance, including "considerable increase in the heart rate and, surprisingly, a simultaneous drop in blood pressure. . . . a drop in the so-called stressors (adrenaline, noradrenaline, and cortisol), while the beta endorphins, the body's own painkillers, began to appear and stayed high even after the end of the trance" (39).
5. I have not found evidence that any of the writers I examine read this text.
6. Describing Christianity as bearing evidence of an "older matriarchal mythology," Frye suggests that the early Church substituted the Queen of Heaven for the earth goddess and replaced the white goddess with the Holy Ghost (7, 30). Marilyn Butler points out that through their depictions of pagan polytheism, Romantic writers rebelled against the Christian God (59).

7. See Shanyn Fiske on Eliot's and Brontë's knowledge of the classics as well as Felicia Bonaparte on Eliot's study (Fiske 64, 119; Bonaparte 16, 18).

8. The note for Job 35:10 reads: "Heb. 'makers' [gods], in the plural number . . . might as well have been put in the singular number, yea, though 'Elohim' be plural" (*Holy Bible*).

9. This includes the time of Jeroboam, when "the goddess shared the temple with Jehovah," and Jezebel "was pro-goddess and anti-Jehovah and had converted King Ahab to her belief in the goddess" (Davis 67).

10. See Kimberly VanEsvald Adams's discussion in "Feminine Godhead, Feminist Symbol."

11. With the rise of armchair antiquarians and professional archaeologists, the notion of deep time had to be faced head-on, especially when the construction of railroads uncovered ancient artifacts (Philippa Levine 5, 7). Some of the works on the Celtic heritage include Stukeley's *Stonehenge* (1740); Blair's preface to *Fragments of Ancient Poetry Collected in the Highlands of Scotland* (1760); Percy's *Reliques of Ancient English Poetry* (1765) and *Northern Antiquities* (1770); and Higgins's *The Celtic Druids* (1827). Works that argue that the Druids came from Noah (Piggott *The Druids*), include Stukeley and Pezron's *The Antiquities of the Nations* (1706); Rowlands's *Mona Antiqua Restaurata* (1723); Cooke's *An Enquiry into the Patriarchal and Druidical Religion* (1754); Jones's *The Origin of Language and Nations* (1764); James's *The Patriarchal Religion of Britain* (1836); and, of course, Edward Davies's works. For further discussion of the influence of the indigenous Celtic heritage on the Romantics see Carruthers and Rawes, *English Romanticism and the Celtic World*.

12. See Dafydd R. Moore's "The Critical Response to Ossian's Romantic Bequest" and Carruthers and Rawes, "Introduction: Romancing the Celt."

13. T. Wemyss Reid notes that Brontë's father loved telling supernatural stories to his children (215). In contributions to *Penzance Natural History and Antiquarian Society*, Richard Edmonds describes the May Day festivals, cromlêhs near Penzance, Druidical altars, and other antiquities of which the Branwells would have been aware.

14. Archaeological finds were within walking distance of the Brontë Parsonage. Ostensible remains of Druid ceremonies were found in 1773 at Rishworth in the West Riding of Yorkshire, and Druidical etymology was traced in Ripon and York, just a few miles from the Brontë residence (Piggott 170; Higgins 195).

15. See Houston, *Royalties: The Queen and Victorian Writers*.

16. Though she notes that the male Romantics' adoration of Mother Nature was founded on a pre-classical period of matriarchy and goddess worship, Margaret Homans in *Bearing the Word* argues that Mother Nature could not be a positive type for the woman writer because nature is a fructifying agent in biological rather than linguistic terms.

17. See Grace M. Jantzen's discussion of the Law of the Father, Freud, and Lacan 32–58.

18. A number of socialist-feminists were writing at this time, including Emma Martin, Eliza Macauley, Margaret Chappellsmith, and Frances Cooper.

19. It is clear that Fourier, Saint-Simon, and Owens ultimately could not break away from sexist views of who was to do the housework and who was to actually lead their utopian efforts.

20. Barbara Taylor maintains that Southcott "laid fertile mental ground in which socialist feminist doctrines could be sown" ("Woman-Power" 130).

21. When feminist-socialist Emma Martin died in 1849, Harriet Martineau was one of the subscribers who helped purchase a headstone for her grave, a fact suggesting how many mainstream Victorian writers may have known and admired Martin and her fellow socialists (Taylor, *Eve* 156).

22. R. Cooper also writes, "Who, possessing the smallest particle of common sense, would suppose for a moment that a God, possessing the attribute of OMNISCIENCE, would place man in a garden, and point out to him a certain tree whose fruits should be of the most alluring character, and yet prohibit him, under the pain of incurring his most bitter and eternal malediction, from eating of them. . . . Such an act, if it was performed by the Deity, . . . evinces a mind which is imbecile, and a disposition which is cruel, rather than a mind which is omniscient, and a disposition which is munificent" (*A Lecture on Original Sin*, 1838, 4).

Chapter 2

1. Barmby writes a similar description in his poem "The Woman-Power."
2. See Kate Lawson's exploration of this theme in "Imagining Eve."
3. Brontë's Angrian pseudonyms include Charles Townshend (otherwise known as Lord Charles Albert Florian Wellesley), Captain "Andrew" Tree, and, of course, Arthur Wellesley, the Marquis of Douro (later named the Duke of Zamorna) (Alexander, *The Oxford Companion* 407).
4. Gaskell writes, "Miss Brontë" had been "as anxious as ever to preserve her incognito in 'Shirley.' . . . and thus, when the earliest reviews were published, and asserted that the mysterious writer must be a woman, she was much disappointed" (322).
5. See Elizabeth A. Johnson on the female writer's need for a female god.
6. In a letter to Lewes in 1848, Brontë notes, "I can understand admiration of George Sand—for though I never saw any of her works which I admired throughout . . . yet she has a grasp of mind which . . . I can very deeply respect" (*Letters* 2:10). In another letter to Lewes in 1848, she says, "It is poetry, as I comprehend the word which elevates that masculine George Sand, and makes out of something coarse, something godlike" (*Letters* 2:14).
7. From the beginning, scholars and biographers have linked Emily with pagan worship. Recalling her conversation with Charlotte about Emily's being the prototype for Shirley, Gaskell uses Shirley's language for depicting a goddess. "Emily," she says, "must have been a remnant of the Titans,—great-grand-daughter of the giants who used to inhabit the earth" (440). Also believing that Charlotte ventriloquized Emily through the character of Shirley, Swinburne writes, "It is into the lips of her representative Shirley Keeldar that Charlotte puts the fervent 'pagan' hymn of visionary praise to her mother nature" (73). Stating that Charlotte did not have "Emily's fine Paganism," May Sinclair claims that Emily was a mystic (133, 224, 173). In 1925 M. P. Willcocks asserted that Charlotte only saw the visionary "world in mere glimpses" while Emily "gave herself gladly to the great breath" (164, 162). Willcocks explains that Emily's "intense consciousness of the Earth" and her "pagan love" for it are distilled in Shirley on the "'Stilbro' Moor'" where "she sees Creative Nature working on the loom as a Woman" (167). David Cecil complains that Charlotte's unrestrained imagination allows Shirley to indulge "in a flight of visionary meditation" (109).

Robert Bernard Martin agrees that Shirley is based on Emily (129). Robert B. Heilman is the first, as far as I can tell, to suggest that Charlotte's work preempts the modern goddess movement (289). Curiously, Heilman does not see this aspect of Brontë's work as crucial, and he drops this line of study to focus instead on how she symbolizes the power of intuition through moon imagery. Late twentieth-century scholarship continues the assertion that Brontë was a conduit for Emily's mysticism. Lyndall Gordon finds that "the prophetic proto-feminism of Charlotte and the visionary nature of Emily, meet in Shirley" (189); Nancy Pell notes that Jane Eyre replaces the male deity with "'the universal Mother, nature'" (402). Her article goes no further on the importance of Brontë's search for a way of embodying a female trope underlying the cosmos. *The Oxford Companion to the Brontës* explains Brontë's mainstream Anglican background, but the editors confirm that Charlotte "also described unconventional epiphanic scenes such as that in *Shirley*," in which there is a "non-Christian religious fable" using the "central figure, Eva" (Alexander 426). In keeping with other scholars, the editors of *The Companion* do not track the meaning of this entity elsewhere in Brontë's work. See also Lisa Wang, "Unveiling the Hidden God."

8. Of their roles as the four Chief Genii, Christine Alexander refers to the children's creation of themselves as "pseudo-gods" in the Angrian tales ("Autobiography" 156).

9. "Psychiatrists most commonly refer to dissociation (or more distantly hysteria); anthropologists to trance, spirit possession, and altered states of consciousness; and religionists to visions, inspiration, mysticism, and ecstasy. These discourses are not simply descriptive, but rather reflect the various historical and explanatory commitments of the disciplines themselves" (Taves 7).

10. Questions that would need to be considered: Did she write her trances down immediately after experiencing them, which would explain the erratic handwriting? Or, as she inscribed her trances in a calmer state, did the mere act of transcribing her epiphaâânic experience invoke a tumultuous response?

11. See Marianne Thormälen as well as Michael Baumber, who examine the evangelical and biblical influences on Brontë.

12. Others not discussed include "Proudly the sun has sunk" (#31), "The Evening Walk" (#34), "Vesper" (#53), "Hearken, O! mortal!" (#61), "Fragment" (#62), "The Bridal" (#65), "We wove a web in childhood" (#106), "Frances" (#190), all in *Poems*.

13. Many critics have noticed the moon imagery in Brontë's work, but none mention that it is a feature in the juvenilia and linked to a female god. See Daley's "The Moons and Almanacs of *Wuthering Heights*"; Kiernan's "The Moon in the Brontë Novels"; Maynard, *Charlotte Brontë;* Heilman's "Charlotte Bronte, Reason, and the Moon"; Lindner in *Romantic Imagery in the Novels of Charlotte Brontë;* Sabol and Bender's *concordance,* which provides numerous references to the moon. See Swinburne's paean to Brontë's description of the moon (*A Note*).

14. See, for example, "Morning By Marquis Douro," lines 37–40, #40; "Song By Lord Wellesley," #42. In "Vesper," Charlotte refers to the moon as "Nights empress" (line 27, #53). In "Reflections on the fate of neglected Genius," Genius is referred to as a "bright-eyed queen" and "Divinity" (lines 17, 24, #56). In "The moon dawned slow on the dusky gloaming," the "crescent moon" is referred to as "her" (lines 21–22, #88); in "Long since as I remember well" the moon is a "her" with "holiest light" (line 364, #108). In regard to the sun as male, see "Sunrise," #12; "The Churchyard," #19; "The Evening Walk," #34; "Morning by Marquis of Douro," #40; "Dream of the West," #138, all in *Poems*.

15. In keeping with this confluence of meanings for the moon, Bachofen notes, "Mother right may be identified with the moon and the night, father right with the sun and the day" (148).

16. Neufeldt believes that only half of the poems Charlotte wrote in the juvenilia are not associated with the Glass Town fantasy world (*Poems* xxxv).

17. At Cambridge, Patrick was enamored of Methodism, which, as J. F. C. Harrison notes, "was essentially a religion of experience. Its appeal was not to specific doctrines as such," but to emotional, mystical experience (*Second Coming* 30). Brontë's trances could have been related to Methodist forms of mystical experience.

18. Regarding the connections between Protestantism and messianic prophets, see the work of Ronald Matthews and Christopher Hill.

19. See Barbara Newman, "Henry Suso and the Medieval Devotion to Christ the Goddess."

20. See Kevin Binfield's "The French, the 'Long-wished-for Revolution.'"

21. Brontë researched the *Leeds-Mercury* for the years 1812–14 in preparation for writing the novel (Alexander, *Oxford Companion* 100, 464–65). She may also have read *The Voice of the West Riding*, a radical newspaper published during the years 1833–34.

22. Other places in *Shirley* (Penguin) that feature the moon in a trancelike moment include pages 202–3, 238–39, 241–42, 249, 373–74, 406, 485. More than any of Brontë's other novels, *Shirley* features many allusions to pagan gods and goddesses while also showing a strong grasp of biblical narrative. Some of these pagan references, as cited in the Penguin edition, include Baal (69), Saturn (166, 315), Medusa (194), Tophet (313), Hyperion (315), Oceanus (315), Prometheus (315), Calypso and Eucharis (455), Juno (462, 491), Thalestris (473), Endymion (485), Moloch (499), Dagon (519), and the "god of Egypt" (575).

23. The criticism on *Shirley* suggests that the schisms are too various to find *concors* in the *discordia*. See the *Edinburgh Review* ("Shirley: a Tale"); *Sharpe's London Journal* ("*SHIRLEY*"). Much modern scholarship typifies Susan Gubar's view that *Shirley* is "muddled in subject and point of view" (5). For example, see Terry Eagleton (*Myths of Power*); Gisela Argyle; Philip Rogers; Miriam Bailin.

Chapter 3

1. The *Quarterly Review* described the rites in Rome: "the cannon of St. Angelo, re-echoed by mortars in the streets, and the bells of all the churches, announce to the city and the world, *urbi et orbi*, that some event of great interest to Christendom is consummated." "The Pope, speaking 'ex cathedrâ,' has dogmatically defined the 'Immaculate Conception of the Virgin Mary'" ("La Croyance" 146). See discussions of the debates about the Immaculate Conception in Carol Engelhardt Herringer 116–43; Maria LaMonaca 160–62, 164–68.

2. See "The Gods of Antiquity" (Saturday 1 August 1868), which reads, "the worship of the Madonna—*Mea Domina, My Lady*, queen of heaven continued to be practised till the introduction and spread of Christianity, when the people still persisting in rendering homage to the revered goddess of their forefathers, in an evil moment, but with perhaps a good intention, the name of Mary was substituted for the Pagan goddess, the latter be-

ing designated as the symbol, throughout all past time, of the Virgin Mary, the Mother of Christ."

3. This argument continued in the nineteenth century. See "Dr. Pusey on Marian Devotion."

4. Ullathorne also writes of Mary, "she is the most wonderful example of exception from the common laws of our nature in so many ways. No mortal, no angel, no creature ever was before, or will be again, the Mother of God. Next to her Divine Son, the created universe has nothing like to her. And from how many laws is she excepted" (40).

5. "The Church of England a portion of Christ's One Holy Catholic Church" in the *Christian Remembrancer* 1866 noted that Pusey's *Eirenicon* sold about 5,000 copies and thus could be said to have been read by twenty to thirty thousand people but that most had not heard of the *Eirenicon* until the *Times* referred to it on 2 December 1866 (176).

6. The press had a field day, and there were barbs enough to go around for both Newman and Pusey. See "Replies to the Eirenicon"; "Doctor Pusey's Eirenicon"; Rev. of "*A Letter to the Rev. E. B. Pusey.*"

7. Further, making her conception immaculate raised issues about the immaculateness of the conception of her mother and father and so on.

8. See the review titled "*Sacred and Legendary Art*": "The treatment is catholic, not roman catholic," for she focuses on the "aesthetic," not "religious" (707). An anonymous review of *Legends of the Madonna* in *Blackwood's Edinburgh Magazine* remarks: "we must not forget we are reviewing Mrs. Jameson's *Legends of the Madonna*, a work which, professing to treat the subject relatively to art, repudiates controversy" (29).

Chapter 4

1. Regarding Barrett's spiritual leanings see Linda M. Lewis's *Elizabeth Barrett Browning's Spiritual Progress;* David G. Riede's "EBB: The Poet as Angel"; Patricia Murphy, "Reconceiving the Mother."

2. See Susan Stanford Friedman's "Gender and Genre Anxiety" regarding how Barrett "reformulated epic conventions to suit [her] female vision and voice" (203). Regarding EBB's knowledge of Greek, see Alice Falk's "Lady's Greek without the Accents," which is a good overview of EBB's immersion in the Greek language and her desire to be both a manly and a womanly poet. Jennifer Wallace's "Elizabeth Barrett Browning: Knowing Greek" also discusses EBB's trope of cross-dressing (346).

3. Regarding EBB and Swedenborgianism, see Lewis and Dorothy Mermin.

4. In her study of Barrett's spiritual life, though Lewis briefly mentions the radical sources of the belief in a female messiah, she does not examine how that tradition structures Barrett's writing (5).

5. Lewis notes that Barrett's work continually refers to the prophetesses "Miriam, Eve, Mary Magdalene, the Pythian, Cassandra, and Godiva" (14, 186).

6. See diary entries in *Diary by E.B.B.* 22, 33, 51, 59, 65, 89, 96, 106, 124, 152, 165, 176, 192, 201, 217, 219, 223, 225, 230, 234, 239.

7. See Lynee Lewis Gaillet's "Reception of Elizabeth Barrett Browning's *Aurora Leigh.*" The majority of critics recognized the brilliance of EBB's writing but criticized her metaphors: her hyperbolic metaphors, said one, "are signs of some deficiency in real strength" (*National Review* 248. One review complained that Romney was a "laughing-

stock" because of his adoration of such an independent woman, noting that "woman was created to be dependent" on "man" ("MRS. BARRETT BROWNING" 33).

8. The breast imagery is also in her "The Seraph and Poet."

9. References to God as "He" are throughout, including 1:204–5, 1134–36; 2:363, 675–76, 1233–34; 3:943; 5:70; 6:159, 1234; 7:753–60; 8:26, 560, 636, 671–72; 9:252, 343–44, 949).

10. See AL 1:551–53, 920–27; 5:139–40. A reference to Juno is found in 3:254–55; and a reference to Druid gods is found in 8:1008.

11. See Anne Ross, *Pagan Celtic Britain*, who writes that "The basic Celtic goddess type was at once mother, warrior, hag, virgin, conveyor of fertility, of strong sexual appetite which led her to seek mates amongst mankind equally with the gods, giver of prosperity to the land, protectress of the flocks and herds" (233).

12. See Terrance Allan Hoagwood and Herbert F. Tucker on this aspect of *Aurora Leigh*.

13. I am grateful to Sandra Donaldson for her insights on this motif.

14. Regarding the Reform Bill of 1832, EBB writes, "I know little or nothing about it—but I do like a nation to be free,—and I do like to belong to a free nation. And if the meaning of freedom is not, that the majority of the nation, called *the people*, should have a proportionate weight and influence in the government of the nation, I confess I do not understand what freedom means" (*EBB to Mr. Boyd* 140). She also writes on 9 June 1832, "The Bill has passed. We may be prouder of calling ourselves English, than we were before it passed,—and stand higher among nations, not only as a freer people, but as a people worthy of being free" (176).

15. The blinding of Romney has been much debated among feminists; see Cora Kaplan, "Introduction," *Aurora Leigh*; Friedman, "Gender and Genre Anxiety"; Steve Dillon and Katherine Frank, "Defenestrations of the Eye"; Carpenter, "Blinding the Hero."

Chapter 5

1. For other correspondence from Concordia, see the following, all in *The Crisis*: 3.32 (5 April 1834): 257–58; 4.4 (3 May 1834): 31–32; 4.9 (7 June 1834): 67–68; 4.10 (14 June 1834): 75.

2. Brontë and Barrett Browning also feature Cassandra in their writings (*Belgian Essays* 348; see also Fiske 98).

3. See Evelyn L. Pugh's "Florence Nightingale and J. S. Mill" regarding a disagreement similar to Owen's and Concordia's about legislation for women. Pugh argues that Mill's *Subjection of Women* was much influenced by Nightingale's 1852 *Suggestions*, which included "Cassandra."

4. Her journals, letters, and jottings held at the British Library indicate a rigorous and, to modern ears, severe sense of being set apart to fulfill a holy mission.

5. Barbara Montgomery Dossey suggests, "In many places, she identifies with major prophets, apostles, and other people on their journeys of faith. She often challenges the masculine imagery of God" (337).

6. Kalton's description of equality typifies this scene in which Eve/Nightingale's relationship with deity is one of horizontal transcendence. A horizontal approach would see humans as entwined with nature, in contrast to the traditional Christian view that human-

kind is the pinnacle of God's creation and the center of and dominating force over nature. If vertical transcendence may be equated with a hierarchical chain of being, horizontal transcendence posits that there can be no spiritual grounding without a material sense of one's interdependence with all life.

7. See also Christopher Hill.

8. In annotations to her Bible she writes in Greek, Latin, Italian, German, and French (Dossey 337).

9. In April 1861, Jowett writes to Nightingale: "do not let Cassandra die, but live & declare the works of God" (Jowett 4).

10. Jowett writes to Nightingale: "I did not exactly take Cassandra for yourself, but I thought that it represented more of your own feeling about the world than could have been the case" (Jowett 8). "But, how to remedy, or even to describe the evil without doing harm it is difficult to conceive. It seems to require a true woman or queen, a female Christ, as you say, to show the way. It seems to demand a nature which unites all feminine sympathies & in a certain sense, graces, with an heroic temper & firmness of soul. There are so many germs of nobleness in the characters of women that I cannot doubt a great deal might be done to ennoble them still more. But at present, the best women suffer more than any one from the degenerate state of religion & are fed or feed themselves on Methodistical or Catholic fancies" (Jowett 6).

Chapter 6

1. In 1851, she mentioned receiving a call from a follower of Owen, a Mr. Conyngham, who wanted to establish a federation between America and England "with an ultimate view of Socialism" (*GEL* 1:375). She also refers to Robert Owen's "Manifesto" in a letter to the Brays (*GEL* 2:88).

2. J. B. Bullen suggests that Romola progressed through the three Comtean phases, beginning in polytheism under her father, turning to monotheism under the tutelage of Savonarola, and finally attaining a positivist state free of superstition at the end of the novel (430). Pauline Nestor views Romola as a "Positivist 'priestess of Humanity'" (334).

3. In the 1820s Saint-Simon was a model for young French intellectuals, who looked for meaning in the post-revolution chaos (Pickering 211). After Comte's rupture with Saint-Simon, Saint-Simon's followers came to Comte for a clear portrayal of Saint-Simon's ideas (216–17).

4. "The theories of the master [St. Simon], particularly as modified by his former secretary August Comte, were avidly studied by such figures as Thomas Carlyle, George Eliot, and John Stuart Mill. Mill singled out Enfantin's movement as the source of many of his own feminist ideas" (Malmgreen 10).

5. Perhaps disingenuously, Eliot put off the repeated appeals from positivist follower Frederic Harrison to create a fictional rendition of a positivist Utopia (see *GEL* 4:448). She allowed that "an ever present dream of mine that the grand features of Comte's world might be sketched in fiction," but in later correspondence explains that her "whole soul goes with your desire that it should be done, and I shall at least keep the great possibility (or impossibility) perpetually in my mind, as something towards which I must strive, though it may be that I can do so only in a fragmentary way" (*GEL* 4:287, 301).

6. The following deal with the dry-as-dust nature of Eliot's scholarship and agree about its embalmment: Bullen (434); Henry James in *Partial Portraits* (88; qtd. in Bullen 434); "Romola," the *Athenaeum* 46; *the Reader* 2.28.

7. Henry Alley notes that Eliot obtains a "synthesis of the pagan and Christian elements" in the epilogue in the figures of Romola and Piero (95).

8. After Eliot's mother lost her twin sons, five-year-old Evans was sent to a boarding school. Though her mother lived until Mary Anne was sixteen, the two never shared a warm relationship (Carpenter, "The Trouble with Romola" 119, 120). To Carpenter, *Romola* is about Evans's rage at being separated from her mother ("Trouble" 120). Carpenter's argument attempts to show, as I do, that Romola became a mixture of two divine female entities, though Carpenter suggests that they are the Madonna and the "woman clothed with the sun" of Revelation ("Trouble").

9. LaMonaca asserts, "Even as Madonna Romola comes across as an essentialist vision of sacred womanhood, it is a vision of womanhood that eclipses male authority" (176).

10. Homans argues that the highest form of translation is that which translates creatively rather than literally and suggests that Eliot grew tired of playing the role of literal translator (*Bearing the Word* 178–79).

11. In her journal of 21 July 1859, Eliot writes in the serio-comic voice of Mary: "From Boulogne homeward. Found a charming letter from Dickens, and pleasant letters from Blackwood: nothing to annoy us. Magnificat anima mea!" [Latin, 'my soul doth magnify the Lord'] (*The Journals* 79).

Bibliography

Abrams, M. H. *The Mirror and the Lamp: Romantic Theory and the Critical Tradition*. New York: Oxford University Press, 1953.

Adams, Kimberly VanEsvald. "Feminine Godhead, Feminist Symbol: The Madonna in George Eliot, Ludwig Feuerbach, Anna Jameson, and Margaret Fuller." *Journal of Feminist Studies in Religion* 12.1 (1996): 41–70. Web. 9 Sept. 2010.

Alexander, Christine. "Autobiography and Juvenilia: The Fractured Self in Charlotte Brontë's Early Manuscripts." Alexander and McMaster 154–72.

———. *The Early Writings of Charlotte Brontë*. Buffalo, NY: Prometheus Books, 1983.

Alexander, Christine, and Juliet McMaster, eds. *The Child Writer from Austen to Woolf*. Cambridge: Cambridge University Press, 2005.

Alexander, Christine, and Margaret Smith. *The Oxford Companion to the Brontës*. Oxford: Oxford University Press, 2003.

Allen, Michael J. B., Valery Rees, with Martin Davies, eds. *Marsilio Ficino: His Theology, His Philosophy, His Legacy*. Leiden: Brill Academic Publishers, 2002.

Alley, Henry. *The Quest for Anonymity: The Novels of George Eliot*. Newark: University of Delaware Press, 1997.

Anderson, Pamela Sue. *A Feminist Philosophy of Religion: The Rationality and Myths of Religious Belief*. Oxford: Blackwell, 1998.

Anzaldúa, Gloria E. *Interviews/Entrevistas*. Ed. AnaLouise Keating. New York: Routledge, 2000.

Argyle, Gisela. "Gender and Generic Mixing in Charlotte Brontë's *Shirley*." *SEL* 35 (1995): 741–56. Web. 9 Sept. 2010.

Arnold, Matthew. *Complete Prose Works of Matthew Arnold. English Literature and Irish Politics*. Ed. R. H. Super. Vol. 9. Ann Arbor: University of Michigan Press, 1973.

———. *Literature and Dogma*: An Essay Towards a Better Apprehension of the Bible," London: Smith, Elder, 1880. Web. 10 Dec. 2011.

———. "The Study of Celtic Literature." Part 3. *The Cornhill Magazine* 13.77 (May 1866): 538–55. Web. 17 Mar. 2009.

———. "The Study of Celtic Literature." Part 4. *The Cornhill Magazine* 14.79 (July 1866): 110–28.

"Aurora Leigh." *The National Review* 8 (April 1857): 239–67.

Bachofen, J. J. *Myth, Religion, and Mother Right: Selected Writings of J. J. Bachofen*. Trans. Ralph Manheim. Princeton: Princeton University Press, 1967.

Bailin, Miriam. "'Varieties of Pain': The Victorian Sickroom and Brontë's *Shirley*." *Modern Language Quarterly: A Journal of Literary History* 48.3 (September 1987): 254–78. Web. 11 Dec. 2010.

Balleine, G. R. *Past Finding Out: The Tragic Story of Joanna Southcott and Her Successors*. New York: Macmillan, 1956.

Barmby, John Goodwyn. "Venus Rising from the Sea: An Ode to the Woman Power." *The Promethean, or Communitarian Apostle* 1.1 (January 1842): 9. Fiche. 12 Nov. 2008.

Barrett Browning, Elizabeth. *Aurora Leigh*. Ed. Margaret Reynolds. New York: W. W. Norton, 1996.

———. *The Brownings' Correspondence, 1809–1826*. Ed. Philip Kelley and Ronald Hudson. Vol. 1. Winfield: Wedgestone Press, 1984.

———. *Charles Dickens and Other "Spirits of the Age": Discussed and Analyzed*. London: Richard Clay and Sons, 1919. 16991. Huntington Museum, San Marino.

———. "A child's thought of God." MS Add. 45982 f.71. British Library, London.

———. *Diary by E. B. B.: The Unpublished Diary of Elizabeth Barrett, 1831–1832*. Ed. Philip Kelley and Ronald Hudson. Athens: The Ohio University Press, 1969. 509 B884 K2. Pierpont Morgan Library, New York.

———. "Edgar Allan Poe: A Criticism With Remarks on the Morals and Religion of Shelley and Leigh Hunt." London: Printed for Private Circulation Only by Richard Clay, 1919.

———. *Elizabeth Barrett to Mr. Boyd: Unpublished Letters of Elizabeth Barrett Browning to Hugh Stuart Boyd*. Ed. Barbara P. McCarthy. New Haven: Yale University Press, 1955.

———. *Elizabeth Barrett Browning: Letters to Her Sister, 1846–1859*. Ed. Leonard Huxley. London: John Murray, 1929.

———. *Essays on the Greek Christian Poets and the English Poets*. 1842. New York: James Miller, 1863. 471983. Huntington Museum, San Marino.

———. *Hitherto Unpublished Poems and Stories with an Inedited Autobiography*. Boston: Bibliophile Society, 1914. 87433 Huntington Museum, San Marino.

———. Juvenile Autobiography of Elizabeth Barrett Browning. MS 4879. Huntington Museum, San Marino.

———. Letter #261. To Anna Jameson. 1860. MS Add. 42231. British Library, London.

———. Letter #465. To Anna Jameson. 2 Feb. 1857. MS Add. 42230. British Library, London.

———. *The Letters of Elizabeth Barrett Browning*. Ed. Frederic G. Kenyon. 4th ed. 2 vols. London: Smith, Elder, 1897.

———. *The Letters of Elizabeth Barrett Browning to Mary Russell Mitford 1836–1854*. 3 vols. Ed. Meredith Raymond and Mary Rose Sullivan. Winfield, KS: Wedgestone Press, 1983.

———. *The Religious Opinions of Elizabeth Barrett Browning As Expressed in Three Letters Addressed to Wm. Merry, Esq., J. P.* Ed. W. Robertson Nicoll. London: Privately Printed, 1896. 22898. Huntington Museum, San Marino.

———. "To my dearest Mama on her birthday." Hope End, 1 May 1817. MS Hope End MS box. Scraps. 18. The Henry W. and Albert A. Berg Collection of English and American Literature. The New York Public Library. Astor, Lenox and Tilden Foundations. New York City.

Baumber, Michael. "William Grimshaw, Patrick Brontë and the Evangelical Revival." *History Today* 42.11 (November 1992): 25–31. Web. 12 Dec. 2010.

Bidney, Martin. *Patterns of Epiphany: From Wordsworth to Tolstoy, Pater, and Barrett Browning*. Carbondale: Southern Illinois University Press, 1997.

Bigwood, Carol. "Renaturalizing the Body (with the Help of Merleau-Ponty)." Welton 99–114.

Billone, Amy Christine. *Little Songs: Women, Silence, and the Nineteenth-Century Sonnet*. Columbus: The Ohio State University Press, 2007.

Binfield, Kevin, "The French, the 'Long-wished-for Revolution,' and the Just War in Joanna Southcott." *Rebellious Hearts: British Women Writers and the French Revolution*. Ed. Adriana Craciun and Kari E. Lokke. New York: SUNY, 2001. 135–59.

Bonaparte, Felicia. *The Triptych and the Cross: The Central Myths of George Eliot's Poetic Imagination*. New York: New York University Press, 1979.

Booth, Alison. ed. *Famous Last Words: Changes in Gender and Narrative Closure*. Charlottesville: University Press of Virginia, 1993.

———. "The Silence of Great Men: Statuesque Femininity and the Ending of *Romola*." Booth 110–34.

Braude, Ann. *Radical Spirits: Spiritualism and Women's Rights in Nineteenth-Century America*. 2nd ed. Bloomington: Indiana University Press, 2001.

Bray, Charles. *The Philosophy of Necessity; or, Natural Law as Applicable to Moral, Mental, and Social Science*. 2nd ed. Rev. London: Longman, Green, Longman & Roberts, 1863.

Brontë, Charlotte. "All this day." H. H. Bonnell. HT 67. Brontë Parsonage Museum, Haworth, England.

———. *The Belgian Essays: Charlotte Brontë and Emily Brontë*. Ed. and trans. Sue Lonoff. New Haven: Yale University Press, 1996.

———. "Gods of the Old Mythology." MS Bonnell 127 #102. HT4. S. B. 1981 (iv). Brontë Parsonage Museum, Haworth, England.

———. *Jane Eyre*. Harmondsworth, England: Penguin, 1966.

———. *The Letters of Charlotte Brontë with a selection of letters by family and friends, 1848–1851*. Ed. Margaret Smith. Vol. 2. Oxford: Clarendon, 2000.

———. "Look into thought & say what dost thou see." October 1836. *The Poems of Charlotte Brontë*. Poem #117.

———. *The Poems of Charlotte Brontë: A New Text and Commentary*. Ed. Victor A. Neufeldt. New York: Garland Publishing, 1985.

———. *Shirley*. George Smith Memorial Bequest. MS Add. 43477. B10. British Library, London.

———. *Shirley*. Ed. Andrew and Judith Hook. New York: Penguin, 1985.

———. *Shirley*. Ed. Herbert Rosengarten and Margaret Smith. Oxford: Clarendon Press, 1979.

———. *Villette*. Ed. Mark Lilly. Harmondsworth, England: Penguin, 1986.

———. "The Violet." MS. Bonnell 127, poem #102. Brontë Parsonage Museum, Haworth, England.

———. Well, here I am at Roe Head." 1836 Feb. 4 and [n.d.]. MS MA 2696. Pierpont Morgan Library, New York.

Brown, Sarah Annes. "*Paradise Lost* and *Aurora Leigh*." *SEL* 37 (1997): 723–40. Web. 10 Feb. 2008.

Brunn, Emilie Zum, and Georgette Epiney-Burgard. *Women Mystics in Medieval Europe*. Trans. Sheila Hughes. New York: Paragon House, 1989.

Bryant, John. "Rewriting *Moby-Dick:* Politics, Textual Identity, and the Revision Narrative." *PMLA* 125.4 (2010): 1043–60.
"THE BUCHANITES." *Chambers's Edinburgh Journal* 153 (5 Dec. 1846): 362–65. Web. 2 Nov. 2010.
Bullen, J. B. "George Eliot's Romola as a Positivist Allegory." *The Review of English Studies* n.s. 26.104 (1975): 425–35. Web. 23 Aug. 2010.
Butler, Marilyn. "Druids, Bards and Twice-Born Bacchus: Peacock's Engagement With Primitive Mythology." Keats-*Shelley Review* 36 (1985): 57–76.
Calabria, Michael D. *Florence Nightingale in Egypt and Greece: Her Diary and 'Visions.'* Albany: State University of New York Press, 1997.
Callinicos, Alex. "Jacques Derrida and the new international." *Derrida's Legacies.* Ed. Simon Glendinning and Robert Eaglestone. London: Routledge, 2008. 80–89.
Carlile, Richard. "IMMACULATE CONCEPTION!" *Republican* 11:16 (22 April 1825): 495–500. Web. 14 June 2010.
Carlyle, Thomas. "Goethe's Helena." *Thomas Carlyle, Ralph Waldo Emerson, and Henry Swasey, Carlyle's Miscellanies.* Vol. 1. Cambridge Press. 1838. 162–219. Web. 13 Dec. 2011.
———. *Sartor Resartus: The Life and Opinions of Her Teufelsdrockh at School.* 1831. Web. 12 Dec. 2011.
Carpenter, Mary Wilson. "Blinding the Hero." *Differences: A Journal of Feminist Cultural Studies* 17.3 (Fall 2006): 52–68. Web. 18 Aug. 2010.
———. *George Eliot and the Landscape of Time: Narrative Form and Protestant Apocalyptic History.* Chapel Hill: University of North Carolina Press, 1986.
———. "The Trouble with Romola." Morgan. 105–28.
Carroll, David. "George Eliot Martyrologist: The Case of Savonarola." Levine and Turner. 105–21.
Carruthers, Gerard, and Alan Rawes. eds. *English Romanticism and the Celtic World.* Cambridge: Cambridge University Press, 2003.
———"Introduction: Romancing the Celt." *Carruthers and Rawes* 1–19
Cecil, David. *Early Victorian Novelists: Essays in Revaluation.* New York: Bobbs-Merrill, 1935.
Chaney, Christine. "The Prophet-Poet's Book." *SEL* 48.4 (2008): 791–99. Web. 9 Nov. 2010.
Chase, Karen. "The Modern Family and the Ancient Image in Romola." *Dickens Studies Annual* 14 (1985): 303–26. Web. 17 Sept. 2011.
Chorley, H. F. "*Aurora Leigh.*" *The Athenaeum* 1517 (22 November 1856): 1425–27. Web. 13 Dec. 2011.
Christ, Carol P. "Why Women Need the Goddess: Phenomenological, Psychological, and Political Reflections." *The Politics of Women's Spirituality.* Ed. Charlene Spretnak. New York: Anchor Books, 1982. 71–86.
"The Church of England a portion of Christ's One Holy Catholic Church, and a Means of restoring visible Unity." *Christian Remembrancer* 51.131 (January 1866): 156–89. Web. 10 Apr. 2009.
Classified Catalogue of the Library of the Mechanics' Institution, Keighley and a List of Apparatus. Keighley: Aked, 1855. Brontë Parsonage Museum, Haworth, England.
Code, Lorraine. *What Can She Know? Feminist Theory and the Construction of Knowledge.* Ithaca: Cornell University Press. 1991.

Concordia. "Letter." *The Crisis* (Saturday 10 August 1833): 254–55. Ed. Robert Owen and Robert Dale Owen. London: J. Eamonson, 1833. *The Crisis, and National Co-operative Trades' Union Gazette.* 2 vols. 1832–1833. New York: Greenwood reprint, 1968.

Cook, Edward Tyas. *The Life of Florence Nightingale.* 2 vols. London: Macmillan, 1913.

Cooper, R. *A Lecture on Original Sin.* Manchester: A Heywood, 1838. Fiche. 10 Apr. 2009.

Corner, Julian. "'Telling the Whole': Trauma, Drifting, and Reconciliation." Levine and Turner. 67–88.

Coward, Rosalind. *Patriarchal Precedents: Sexuality and Social Relations.* London: Routledge & Kegan Paul, 1983.

The Crisis. Vol. 3. London: B. D. Cousins, 1834. *The Crisis, and National Co-operative Trades' Union Gazette.* Vols. 3–4. 1833–34. New York: Greenwood, 1968.

Dale, R. W. "The Truth and Office of the English Church; or, the Church of England a Portion of Christ's One Holy Catholic Church, and a Means of Restoring Visible Unity." *The British Quarterly Review* 86 (April 1866): 281–290. Web. 22 Sept. 2010.

Daley, A. Stuart. "The Moons and Almanacs of *Wuthering Heights*." *Huntington Library Quarterly: A Journal for the History and Interpretation of English and American Civilization* 37 (1974): 337–53.

Dalley, Lana L. "'The least 'Angelical' poem in the language': Political Economy, Gender, and the Heritage of Aurora Leigh." *Victorian Poetry* 44.4 (2006): 525–42. Web. 22 Sept. 2010.

David, Deirdre. *Intellectual Women and Victorian Patriarchy: Harriet Martineau, Elizabeth Barrett Browning, George Eliot.* New York: Cornell University Press, 1987.

Davies, Edward. *The Mythology and Rites of the British Druids, Ascertained by National Documents; and Compared with the General Traditions and Customs of Heathenism, as Illustrated by the Most Eminent Antiquaries of Our Age.* London: J. Booth, 1890. 489330. Huntington Museum, San Marino.

Davies, Peter. "Myth and Maternalism in the Work of Johann Jakob Bachofen." *German Studies Review* 28.3 (2005): 501–18.

Davis, Elizabeth Gould. *The First Sex.* New York: Penguin, 1971.

DeShazer, Mary K. *Inspiring Women: Reimagining the Muse.* New York: Pergamon Press, 1986.

Dickens, Charles. *A Tale of Two Cities.* Ed. Richard Maxwell. New York: Penguin, 2003.

Dillon, Steve, and Katherine Frank. "Defenestrations of the Eye: Flow, Fire, and Sacrifice in 'Casa Guidi Windows.'" *Victorian Poetry* 35.4 (1997): 471–92. Web. 15 Nov. 2010.

"Doctor Pusey's Eirenicon." *Eclectic Review* 10 (1866): 77–86. Web. 20 Aug. 2010.

"The Doctrine of the Immaculate Conception." *Rambler* 3 (March 1849): 547. Web. 8. Sept. 2009.

Dolin, Tim. "Fictional Territory and a Woman's Place: Regional and Sexual Difference in *Shirley.*" *ELH* 62.1 (1995): 197–212. Web. 20 Feb. 2011.

Dossey, Barbara Montgomery. *Florence Nightingale: Mystic, Visionary, Healer.* Springhouse, PA, 2000.

"Dr. Pusey on Marian Devotion." *Dublin Review* 7:13 (1866): 142–99. Web. 20 Aug. 2010.

Dyer, Mary M. *The Rise and Progress of the Serpent from the Garden of Eden, to the Present Day: With A Disclosure of Shakerism.* Concord, NH. Printed for the author, 1847. Web. 13 Aug. 2010.

Eagles, John. Rev. of "*Legends of the Madonna* by Mrs. Jameson." *Blackwood's Edinburgh Magazine* 74.453 (1853): 23–38. Web. 19 June 2010.

Eagleton, Terry. *Myths of Power: A Marxist Study of the Brontës*. London: Macmillan, 1975.

Edmonds, Richard. "An Account of some ancient Barrows, Urns, and other Sepulchral Remains, found near Penzance." *Penzance Natural History and Antiquarian Society Report for 1845*. Penzance: F. T. Vibert, 1851. AC 3011. British Library, London. 229–36.

———. "On the remains of Druidical Temples near Penzance." *Penzance Natural History and Antiquarian Society Report for 1845*. Penzance: F. T. Vibert, 1851. AC 3011. British Library, London. 381–86.

———. "On some Ancient Customs in the western extremity of Cornwall." *Penzance Natural History and Antiquarian Society Report for 1844*. Penzance: F. T. Vibert, 1851. AC 3011. British Library, London. 69–82.

Eliot, George. *The George Eliot Letters*. 9 vols. Ed. Gordon S. Haight. New Haven: Yale University Press, 1954–78.

———. *The Journals of George Eliot*. Ed. Margaret Harris and Judith Johnston. Cambridge: Cambridge University Press, 1998.

———. "Margaret Fuller and Mary Wollstonecraft." *The Leader* 6.290 (13 October 1855): 988–89. Web. 10 Dec 2011.

———. *Romola*. Ed. Robert Kiely. New York: Modern Library, 2003.

"EMMA MARTIN." *The Leader* 2:82 (October 1851): 985–86. Web. 18 June 2010.

"EPIGRAMS ON "ROMOLA." *New Monthly Magazine* 148: 601 (January 1871): 32. Web. 22 Aug. 2010.

Evans, Frederick William. "A Short Treatise on the Second Appearing of Christ in and through the order of the Female." Boston: Bazin & Chandler, 1853. 287833. Huntington Museum, San Marino.

"Extract from Dr. Holley's Review of Professor Silliman's Journal." *Account of Some of the Proceedings of the Legislatures of the States of Kentucky and New Hampshire, 1828 &c in Relation of the People Called Shakers*. Western Review 3: 203. Rpt. New York, 1846. 4182 b4. British Library, London.

Faber, Frederic William. *The Precious Blood: or, the Price of Our Salvation*. London: Thomas Richardson & Son, 1860. Web. 13 Dec. 2011.

Falk, Alice. "Lady's Greek Without the Accents: Aurora Leigh and Authority." *Studies in Browning and His Circle: A Journal of Criticism, History, and Bibliography* 19 (1991): 84–92. 13 Dec. 2011.

Fanon, Frantz. *Black Skin, White Masks*. Trans. Charles Lam Markmann. New York: Grove Press, 1967.

Feuerbach, Ludwig. *The Essence of Christianity*. Trans. George Eliot. Amherst, NY: Prometheus Books, 1989.

"A Few More Odd Women." *All the Year Round* 13.316 (19 December 1874): 222–25. Web. 22 June 2010.

Fiorenza, Elisabeth Schüssler. "G*d—The Many-Named: Without Place and Proper Name." *Transcendence and Beyond: A Postmodern Inquiry*. Ed. John D. Caputo and Michael J. Scanlon. Bloomington: Indiana University Press, 2007. 109–26. Web. 7 Sept. 2010.

———. *In Memory of Her: A Feminist Theological Reconstruction of Christian Origins*. New York: Crossroad, 1983.

Fiske, Shanyn. *Heretical Hellenism: Women Writers, Ancient Greece, and the Victorian Popular Imagination.* Athens: The Ohio University Press, 2008.
Friedman, Susan Stanford. "Gender and Genre Anxiety: Elizabeth Barrett Browning and H. D. as Epic Poets." *Tulsa Studies in Women's Literature* 5.2 (1986): 203–28. Web. 10 Dec. 2010.
Frye, Northrop. *A Study of English Romanticism.* Chicago: University of Chicago Press, 1982.
Fuller, Margaret. *Woman in the Nineteenth Century.* American Transcendentalism. Web. 8 Dec. 2011.
Gaillet, Lynee Lewis. "Reception of Elizabeth Barrett Browning's *Aurora Leigh:* An Insight into the Age's Turmoil Over the Representation of Gender and Theories of Art." *Studies in Browning and His Circle* 20 (1993): 115–22. 3 Nov. 2010.
Gaskell, Elizabeth. *The Life of Charlotte Brontë.* Ed. Angus Easson. Oxford: Oxford University Press, 1996.
Geertz, Clifford. "Religion as a Cultural System." *The Interpretation of Cultures: Selected Essays.* Waukegan, IL: Fontana Press, 1993. 87–125. 7 Oct. 2010.
Gelpi, Barbara Charlesworth. "*Aurora Leigh:* The Vocation of the Woman Poet." *Victorian Poetry* 19.1 (1981): 35–48.
Gilbert, Sandra M., and Susan Gubar. *The Madwoman in the Attic: The Woman Writer and the Nineteenth-Century Literary Imagination.* New Haven: Yale University Press, 1984.
Glendinning, Simon, and Robert Eaglestone, eds. *Derrida's Legacies: Literature and Philosophy.* London: Routledge, 2008.
"Goddess Worship." *The Dictionary of the History of Ideas* maintained by *The Electronic Text Center* at the University of Virginia Library, Gale Group. Web. 1 May 2009.
"Goddess Worship: Theoretical Perspectives." *The Encyclopedia of Religion.* Mircea Eliade. 6:53. Web. 20 Apr. 2007.
"The Gods of Antiquity." *The Treasury of Literature and The Ladies' Treasury* (Saturday 1 August 1868): 65. Web. 6 May 2010.
Goldstein, Leslie F. "Early Feminist Themes in French Utopian Socialism: The St.-Simonians and Fourier." *Journal of the History of Ideas* 43.1 (1982): 91–108.
Goodman, Felicitas D. *Ecstasy, Ritual, and Alternate Reality: Religion in a Pluralistic World.* Bloomington: Indiana University Press, 1988.
Gordon, Lyndall. *Charlotte Brontë: A Passionate Life.* London: Chatto & Windus, 1994.
Goslee, Nancy Moore. *Scott: The Rhymer.* Lexington: University Press of Kentucky, 1988.
Gregory, Richard L., ed. *Oxford Companion to the Mind.* New York: Oxford University Press, 1987.
Griffin, Susan M. *Anti-Catholicism and Nineteenth-Century Fiction.* Cambridge: Cambridge University Press, 2004.
Gubar, Susan. "The Genesis of Hunger according to *Shirley.*" *Feminist Studies* 3.3/4 (1976): 5–21. Web. 10 Dec. 2011.
Gunton, Colin E. *The One, the Three and the Many.* Cambridge: Cambridge University Press, 1993.
Haight, Gordon S. *George Eliot: A Biography.* New York: Oxford University Press, 1968.
Harrison, J. F. C. *The Second Coming: Popular Millenarianism, 1780–1850.* London: Routledge & Kegan Paul, 1979.
———. "Thomas Paine and Millenarian Radicalism." *Citizen of the World: Essays on Thomas Paine.* New York: St. Martin's Press, 1988.

Haskett, William J. *Shakerism Unmasked or the History of the Shakers*. Pittsfield: B. H. Walkley, Printer, 1828. Web. 14 July 2010.

Heilman, Robert B., "Charlotte Bronte, Reason, and the Moon." *Nineteenth-Century Fiction* 14.4 (1960): 283–302.

Herringer, Carol Engelhardt. *Victorians and the Virgin Mary: Religion and Gender in England, 1830–85*. Manchester: Manchester University Press, 2008.

Hewlett, Dorothy. *Elizabeth Barrett Browning: A Life*. New York: Alfred A. Knopf, 1952.

Higgins, Godfrey. *The Celtic Druids*. London: R. Hunter, 1827. 144210. Huntington Museum, San Marino.

Hill, Christopher. *The World Turned Upside Down: Radical Ideas During the English Revolution*. London: Penguin, 1991.

Hill, Susan E. "Translating Feuerbach, Constructing Morality: The Theological and Literary Significance of Translation for George Eliot." *Journal of the American Academy of Religion* 65.3 (1997): 635–53. Web. 22 Aug. 2010.

Hirsch, Pam. "Charlotte Brontë and George Sand: The Influence of Female Romanticism." *Brontë Society Transactions* 21.6 (1996): 209–18.

"Histoire de l'Eglise de France." *Christian Remembrancer* 32.94 (October 1856): 423–50. Web. 22 Aug. 2010.

Hoagwood, Terence Allan. "Biblical Criticism and Secular Sex: Elizabeth Barrett's *A Drama of Exile* and Jean Ingelow's *A Story of Doom*." *Victorian Poetry* 42.2 (2004): 165–80.

Hodgson, Peter C. *The Mystery beneath the Real: Theology in the Fiction of George Eliot*. Minneapolis: Fortress Press, 2000.

Holmes, Alicia E. "Elizabeth Barrett Browning: Construction of Authority in *Aurora Leigh* by Rewriting Mother, Muse, and Miriam." *The Centennial Review* 36.3 (1992): 593–606.

The Holy Bible; containing the Sacred Texts of the Old and New Testaments and the Apocrypha at Large; with Practical Observations by Rev. Mr. Ostervald. Newcastle-upon-Tyne: M. Brown, 1811. SB1923. Haworth Parsonage Museum, Haworth, England.

Homans, Margaret. *Bearing the Word: Language and Female Experience in Nineteenth-Century Women's Writing*. Chicago: University of Chicago Press, 1986.

———. *Women Writers and Poetic Identity: Dorothy Wordsworth, Emily Brontë, and Emily Dickinson*. Princeton: Princeton University Press, 1980.

Homes, Elsie B. "George Eliot's Wesleyan Madonna." *The George Eliot Fellowship Review* 18 (1987): 52–59.

Horne, R. H., ed. *A New Spirit of the Age*. Vol. 2. London: Smith, Elder, 1844.

Houston, Gail Turley. *Royalties: The Queen and Victorian Writers*. Charlottesville: University Press of Virginia, 1999.

"'Immaculate Conception' of the Virgin Mary." *Wesleyan-Methodist Magazine* 13 (July 1867): 595–601. Web. 22 Oct. 2008.

Irigaray, Luce. *Sexes and Genealogies*. Trans. Gillian C. Gill. New York: Columbia University Press, 1993.

Jameson, Anna. *A Commonplace Book of Thought*. London: Longman, Brown, Green, and Longmans, 1854. 8406 e 24. British Library, London.

———. *The History of Our Lord: As Exemplified in Works of Art*. Cont. and Completed by Lady Eastlake. Vol. 1. London: Longman, Green, Longman, Roberts, & Green, 1864. 7801 aa10. British Library, London.

———. *Legends of the Madonna, as Represented in the Fine Arts*. London: Longman, Brown, Green, and Longmans, 1852. 109489. Huntington Musueum, San Marino.

———. *The Relative Position of Mothers and Governesses.* 2nd ed. London: Spottiswoode and Shaw. n.d. "Reprinted for the Benefit of the Asylum for Aged Governesses. 1509 261. British Library, London.

———. *Sacred and Legendary Art.* 2nd ed. London: Longman, Brown, Green, and Longmans, 1850. 1401 h6. British Library, London.

———. "'Woman's Mission,' and Woman's Position." *Memoirs and Essays Illustrative of Art, Literature, and Social Morals.* London: Richard Bentley, 1846. 207–48. 1401 c.17. British Library, London.

Jantzen, Grace M. *Becoming Divine: Towards a Feminist Philosophy of Religion.* Bloomington: Indiana University Press, 1999.

Jeffrey, Francis. Rev. of *"A Warning to the whole World, from the Sealed Prophecies of Joanna Southcott, and other Communications given since the Writings were opened on the 12th of January 1803."* *The Edinburgh Review* 24.48 (1815): 452–71. Web. 1 Sept. 2010.

Jenkins, Ruth Y. *Reclaiming Myths of Power: Women Writers and the Victorian Spiritual Crisis.* Lewisburg: Bucknell University Press, 1995.

———. "Rewriting Female Subjectivity: Florence Nightingale's Revisionist Myth of Cassandra." *Weber Studies: An Interdisciplinary Humanities Journal* 11.1 (1994): 16–26.

Johnson, Elizabeth A. *She Who Is: The Mystery of God in Feminist Theological Discourse.* New York: Herder & Herder, Crossroad Publishing, 2005.

Jowett, Benjamin. *Dear Miss Nightingale: A selection of Benjamin Jowett's Letters to Florence Nightingale, 1860–1893.* Ed. Vincent Quinn and John Prest. Oxford: Clarendon Press, 1987.

Julian of Norwich. *Sixteen Revelations of Divine Love.* 1640; London: S. Clarke, 1843. Web. 18 June 2010.

Kalton, Michael C. "Green Spirituality: Horizontal Transcendence." *The Psychology of Mature Spirituality: Integrity, wisdom, transcendence.* Ed. Polly Young-Eisendrath and Melvin E. Miller. London: Routledge, 2000. 187–200.

Kaplan, Cora. "Introduction." *Aurora Leigh with Other Poems.* London: Women's Press, 1978. 5–36.

Keats, John. *Poetical Works and Other Writings of John Keats.* Ed. H. Buxton Forman. Vol. 7. New York: Charles Scribner's Sons, 1939.

Keightley, Thomas. *The Mythology of Ancient Greece and Rome.* London: Whittaker, 1838.

Kiernan, N. S. "The Moon in the Brontë Novels." Part 91. *Brontë Society Transactions* 18.91: 36–38.

Knight, Mark, and Emma Mason. *Nineteenth-Century Religion and Literature: An Introduction.* Oxford: Oxford University Press, 2006.

Kristeva, Julia. *The Portable Kristeva.* Ed. Kelly Oliver. New York: Columbia University Press, 1997.

———. "Stabat Mater." *The Portable Kristeva.* Ed. Kelly Oliver. New York: Columbia University Press, 1997. 308-31.

———. *Strangers to Ourselves.* Trans. Leon S. Roudiez. New York: Columbia University Press, 1991.

Krueger, Christine L. *The Reader's Repentance: Women Preachers, Women Writers, and Nineteenth-Century Social Discourse.* Chicago: University of Chicago Press, 1992.

"La Croyance à l'immaculée Conception de la Sainte Vierge ne peut devenir dogme de foi." *Quarterly Review* 97.193 (June 1855): 143–83. Web. 29 Aug. 2010.

LaMonaca, Maria. *Masked Atheism: Catholicism and the Secular Victorian Home.* Columbus: The Ohio State University Press, 2008.

Larson, Janet L. "'Who is Speaking?': Charlotte Brontë's Voices of Prophecy." Morgan 66–86.
Lawson, Kate. "The Dissenting Voice: *Shirley*'s Vision of Women and Christianity." *SEL* 29 (1989): 729–43.
———. "Imagining Eve: Charlotte Bronte, Kate Millett, Hélène Cixous." *Women's Studies* 24 (1995): 411–26.
Lefkowitz, Mary R. "The New Cults of the Goddess." *The American Scholar* 62.2 (1993): 261–68.
"*Legends of the Madonna* by Mrs. Jameson." *Blackwood's Edinburgh Magazine* 74.453 (July 1853): 23–38.
Leonard, William. "A Discourse on the Order and Propriety of Divine Inspiration and Revelation, Showing the Necessity thereof, in all Ages, to Know the Will of God, also, A Discourse on The Second Appearing of Christ, in and through the Order of the Female, and A Discourse on the Propriety and Necessity of a United Inheritance in all Things, in Order to Support a True Christian Community." Harvard: United Society, 1853. 4182 b4. British Library, London.
Lerner, Gerda. *The Creation of Patriarchy.* New York: Oxford University Press, 1986.
Levine, Caroline, and Mark W. Turner, eds. *From Author to Text: Re-reading George Eliot's Romola.* Aldershot: Ashgate, 1998.
Levine, Philippa. *The Amateur and the Professional: Antiquarians, Historians, and Archaeologists in Victorian England, 1838–1886.* Cambridge: Cambridge University Press, 1986.
Lewes, G. H. Rev. of "Shirley: a Tale." *The Edinburgh Review* 91.183 (January 1850): 153–73. Web. 27 Apr. 2009.
Lewis, Linda M. *Elizabeth Barrett Browning's Spiritual Progress: Face to Face with God.* Columbia: University of Missouri Press, 1998.
Liddington, Jill. "Anne Lister and Emily Brontë, 1838–39: Landscape with Figures." *Brontë Society Transactions* 26.1 (2001): 46–58.
Lindner, Cynthia A. *Romantic Imagery in the Novels of Charlotte Brontë.* London: Macmillan, 1978.
Lipshitz, Susan, ed. *Tearing the Veil: Essays on Femininity.* London: Routledge & Kegan Paul, 1978.
"The 'London Review' Irish Church Commission." *London Review of Politics, Society, Literature, Art, and Science* 12.309 (2 June 1866): 616–19. Web. 27 Aug. 2010.
Macpherson, James. *The Poems of Ossian.* Trans. James Macpherson. London: J. Walker, 1819. 206 (1222H). Brontë Parsonage Museum, Haworth, England.
Maguire, Edward. *The New Romish Dogma of the Immaculate Conception or, Trial of the Church of Rome, Before a Jury of Roman Catholics.* New York: T.L. Magagnos, 1855.
Mallock, W. H. "*Impressions of Theophrastus Such.*" *The Edinburgh Review* 150.308 (October 1879): 557–86. Web. 10 Dec 2011.
Malmgreen, Gail. *Neither Bread nor Roses: Utopian Feminists and the English Working Class, 1800–1850.* 2nd ed. Marion, IN: The Chronicle Co., 1983.
"Mariolatry: Dr. Pusey's Testimony Against Rome." *Wesleyan-Methodist Magazine* 1 (November 1866): 500–505. Web. 8 Sept. 2009.
Martin, Robert Bernard. *The Accents of Persuasion: Charlotte Brontë's Novels.* London: Faber & Faber, 1966.
Marx, Karl. "Theses on Feuerbach." *On Religion.* Ed. Karl Marx and Friedrich Engels. New York: Schocken, 1964. 69–72.
Marx, Karl, and Friedrich Engels. *On Religion.* New York: Schocken, 1964.

"Mary.—The Rise, Progress, and Development of a Theological Illusion." *Eclectic Review* 13 (July 1867): 25–36. Web. 18 Aug. 2010.
Matthews, Ronald. *English Messiahs; Studies of Six English Religious Pretenders, 1656–1927*. London: Methuen, 1936.
May, Chad. "Reforming History: George Eliot's *Romola*." *Gender and Victorian Reform*. Newcastle upon Tyne: Cambridge Scholars, 2008. 12–25.
Mayberry, Nancy. "The Controversy Over the Immaculate Conception in Medieval and Renaissance Art, Literature, and Society." *Journal of Medieval and Renaissance Studies* 21.2 (1991): 207–24.
Maynard, John. *Charlotte Brontë and Sexuality*. Cambridge: Cambridge University Press, 1984.
Mermin, Dorothy. *Elizabeth Barrett Browning: The Origins of a New Poetry*. Chicago: University of Chicago Press, 1989.
Miller, J. Hillis. *The Disappearance of God: Five Nineteenth-Century Writers*. Cambridge, MA: Belknap Press, 1963.
Milman, Henry Hart. *The History of Christianity: From the Birth of Christ to the Abolition of Paganism in the Roman Empire*. 3 vols. 1840; New York: A. C. Armstrong, n.d.
Mollenkott, Virginia Ramey. *The Divine Feminine: The Biblical Imagery of God as Female*. New York: Crossroad, 1994.
Moore, Dafydd R. "The Critical Response to Ossian's Romantic Bequest." Carruthers and Rawes 38–53.
Morgan, Thaïs E., ed. *Victorian Sages and Cultural Discourse: Renegotiating Gender and Power*. New Brunswick: Rutgers University Press, 1990.
Morris, Pam. *Imagining Inclusive Society in Nineteenth-Century Novels: The Code of Sincerity in the Public Sphere*. Baltimore: Johns Hopkins University Press, 2004.
Moses, Claire G. "Saint-Simonian Men/Saint-Simonian Women: The Transformation of Feminist Thought in 1830s' France." *The Journal of Modern History* 54.2. *Sex, Science, and Society in Modern France* (1982): 240–67.
"MRS. BARRETT BROWNING-AURORA LEIGH." *Blackwood's Edinburgh Magazine* 81.495 (January 1857): 23–41. Web. 22 Nov. 2010.
Murphy, Patricia. "Reconceiving the Mother: Deconstructing the Madonna in *Aurora Leigh*." *Victorian Newsletter* 91 (1997): 21–27.
Nestor, Pauline. "Leaving Home: George Eliot and *Romola*." *Women's Writing* 10.2 (2003): 329–42.
"The New Catholic Goddess." *UNA: a Paper Devoted to the Elevation of Woman* 3.3 (April 1855): 41–42. Web. 10 May 2010.
The New Moral World or Millennium: A London Weekly Publication Developing the Principles of The Rational System of Society. Vol. 2. London: Thomas Stagg, 1836. *The New Moral World*. Vol. 2. 1835–36. New York: Greenwood Reprint, 1969.
Newman, Barbara. "Henry Suso and the Medieval Devotion to Christ the Goddess." *Spiritus: A Journal of Christian Spirituality* 2.1 (2002): 1–14.
Newman, John Henry. "A Letter to the Rev. E. B. Pusey, D. D., on his recent Eirenicon." London: Longmans, Green, Reader, and Dyer. Web. 22 Oct. 2008.
Nietzsche, Friedrich. *The Birth of Tragedy and the Genealogy of Morals*. Trans. Francis Golffing. New York: Doubleday, 1956.
———. "On Truth and Lie in an Extra-Moral Sense." *The Portable Nietzsche*. Ed. and trans. Walter Kaufmann. 1954; New York: Viking, 1968. 42–47.
Nightingale, Florence. "Cassandra." Add. 45839. British Library, London.

———. "Cassandra." *Suggestions for Thought: To Searchers After Religious Truth.* London: George E. Eyre and William Spottiswoode, 1860.

———. *Ever Yours, Florence Nightingale: Selected Letters.* Ed. Martha Vicinus and Bea Nergaard. London: Virago, 1989.

———. *Florence Nightingale in Rome: Letters Written by Florence Nightingale in Rome in the Winter of 1847–1848.* Ed. Mary Keele.. Philadelphia: American Philosophical Society, 1981.

———. *Florence Nightingale's Spiritual Journey: Biblical Annotations, Sermons, and Journal Notes.* Vol. 2. Ed. Lynn McDonald. Waterloo, ON: Wilfred Laurier University Press, 2001.

———. Nightingale Papers XII MS Adds. 45750, 45783, 45839, 45840, 45841, 45843, 45844, 45845, 45846, 45847. British Library, London.

———. *Suggestions for Thought by Florence Nightingale: Selections and Commentaries.* Ed. Michael D. Calabria and Janet A. Macrae. Philadelphia: University of Pennsylvania Press, 1994.

Novalis (Georg Friedrich Philipp von Hardenberg). *Henry Von Ofterdingen.* Trans. Palmer Hilty. New York: Frederick Ungar, 1964.

O'Malley, Patrick R. *Catholicism, Sexual Deviance, and Victorian Gothic Culture.* Cambridge: Cambridge University Press, 2006.

Omer, Ranen. "Elizabeth Barrett Browning and Apocalypse: The Unraveling of Poetic Autonomy." *Texas Studies in Literature and Language* 39.2 (1997): 97–124.

Otto, Rudolph. *The Idea of the Holy: An Inquiry into the Non-Rational Factor in the Idea of the Divine and Its Relation to the Rational.* Trans. John W. Harvey. London: Oxford University Press, 1968.

Owen, Robert. "Sunday Evening." *The Crisis.* Vol. 3. London: B. D. Cousins, 1834. *Crisis, and National Co-operative Trades' Union Gazette.* Vols. 3–4. 1833–1834. New York: Greenwood, 1968. 1 (7 Sept. 1877): 2–4.

Parrinder, Geoffrey. *Sex in the World's Religions.* London: Sheldon, 1980.

Peake, R. B. "Pope Joan." *Bentley's Miscellany* 12 (July 1842): 148–56. Web. 12 Oct. 2008.

Pell, Nancy. "Resistance, Rebellion, and Marriage: The Economies of *Jane Eyre.*" *Nineteenth-Century Fiction* 31.4 (1977): 397–420.

Penzance Natural History and Antiquarian Society. Report for 1844. Penzance: F. T. Vibert, 1851. Vol. I, 1845–50. AC 3011. British Library, London.

———. Report for 1845. Penzance: F. T. Vibert, 1851. Vol. I, 1845–50. AC 3011. British Library, London.

Petroff, Elizabeth Alvilda. *Body and Soul: Essays on Medieval Women and Mysticism.* New York: Oxford University Press, 1994.

Pickering, Mary. "Auguste Comte and the Saint-Simonians." *French Historical Studies* 18.1 (1993): 211–36. Web. 9 July 2010.

Piggott, Stuart. *The Druids.* 1968; New York: Thames and Hudson, 1973.

Pionke, Albert D. "Reframing the Luddites: Materialist and Idealist Modes of Self in Charlotte Brontë's *Shirley.*" *Victorian Review* 30.2 (2004): 81–102. Web. 27 Nov. 2010.

Piquet, François. "Shadows of Prophecy: Blake and Millenarian Ideology." *The Yearbook of English Studies* 19: *The French Revolution in English Literature and Art Special Number 19* (1989): 28–35.

"Pope Joan: a Study of the Middle Ages." *Athenaeum* (16 January 1869): 91–92. Web. 22 Oct. 2008.

Prickett, Stephen. *Origins of Narrative: The Romantic Appropriation of the Bible.* Cambridge: Cambridge University Press, 1996.
Pugh, Evelyn L. "Florence Nightingale and J. S. Mill Debate Women Rights." *Journal of British Studies* 21.2 (1982): 118–38.
Pusey, E. B. "The Church of England A Portion of Christ's One Holy Catholic Church, And a Means of Restoring Visible Unity: An Eirenicon. In a Letter to the Author of 'The Christian Year.'" New York: D. Appleton, 1866. Web. 1 Dec. 2010.
Qualls, Barry. "George Eliot and Religion." *The Cambridge Companion to George Eliot.* Ed. George Levine. Cambridge: Cambridge University Press, 2001. 119–37.
———. *The Secular Pilgrims of Victorian Fiction: The Novel as Book of Life.* Cambridge: Cambridge University Press, 1982.
"The Recent Decree on the Immaculate Conception of the Blessed Virgin Mary: A Sign of the Present Time." Preached at Albury on 25 December 1854. London: Thomas Bosworth, 1855.
Reid, T. Wemyss. *Charlotte Brontë: A Monograph.* New York: Charles Scribner's Sons, 1877.
"The Religion of the New Moral World." Vol. 2 (Saturday 21 May 1836): 237. *The Millennium: A London Weekly Publication Developing the Principles of The Rational System of Society.* London: Thomas Stagg, 1836. *New Moral World.* Vol. 2. 1835–36. New York: Greenwood Reprint, 1969.
Renk, Kathleen. "Resurrecting the Living Dead: Elizabeth Barrett Browning's Poetic Vision in *Aurora Leigh.*" *Studies in Browning and his Circle* 23 (May 2000): 40–49.
"Replies to the Eirenicon." *London Review of Politics, Society, Literature, Art, and Science* 12.313 (30 June 1866): 736–37. Web. 10 Oct. 2010.
Rev. of "*The Buchanites From First to Last.*" *New York Observer and Chronicle* 25.7 (13 February 1847): 28. Web. 16 Oct. 2010.
Rev. of "*The Buchanites, From First to Last.* *Tait's Edinburgh Magazine* 14.157 (January 1847): 60-62. Web. 16 Oct. 2010.
Rev. of "The Glories of Mary." *Christian Remembrancer* 30.90 (1855): 417–67. Web. 22 Aug. 2010.
Rev. of "*A Letter to the Rev. E. B. Pusey, D. D. on His Recent Eirenicon.*" *London Quarterly Review* 26.51 (April 1866): 255–57. Web. 22 Feb. 2008.
Rev. of "*Sacred and Legendary Art.*" *Examiner* 2127 (November 1848): 707–8. Web. 12 Sept. 2009.
Rickard, Suzanne. "Victorian Women with Causes: Writing, Religion and Action." *Women, Religion and Feminism in Britain 1750–1900.* Ed. Sue Morgan. Houndmill, Basingstoke, Hampshire: Palgrave Macmillan, 2002. 139–57.
Riede, David G. "Elizabeth Barrett: The Poet as Angel." *Victorian Poetry* 32.2 (1994): 121–39.
Rigby, Catherine E. *Topographies of the Sacred: The Poetics of Place in European Romanticism.* Charlottesville: University Press of Virginia, 2004.
Robinson, Carole. "'Romola': a Reading of the Novel." *Victorian Studies* 6.1 (1962): 29–42. Web. 23 Aug. 2010.
Rogers, Philip. "Tory Brontë: Shirley and the 'MAN.'" *Nineteenth-Century Literature* 58.2 (2003): 141–75. Web. 18 Sept. 2008.
"Romola." *The Athenaeum* 1863 (11 July 1863): 46. Web. 23 Aug. 2010.
"Romola." *The British Quarterly Review* 76: 448–65. Web. 23 Aug. 2010.
"Romola." *Reader* 2.28 (11 July 1863): 28–29. Web. 23 Aug. 2010.

"ROMOLA." *Saturday Review of Politics, Literature, Science and Art* 16.404 (25 July 1863): 124–25. Web. 23 Aug. 2010.

"Romola." *Westminster Review* 24.2 (October 1863): 344–52. Web. 23 Aug. 2010.

Ross, Anne. *Pagan Celtic Britain: Studies in Iconography and Tradition.* London: Routledge & Kegan Paul, 1967.

Rountree, Kathryn. "Archaeologists and Goddess Feminists at Çatalhöyük: An Experiment in Multivocality." *Journal of Feminist Studies in Religion* 23.2 (2007): 7–26.

Rousseau, Jean-Jacques. *Émile, or Education.* Trans. Barbara Foxley. London: J. M. Dent, 1921. Web. 9 Sept. 2011.

Ruskin, John. "Fiction, Fair and Foul." *On the Old Road Vol. 2: essays by John Ruskin.* 265–90. Web. 25 Sept. 2010.

Sabol, C. Ruth, and Todd K. Bender. *A concordance to Brontë's Jane Eyre.* New York: Garland Publishing, 1981.

Schiller, Friedrich. "Gods of Greece." *The Poems of Schiller.* Trans. E. P. Arnold-Forster. London: William Heinemann, 1901. 72–76. Web. 10 Dec. 2011.

———. "On Naïve and Sentimental Poetry." Trans. William F. Wertz, Jr. Web. 11 Dec. 2011.

Scholl, Lesa. "Translating Authority: *Romola*'s Disruption of the Gendered Narrative." *The Victorian Newsletter* 112 (Fall 2007): 6–18. Web. 23 Aug. 2010.

Sharples, Eliza. "Dedication: To the Young Women of England for Generations to Come, or Until Superstition is Extinct." *The Isis* 1.1 (11 February 1832): iii–iv. Fiche. 20 Oct. 2008.

———. "Editor's Response." *The Isis* 8.1 (31 March 1831): 128. Fiche. 20 Oct. 2008.

———. "First Discourse." *The Isis* 1.1 (11 February 1832): 1–5. Fiche. 20 Oct. 2008.

———. "The Second Person of the Trinity." *The Isis* 39.1 (15 December 1832): 611–17. Fiche. 20 Oct. 2008.

———. "The Sixteenth Discourse." *The Isis* 15.1 (19 May 1832): 225–31. Fiche. 20 Oct. 2008.

———. "The Tenth Discourse." *The Isis* 9.1 (7 April 1832): 129-34. Fiche. 20 Oct. 2008.

———. "The Thirteenth Discourse." *The Isis* 12.1 (Saturday, 28 April 1832): 177–83. Fiche. 20 Oct. 2008.

———. "To Correspondents." *The Isis* 12.1 (28 April 1832): 190–91. Fiche. 20 Oct. 2008.

———. "To the Lady of the Rotunda." *The Isis* 8.1 (31 March 1832): 112. Fiche. 20 Oct. 2008.

Shine, Hill. "J. S. Mill and an Open Letter on the Saint-Simonian Society in 1832." *Journal of the History of Ideas* 6.1 (1945): 102–8. Web. 18 Feb. 2008.

"SHIRLEY." *Sharpe's London Journal* 11 (January 1850): 370–73. Web. 9 Dec. 2009.

"Shirley: A Tale." *The Edinburgh Review* 91.183 (January 1850): 153–73. Web. 9 Dec. 2009.

Showalter, Elaine. "Florence Nightingale's Feminist Complaint: Women, Religion, and 'Suggestions for Thought.'" *Signs* 6.3 (1981): 395–412. Web. 20 Apr. 2007.

———. *A Literature of Their Own: British Women Novelists from Brontë to Lessing.* Princeton: Princeton University Press, 1977.

Simpson, Shona Elizabeth. "Mapping *Romola*: Physical Space, Women's Place." Levine and Turner. 53–66.

Sinclair, May. *The Three Brontës.* London: Hutchinson, 1912. Web. 12 Dec. 2011.

Smith, W. Anderson. *"Shepherd" Smith the Universalist: The Story of a Mind.* London; Sampson, Low, Marston, 1892. Web. 21 Apr. 2010.
Southcott, Joanna. *COMMUNICATIONS to Joanna Southcott, accounts of her visions, etc. 1792–1814.* 5 vols. MS Add. 32633–32637. ff.269, 305, 204, 211, 206. British Library, London.
Spretnak, Charlene, ed. *The Politics of Women's Spirituality: Essays on the Rise of Spiritual Power Within the Feminist Movement.* New York: Anchor Books, 1982.
Steinmetz, Virginia V. "Images of 'Mother-Want' in Elizabeth Barrett Browning's 'Aurora Leigh.'" *Victorian Poetry* 21.4 (1983): 351–67.
Stockton, Kathryn Bond. *God Between Their Lips: Desire Between Women in Irigaray, Brontë, and Eliot.* Stanford: Stanford University Press, 1994.
Stone, Marjorie. "Genre Subversion and Gender Inversion: 'The Princess' and 'Aurora Leigh.'" *Victorian Poetry* 25.2 (1987): 101–27.
"SUPERSTITION AND FOLLY!" *Literary Gazette* 1557 (21 November 1846): 977–79. Web. 11 Oct. 2009.
Swinburne, Algernon Charles. *"A Note on Charlotte Bronte."* London: Chatto & Windus, 1877. Web. 10 Dec. 2011.
Taves, Ann. *Fits, Trances, & Visions: Experiencing Religion and Explaining Experience from Wesley to James.* Princeton: Princeton University Press, 1999.
Taylor, Barbara. *Eve and the New Jerusalem: Socialism and Feminism in the Nineteenth Century.* London: Virago, 1983.
———. "The Woman-Power: Religious Heresy and Feminism in early English socialism." *Tearing the Veil.* Ed. Susan Lipshitz. London: Routledge & Kegan Paul, 1978. 117–44.
Taylor, Irene. *Holy Ghosts: The Male Muses of Emily and Charlotte Brontë.* New York: Columbia University Press, 1990.
Taylor, Jeremy. *The Golden Grove: A Choice Manual, Containing What is to be Believed, Practised, and Desired or Prayed for.* 1655; Oxford: John Henry Parker, 1847. RB.23a.12865. British Library, London.
Taylor, Olivia Gatti. "Written in Blood: The Art of Mothering Epic in the Poetry of Elizabeth Barrett Browning." *Victorian Poetry* 44.2 (2006): 153–64. Web. 11 Nov. 2010.
Thacker, Christopher. *The Wildness Pleases: The Origins of Romanticism.* London: Croom Helm, 1983.
Thormählen, Marianne. *The Brontës and Religion.* Cambridge: Cambridge University Press, 1999.
Trudgill, Eric. *Madonnas and Magadalens: The Origins and Development of Victorian Sexual Attitudes.* London: Heinemann, 1976.
Tucker, Herbert F. "'Aurora Leigh': Epic Solutions to Novel Ends." Booth 62–85.
Tuveson, Ernest L. "The Millenarian Structure of *The Communist Manifesto.*" *The Apocalypse in English Renaissance Thought and Literature: Patterns, Antecedents, and Repercussions.* Ed. C. A. Patrides. Ithaca: Cornell University Press, 1984. 323–41.
Ullathorne, William Bernard. *The Immaculate Conception of the Mother of God: An Exposition.* London: Richardson and Son, 1855.
Valéry, Paul. *Charmes.* Paris: Gallimard, 1952.
Vanita, Ruth. *Sappho and the Virgin Mary: Same Sex Love and the English Literary Imagination.* New York: Columbia University Press, 1996.
Vargish, Thomas. *The Providential Aesthetic in Victorian Fiction.* Charlottesville: University Press of Virginia, 1985.

Wallace, Jennifer. "Elizabeth Barrett Browning: Knowing Greek." *Essays in Criticism: A Quarterly Journal of Literary Criticism* 50.4 (2000): 329–53.

Wang, Lisa. "Unveiling the Hidden God of Charlotte Brontë's *Villette*." *Literature and Theology* 15.4 (2001): 342–57.

Warner, Marina. *Alone of All Her Sex: The Myth and the Cult of the Virgin Mary.* New York: Alfred A. Knopf, 1976.

Welton, Donn, ed. *Body and Flesh: A Philosophical Reader.* Malden, MA: Blackwell, 1998.

Whitfield, H. J. *Scilly and its Legends.* Penzance: F. T. Vibert, 1852. 10350. British Library, London.

Wihl, Gary. "Republican Liberty in George Eliot's *Romola*." *Criticism: A Quarterly for Literature and the Arts* 51.2 (2009): 247–62. Web. 3 Aug. 2010.

Willcocks, M. P. "Charlotte and Emily Brontë." *Between the Old World and the New: Being Studies in Literary Personality From Goethe and Balzac to Anatole France and Thomas Hardy.* London: George, 1925. 157–68.

William of St. Thierry. *De natura et dignitate amoris.* Migne, *Patrologia Latina,* Paris. 1121–24.

Wilson, John. "The Moors." *Blackwood's Edinburgh Magazine* 28.172 (October 1830): 575–607. Web. 18 Oct. 2008.

"WOMAN AND THE SOCIAL SYSTEM." *Fraser's Magazine for Town and Country* 21.126 (June 1840): 689–702. Web. 17 Apr. 2009.

Wright, Frances. "Lecture I: On the Nature of Knowledge." *Course of Popular Lectures, as delivered by Frances Wright.* New York: Free Enquirer, 1829. 17–40. Fiche. 2 Sept. 2008.

———. "Lecture III: Of the More Important Divisions and Essential Parts of Knowledge." *Course of Popular Lectures, as delivered by Frances Wright.* New York: Free Enquirer, 1829. 63–84. Fiche. 2 Sept. 2008.

Yeazell, Ruth Bernard. "Why Political Novels Have Heroines: *Sybil, Mary Barton,* and *Felix Holt*." *NOVEL: A Forum on Fiction* 18.2 (1985): 126–44.

Young, Katherine K. "Goddesses, Feminists, and Scholars." *The Annual Review of Women in World Religions* 1 (1991): 105–79.

Zlotnick, Susan. "Luddism, Medievalism and Women's History in *Shirley*: Charlotte's Revisionist Tactics." *NOVEL: A Forum on Fiction* 24.3 (Spring 1991): 282–95. Web. 17 Apr. 2009.

Zonana, Joyce. "The Embodied Muse: Elizabeth Barrett Browning's *Aurora Leigh* and Feminist Politics." *Tulsa Studies in Women's Literature* 8.2 (1989): 241–62.

Index

Abrams, M. H., artist as creator and, 12
Adams, Kimberly VanEsvald, Feuerbach's notion of the feminized Savior and, 64
Alexander, Christine: adolescent Brontë as "self-conscious author" and, 26; Brontë's sophisticated repertoire of male voices and, 25
Allen, Michael J. B., Marsilio Ficino and, 129
Alley, Henry, Eliot's Romola and Piero, 153n7
Althusserian perspective, religion as disciplinary apparatus and, 2
Anderson, Pamela Sue: concept of the goddess and, 127; deft feminist epistemology and, 13; meaning of "exist" and, 13; mythoi surrounding the Virgin and, 62; patriarchal version of the Adam and Eve story, 37
Anthony, Susan B., 74
Anzaldúa, Gloria, aesthetic of, 4
Arnold, Matthew: Celtic strain of "natural magic" and, 9; English physical and primordial mark on bodies and, 9; *Literature and Dogma* and, 3; meaning of "God" and, 3
Aurora Leigh (Barrett Browning), 1, 6, 18, 22–23, 41, 73–75, 78–82, 85–86, 90–92, 94, 96–97, 150n7

Bachofen, J. J.: matriarchy preceded patriarchy and, 12; meanings for the moon and, 149n15
Barmby, John Goodwyn: Communist Church and, 17; poem for female savior and, 17
Barrett Browning, Elizabeth: "The Dead Pan" and, 75; description of Eve and, 41; double-seeing female poet and, 6; Edward Irving and, 18; *Essays on the Greek Christian Poets and the English Poets* and, 73, 79–80, 91; Eve and, 65; expansive spirituality and, 77; gender bending and, 108; gender bending via homoeroticism and, 92; "Glimpses into My Own Life and Literary Character" and, 76; hyperbolic metaphors and, 150–151n7; *Iliad* and, 76; letters of, 1; Mother Nature and, 13; Owenite principles and, 94; polytheism and, 23; polytheistic imagery and, 91; quotes from, 73; Reform Bill of 1832 and, 151n14; sectarianism of the National Churches and, 79; Swedenborgian immanence of the eternal and, 85
Beatrijs, Beguine, 4, 123
Bentley's Miscellany, Pope Joan and, 78
Bidney, Martin, literary epiphanies and, 3
Bigwood, Carol, connatural body and, 4

171

Billone, Amy Christine: female writer's masking and, 21; Victorian women writers and, 21
Blackwood, John, letter from George Eliot and, 138–39
Blackwood's Edinburgh Magazine: Aurora Leigh and, 81; Barrett Browning's vulgar tropes and, 96; "The Moors" and, 30; review of *Legends* in, 70; Thomas Aird and, 24
Blagden, Isa, Fourierism and, 95
Blair, Hugh, *Ossian* and, 31
Blake, William, millenarians and, 17
Bodichon, Barbara, 74; Florence Nightingale and, 129; George Eliot and, 74, 124–25, 129, 138; Romola as rebel in disguise and, 138
Bonaparte, Felicia: Christian and classical culture, 127; *Romola's* mise-en-scène and, 127
Booth, Alison, *Romola's* astonishing amount of freedom and, 138
Bray, Caroline, 125
Bray, Charles, 125
Brigham Young University, 143
British Library, Brontë's *Shirley* and, 40, 151n4
British Quarterly Review: Cardinal Manning's enthusiasm for Madonna and, 60; Manning as effeminate and, 60
Brontë, Anne, 40
Brontë, Charlotte: Angrian pseudonyms and, 147n3; brilliant use of masking and, 35–36; censoring of her fictional heroine and, 42; Condition of England novel and, 35; description of a female divinity and, 27; epiphany in early poetry and, 31; feminist religious symbolic and, 29; masking the female deity and, 40; "MILTON'S EVE" and, 64; moon imagery and, 148n13; Mother Nature and, 13; omnipotent feminine essence and, 26; ritual summons of the divine and, 30; solution to class warfare and, 45; symbolic female divinities and, 2; titanic goddess and, 18; trances and, 22, 28, 30, 32–33, 39–43, 45, 77; treatment of religion and, 25; view of literary genius and, 28; *Villette* and, 29, 49; "The Violet" and, 24–26, 31, 38; Woman Question and, 27, 33, 44
Brontë, Emily, 36, 40
Brontë, Patrick, 34
Browning, Elizabeth Barrett. *See* Barrett Browning, Elizabeth
Brunn, Emilie Zum, love and divine knowledge, 4
Bryant, John, revisions of manuscripts and, 41
Buchan, Luckie, 15, 20, 109; journalistic assaults made on, 78; spiritual breathings and, 21
Bullen, J. B., Eliot's *Romola* and, 128, 152n2
Burns, Robert, Buchan's spiritual breathings and, 21
Butler, Marilyn, pagan polytheism and, 145n6
Byron, Lord, Astarte and, 7

Callixtus, Nicephorus, 71
Carlile, Richard: freethinking and, 17; Immaculate Conception and, 52
Carlyle, Thomas, 9–10; co-optation of nature and, 13; new language for nature and, 12; Saint-Simonians and, 152n4; *Sartor Resartus* and, 11; sinister effects of rising capitalism and, 93
Carpenter, Mary: *Aurora Leigh* and, 90; Eliot's *Romola* and, 130; Romola as mixture of two divine female entities and, 153n8
Cassandra (Nightingale), 22–23, 98–99, 101, 104–5, 111–14, 116, 120, 151n3, 152nn9–10
Cecil, David, Brontë's unrestrained imagination in *Shirley* and, 147n7
Celtic gods: Anne Ross and, 151n11; "feminine idiosyncrasy" and, 9; Thomas Macpherson and, 9; variant mythologies and, 7; works on, 146n11

Chadwick, Edwin, Nightingale on Mill's death and, 108
Chaney, Christine, *Aurora Leigh* and, 92
Chase, Karen: Christian and classical culture, 127; *Romola*'s mise-en-scène and, 127
Christian Remembrancer, Immaculate Conception and, 52
Cobbe, Frances Power, 74
Coleridge, H. Nelson: "discordia concours" and, 83; female and male models of divinity, 69; Mary and new ideas about gender, 70
Coleridge, Samuel Taylor, 18, 83
Comte, Auguste: all-but-divine goddess and, 10; George Eliot and, 126; Saint-Simonians and, 152n3; women and self-sacrificing love, 127
Congressional Library, Susan B. Anthony and, 74
Cook, Edward, Nightingale's biographer and, 116
Corner, Julian: Eliot's *Romola* and, 128; Romola's loss of mother and, 135
Coward, Rosalind, original social system and, 12
Creation of Adam and Eve (Michelangelo), 110
The Creation of Patriarchy (Lerner), 145n3
The Crisis, 17: feminist socialists and, 98; legitimacy of religion and, 92–93

Dalley, Lana L., Browning's rejection of socialism and, 95
Daumer, Georg Friedrich, *The Religion of the New Age* and, 141
Davies, Edward, 9
della Mirandola, Pico, "heterodox theses" of, 129
de'Medici, Cosimo, Marsilio Ficino and, 129
Derrida, Jacques, definition of empirical events and, 62
de Saint-Simon, Henri, radical socialist reformer and, 126

DeShazer, Mary K., Mother Nature's son and, 13
de Thierry, William, Beguine mysticism and, 106
Dickens, Charles, sinister effects of rising capitalism and, 93
The Dictionary of the History of Ideas, notion of a "Great Goddess" and, 145n3
Dolan, Tim, Brontë's *Shirley* and, 45
Dossey, Barbara Montgomery: masculine imagery of God and, 151n5; Nightingale's mysticism and, 115
Dublin Telegraph, Immaculate Conception and, 49
Dufour, M. Ariès, 125

Eclectic Review, bleeding deity and, 59
Ecstasy, Ritual, and Alternate Reality (Goodman), 145n4
Edinburgh Journal, Luckie Buchan and, 21
Eirenicon (Pusey), 55, 59, 150nn5–6
Eliot, George: conditions necessary for Utopia and, 131; essay on Wollstonecraft and Fuller, 137; foundations of Marxism and, 18; John Bull and, 126; letter to John Blackwood and, 138–39; Madonna and, 8; *Madwoman in the Attic* and, 129; millennial politics of Victorian Britain and, 18; "moral glow" of positivism and, 126; mother's loss of twin sons and, 153n8; painting of Madonna and, 3; positivist Utopia and, 152n5; preserving the essence of Christian self-sacrifice and, 128; Raphael's *Sistine Madonna* and, 123, 127; rationale for seeing women as part of the Christian godhead and, 64; response to Richard Holman Hutton's review of *Romola* and, 130; *Romola* and, 8, 22–23, 90, 121–24, 127–42, 152n2, 153n6, 153nn8–9; Saint-Simonians and, 152n4; serio-comic voice of Mary and, 153n11; suffrage and,

137; symbolic female divinities and, 2; trajectory of Eliot's theological heuristics and, 124; "truth of feeling" and, 122; W. H. Mallock and, 121; women and self-sacrificing love, 127

Émile (Rousseau), 7

English Civil War, heretical notion of the female savior and, 34

Epiney-Burgard, Georgette, love and divine knowledge, 4

Essays on the Greek Christian Poets and the English Poets (Barrett Browning), 73, 79–80, 91

Essence of Christianity (Feuerbach), 122–23, 129

Eternal Feminine, *Faust* and, 10

Evans, Mary Ann, study of unfulfilled prophecy and, 124

Eve: as godlike being and, 23; as powerful, semi-divine figure and, 34; Brontë's depiction of, 101; Brontë's subversive chapter on, 35; Charlotte Brontë and, 38–40; Christian creation story and, 110–11; Christian view of, 38; curse of, 58; Eliza Sharples and, 19; feminist efforts to recuperate and, 34; Florence Nightingale and, 120; heretical incarnations of, 45; independent, separate identity from Adam and, 66; Jameson's representation of, 64; litany of the goddesses and, 68; Mary Wollstonecraft and, 99; masculine obliteration of Eve's body and, 90; "Milton's Eve" and, 64–65; models of femininity and, 64; "Mother of all living" and, 57; New Jerusalem and, 89; Nightingale's radical grandmothers and, 100; patriarchal version of the Adam and Eve story, 37; relationship with deity and horizontal transcendence, 151–52n6; Sharples's merging of Isis and Eve, 109; stark imagery of, 97; the Fall and, 16, 19–20, 34, 39, 54, 57, 65–66, 78, 89, 110; woman-centered mythology and, 13

Faber, Frederick William, sharing of blood when Christ was in Mary's womb and, 59

Fanon, Frantz: Charlotte Brontë and, 27; mastery of language and, 14

Fawcett, Millicent Garrett, 74

Felski, Rita, Victorian women writers and, 21–22

feminine, resacralizing and, 6–14

feminine images of God, Bible and, 7

Feuerbach, Ludwig: all-but-divine goddess and, 10; Auguste Comte and, 126; Christ's passion and, 123; *Essence of Christianity* and, 122–23, 129; German language and, 129; irrationality of a heavenly Trinity and, 123; suffering and gods' inferiority to humankind and, 142; women and self-sacrificing love, 127

Ficino, Marsilio, Platonism of, 129

Fiorenza, Elizabeth Schussler, feminist religious studies and, 3

Fletcher, Mary Bosanquet, 14

Foucauldian perspective, religion as disciplinary apparatus and, 2

Fourier, Charles, social progress and, 17

Fourierism, 94–95, 112

Fraser's Magazine: Patrick Brontë and, 34; "Women and the Social System" and, 21

freethinking, 81; Frances Wright and, 20; Richard Carlile and, 17

French Revolution, 17–18, 34, 52, 64, 99, 111–12, 115, 124–25, 130

Friedman, Susan Stanford, "Gender and Genre Anxiety" and, 150n2

Frye, Northrop: major male Romantics and, 7; view of God and, 11

Fuller, Margaret: Egyptian Isis and, 124; rationale for seeing women as part of the Christian godhead and, 64; *Woman in the Nineteenth Century* and, 124

Gaskell, Elizabeth: Brontë's father and,

25; *Shirley*'s language for depicting a goddess and, 147n7
Gelpi, Barbara Charlesworth, stereotypes of women in art and literature, 84
Gladstone, William, review of "The Glories of Mary" and, 53
God as metaphor: acceptance of the masculine metaphor and, 12; Brontë's *Shirley* and, 22; Charlotte Brontë and, 27; Elizabeth Barrett Browning and, 87; how society constructs the divine and, 33; Judeo-Christian metaphor of the jealous Father and, 119; Julian of Norwich and, 5; male yearning for the erotic and, 54; Nightingale's theology and, 103; Romantics and, 13; women as omnipotent beings and, 14
goddess, 2, 6–7, 9–13, 18–19, 24–27; and Barrett Browning, 73, 75–76, 79, 86; and Charlotte Brontë, 37–38, 41, 43–44, 51; and Nightingale, 108–11, 118; and Eliot, 121, 126–27, 132, 140
Gordon, Lyndall, prophetic proto-feminism of Brontë and, 148n7
Goslee, Nancy, male Romantic poetry and, 13
Great Mother, 142; Brontë lyric poem and, 24; Brontë's early writings and, 22
Gunton, Colin A., problem with monotheistic religions and, 6

Haight, Gordon, George Eliot and, 124
Harrison, J. F. C., boundary between millenarians and radicals, 17
Haskett, William J., 21
Heilman, Robert B., modern goddess movement and, 148n7
Henry von Ofterdingen (Novalis), 10
Herringer, Carol, Madonna's identity and, 50
Higgins, Godfrey, female progenitor of the gods and, 9

Hill, Susan E., 122
Hirsch, Pam, George Sand and, 26–27
History of Christianity (Milman), 8, 51
The History of Our Lord (Jameson), 65–66
Hodgson, Peter C., George Eliot and, 122
Holy Ghosts (Taylor), 27
Homans, Margaret: critiquing *Romola*'s ending and, 137; highest form of translation and, 153n10; Mother Nature and, 146n16; *Romola*'s self-renunciation and, 135; Western canon and, 13; women's exclusion from and silencing within literature and, 129
Horne, R. H., Barrett Browning's writing and, 73
Hutton, Richard Holman, Eliot's response to Hutton's review of *Romola* and, 130

Immaculate Conception: 1854 endorsement of, 69; consolidation of Mary's power and, 56; establishing the doctrine of, 55; feast of, 58; female blood and, 66; gender concerns and, 52; Jameson's writings and, 64; Papal Bull and, 22; potentiality for divine womanhood and, 61; Romish dogma and, 49; slippage between what is considered human and divine, 53; Victorian debates and, 6; vitriolic arguments between men about, 71; Woman Question and, 63
Irving, Edward, 18
Isis: female prophets and, 90; nursing Horus of the Egyptians and, 68; Protestants and, 51; Sharples's merging of Isis and Eve, 109; Sharples's references to, 23; "Shekinah" and, 129; Veil of Isis and, 118
The Isis, Eliza Sharples and, 19
Isis Unveiled (Blavatsky), 9

Jameson, Anna: art criticism and, 109; difference between the Nestorians and Monophysites, 70; Eve as holy entity in Christian works of art and, 66; *The History of Our Lord* and, 65–66; *Legends of the Madonna* and, 22, 49–50, 64, 67, 71, 150n8; Madonna as dominant motif in Renaissance and Medieval art, 68; "Milton's Eve" and, 64–65; moral regeneration of the whole human race and, 68; pagan worship and, 69; rhetorical gifts of, 64; symbolic female divinities and, 2; "unchristian confusion" about behavior and, 69; Victorian debates about Immaculate Conception and, 6; Victorian verities about motherhood and, 64; Woman Question and, 62–63

Jane Eyre (Brontë), 12, 22, 31, 33, 40, 148n7

Jantzen, Grace M.: being "divine" for others and, 108; Christian God as necrophiliac and, 14; "divine horizon" of potentiality for women and, 62; "feminist symbolic" of "becoming divine" and, 29; feminist theology and, 31

Jenkins, Ruth Y.: Brontë's *Shirley* and, 37; evangelical expectations and Brontë, 26; Florence Nightingale and, 98; women as holy martyrs and, 113

Joan of Arc, 78

John the Baptist, 99, 116, 138

Jowett, Benjamin, 103, 112–13, 116, 152nn9–10

Julian of Norwich: Florence Nightingale and, 109; multi-gendered god and, 87; *Sixteen Revelations of Divine Love* and, 5

Keats, John: Celtic heritage and, 9; goddess and, 7

Keele, Mary, Nightingale's open-minded approach to spirituality and, 101

Keightley, Thomas, 6–7

Kenyon, Frederic G., *The Letters of Elizabeth Barrett Browning* and, 1

Kenyon, John, 75

Kingsley, Charles: sexual abstinence and, 51; *Yeast* and, 8

Kristeva, Julia: critical theories about "gestation and birth of children" and, 82; male-defined Virgin Mary and, 139; mother Goddess and, 121; need for goddesses and, 141

Krueger, Christine L.: early nineteenth-century women preachers and, 14; "evangelical ideolect" and, 15; evangelical rhetoric and, 21

LaMonaca, Maria: Eliot's *Romola* and, 128, 142; Protestant Victorian women writers and, 61

The Language of the Goddess (Gimbutas), 145n3

Larson, Janet L., Brontë's use of "female messianism" and, 27

Lawson, Kate, "Mother/Eve/Nature" as the heart of "feminist dissent" and, 27

Lee, Ann, 15, 20–21, 109, 112

Legends of the Madonna (Jameson), 22, 49–50, 64, 67, 71, 150n8

Le Globe, John Stuart Mill and St. Simonians, 112

Leonard, William, 15

Lewes, G. H.: Brontë letter and, 28; Brontë's pseudonym and, 25; conversation with Eliot and Simcox, 139; George Eliot and, 121; Madonna and, 8

Lewis, Linda: Barrett Browning's hypothetical Christian ideal and, 95; female messiah and, 111

Lewis, Maria, 124

Liddington, Jill, Brontë's *Shirley* and, 36

Literature and Dogma (Arnold), 3

London Review: distaste for the Virgin and, 53–54; Immaculate Conception and, 52; Virgin becoming the omnipotent mediator and, 53

Luddites, 33–36

Ludovisi Gallery, 109

Macpherson, Thomas, *Ossian* and, 9
Madonna: amalgamated with other feminine icons and, 68; appeal of, 119; as cover for Ariadne and, 141; as entity uniting all humans and, 135; *Aurora Leigh* and, 91; Cardinal Manning's enthusiasm for, 60; Catholic and Protestant interpretations of, 50–51; culture's constructions of gender and, 22; divine femininity and, 63; dominant motif in Renaissance and Medieval art, 68; Eliot's *Romola* and, 128; Eliza Sharples and, 135; George Eliot and, 121, 124, 132, 137–39; Jameson's idea of the horizon of woman's divinity and, 71; Kristeva and the cult of the Madonna, 141; male yearning for the erotic and, 54; Mary included in Christ's divinity and Incarnation, 70; "miraculous virginity" and, 51; models of femininity and, 64; Nightingale's theological understanding of, 118; painting of, 3; popular renditions of, 8; Romola as mixture of two divine female entities and, 153n8; secularizing and, 19; sexuality and, 58; "site of free signification" and, 61; unofficial dogma and, 49–50; value system and, 23
Madwoman in the Attic, Eliot's view of herself as an editor and, 129
Maguire, Edward: Mary's postpartum cleanliness and, 59; *The New Romish Dogma of the Immaculate Conception* and, 49
Mallock, W. H., George Eliot and, 121
Malmgreen, Gail, joining socialism with the emancipation of women and, 21
Martin, Robert Bernard, Brontë's *Shirley* and, 148n7
Martineau, Harriet: death of Emma Martin and, 147n21; George Eliot and, 125
Marxism: as millenarian and, 118; influences of, 18; Karl Marx and, 114
matriarchy: as underlying Greek and Jewish culture, 141; Bachofen hypothesis and, 12; goddess worship and, 2; questions about its ancient prevalence, 145n3
May, Chad, conflation of Romola with the Virgin Mary and, 128
Mayberry, Nancy, Mary's virginal integrity and, 59
Merleau-Ponty, Maurice, body's hermeneutic aptitudes and, 4
millenarianism, 2, 6, 13–18, 22–23, 34, 44, 47–48, 50, 74, 85, 89–90, 93, 96–97, 99–100, 111–14, 124–26, 130–31, 142
millenarians, 93, 142; revaluation of the term "God" and, 13; utopian feminists and, 14–23
Miller, J. Hillis: artist as the "creator" and, 12; sacramental heritage and the Romantics, 11
Mill, John Stuart: arguments for women's rights and, 98; as gender bending and, 108; death of, 108; Florence Nightingale and, 101; Saint-Simonians and, 112, 152n4; *Subjection of Women* and, 151n3
Milman, Henry Hart, 8; debased female body and, 21; depicting gods in female form and, 9; early Church's intermixture of pagan elements with the Virgin Mary, 117; female reproductive anatomy and, 59; *History of Christianity* and, 51; Immaculate Conception and, 52; primitive nature of women's breasts and, 78; views of women and divinity, 86
Mohl, Julius, letter from Nightingale and, 100–101
Monophysites, 70
Moore, Louis, Brontë's *Shirley* and, 38–39, 42–43
Morris, Pam: human suffering transforming the maternal into a site of love and, 136; material entity that unites all human beings and, 82
mother-god-want: as site of intense desire and, 13; *Aurora Leigh* and, 81–83, 90; Brontë's *Shirley* and, 37; dynam-

ics of, 6; Elizabeth Barrett Browning and, 88; fictional renditions of, 8; late Western patriarchy and, 14; Luckie Buchan and, 15; Mother Nature and, 88; mother-want and, 1; repressions and, 22; study of, 13

Mother Nature: *Aurora Leigh* and, 83, 88, 90, 97; Bronte and, 26–27, 33, 148n7; male Romantics' adoration of, 146n16; Romanticism and, 11; sanctification of, 7, 13; stark imagery of, 97

Mother Right (Bachofen), 12

mother-want: *Aurora Leigh* and, 82–83; Bronte's *Shirley* and, 37; Charlotte Bronte and, 27; Elizabeth Barrett Browning and, 1; George Sand and, 26–27; mother-god-want and, 1

Murphy, Patricia, "sinister potentiality of maternity" and, 84

mysticism, 106; Barrett Browning and, 148n7; epistemology of, 3–6; Nightingale and, 100–101, 115

mythology: Barrett Browning and, 73, 91; Christianity and, 69, 145n6; revised by women writers and, 3; Sharples and, 19; *Shirley* and, 38; woman-centered and, 13–14

The Mythology of Ancient Greece and Italy, problem with monotheistic religions and, 6–7

Nature: as objective correlative, 26; Bronte's heroines and spiritual inspiration, 38; Bronte's *Shirley* and, 36, 38; Celtic imagination and, 9; Charlotte Bronte's trances and, 22, 28, 30, 32–33, 39–43, 45, 77; Christianity and, 19, 151–52n6; cooptation of, 13; Elizabeth Barrett Browning and, 73, 75, 85, 87–89; hardheaded literalism and, 35; *Jane Eyre* and, 12; pagan worship and, 27; resacralizing and, 7; Romantics and, 11; Thomas Carlyle and, 10–11

Nestorians, 70

Neufeldt, Victor A.: Bronte's Angrian saga and, 30; Bronte's "The Violet" and, 25–26

The New Moral World, legitimacy of religion and, 92–93, 125

Newman, John Henry, 57–58, 60, 150n6

Nietzsche, Friedrich, truth as mobile army of metaphors and, 3

Nightingale, Florence: amorphous understanding of divinity and, 108; belief in horizontal transcendence and, 115; Benjamin Jowett and, 103, 112–13, 116, 152nn9–10; "Cassandra" and, 22–23, 98–99, 101, 104–5, 111–14, 116, 120, 151n3, 152nn9–10; concept of the female Christ and, 114; descriptions of spiritual ecstasy and, 104; divine inspiration and, 100; Eve as precursor for the female messiah and, 111; female Christ and, 18, 115, 152n10; God "is always descending into hell" and, 108; God's meaning and daily lives of the sick and needy, 107; Hermes Trismegistus and, 102, 111, 129; Holy Family and, 113–14; interpretation of Eve and, 110; *The Isis* and, 113; Judeo-Christian metaphor of the jealous Father and, 119; longing for a female savior and, 6; Lord's Prayer and, 105, 109; Mill as "Goddess" and, 109; mystical Christianity and, 23; Nightingale Papers XII and, 98; radical horizontal transcendence and, 116; relationship with deity and horizontal transcendence, 151–52n6; Romola as rebel in disguise and, 138; symbolic female divinities and, 2; theological understanding of the Madonna and, 118; theology of, 101–2; Virgin Mary and, 116–17

Nussey, Ellen, Bronte letter and, 29

Oliphant, Margaret; Madonna and, 8

Oliver, Kelly, 141

Ossian (Macpherson), 9, 31

Owen, Robert: Barrett Browning's vulgar tropes and, 96; English brand of socialism and, 92; female equality and, 17; George Eliot and, 18, 125; "Manifesto" and, 152n1; material effects of the Industrial Revolution and, 93; socialist feminists and, 98

Pagan Celtic Britain (Ross), 151n11
Paine, Thomas, 17
Papal Bull, 22
Parkes, Bessie Raynor, 74
Peake, R. B., 78
Pell, Nancy, *Jane Eyre* and "the universal Mother, nature" and, 148n7
Perkins, Erasmus, 17
Petroff, Alvilda, aesthetic of, 4
The Philosophy of Necessity (Bray), 125
Piquet, François, millenarians and, 17–18
Pius IX, 49–50
polytheistic imagination: Anna Jameson and, 68; Barrett Browning and, 73–75, 79, 81–82, 84–85, 88, 91–92, 97; Charlotte Brontë and, 38; major male Romantics and, 7
The Portable Kristeva (Oliver), 141
Pusey, E. B., 55–59, 150n3, 150nn5–6

Qualls, Barry: discussion of *Jane Eyre* and, 12; *The Secular Pilgrims of Victorian Fiction* and, 24
Quarterly Review: Immaculate Conception and, 52; rites in Rome and, 149n1; schism within the Church and, 52
Queen Victoria, 11–12

radical feminists, 18–21 (*see also* socialist feminists; utopian feminists); Anna Jameson and, 15, 66; Barrett Browning and, 74, 97; Brontë's *Shirley* and, 36; female savior figures and, 90; Nightingale and, 13, 100, 111; Nightingale's representation of the female savior and, 114
Ramses II, 101
Reid, T. Wemyss, Brontë's father and supernatural stories, 146n13
The Religion of the New Age (Daumer), 141
Renk, Kathleen, stereotypes of women in art and literature, 84
Rigby, Kate, resacralizing nature and, 7
Rogers, Philip, "Brontë's proto-feminism" and, 44
Romanticism: Charlotte Brontë and, 24; Continental writers and, 10; God's creativity and, 12; Mother Nature and, 88–89; resacralizing and, 6; re-tailoring culture with female equality and, 13; viewing divinity as in part female and, 12; view of poets and, 11
Romola (Eliot), 8, 22–23, 90, 121–24, 127–42, 152n2, 153n6, 153nn8–9
Rosehill Circle, 125
Rosengarten, Herbert: Brontë's grief and, 40; Brontë's *Shirley* and, 41
Ruskin, John; fictional renditions of mother-god-want and, 8

Sacred and Legendary Art (Jameson), 67
Saint-Simonians, 17, 112, 125–26, 152n3
Sand, George: Brontë's letter to Lewes and, 147n6; female portraits of, 81; influence on Brontë and, 26
Sartor Resartus (Carlyle), 11
Saturday Review, Eliot's *Romola* and, 140
Scenes of Clerical Life (1858), 8
Schiller, Friedrich: co-optation of nature and, 13; "Gods of Greece" and, 75; "On Naïve and Sentimental Poetry" and, 10
Scholl, Lesa, Romola immersed in masculine ideologies and, 137
Scott, Walter, recuperation of Scottish artifacts and, 9
secular feminists, Mary Wollstonecraft and, 120

Seven Manners of Loving (Beatrijs of Nazareth), 4
Shakers, 15, 21
Sharp, William, millenarians and, 17
Sharples, Eliza: *Aurora Leigh* and, 95; brutal press and, 20; Christianity and, 45; Christ's self-sacrifice and, 114; Eliot's *Romola* and, 140; Eve as a powerful, semi-divine figure and, 34; George Eliot and, 132; God's meaning and daily lives of the sick and needy, 107; Madonna and, 135; moral regeneration of the whole human race and, 68; revision of the Genesis text and, 90; rhetoric and, 37; Richard Carlile and, 52; Savior's return and feminist goals, 19; Second Coming and political equality, 115; secular Eden and, 18; secular Millennium and, 16; secular vision of a new world order and, 20; society's aim to keep women ignorant and, 137; symbolic female divinities and, 2; transformation of sociopolitical systems and, 120; Virgin/Isis as the horizon for female perfection and, 121
Shibden Hall, 36
Shirley (Brontë), 22, 24, 27, 33, 35–49, 101, 105, 147–49
Showalter, Elaine, 105; Nightingale's "Cassandra" and, 99
Sibree, Jr., John, George Eliot and, 125
Simcox, Edith, Eliot's influence by men and, 139
Simpson, Elspeth (Luckie Buchan), 15, 109
Simpson, Shola Elizabeth, Eliot's *Romola* and, 137–38
Sistine Madonna (Raphael), 23, 121–23, 127
Sixteen Revelations of Divine Love (Julian of Norwich), 5
Smith, Blanche, Nightingale's letter to, 101
Smith, James Elishma, 112; female prophets appearing in England and, 17
Smith, Margaret: Brontë's grief and, 40; Brontë's *Shirley* and, 41
Snowe, Lucy, masochistic "Reason" and, 29
socialist feminists, 50 (*see also* radical feminists; utopian feminists); Anna Jameson and, 64; Brontë rewrites the fall and, 39; *The Crisis* and, 98; death of Emma Martin and, 147n21; earthly paradise and, 2; Elizabeth Barrett Browning and, 78, 90, 93, 99; female savior figures and, 90; *Fraser's Magazine* and, 21; George Eliot and, 142; Romantic-era and, 14
Southcott, Joanna, 2, 14–16, 18–21, 23, 33–34, 42, 65–66, 78, 89–90, 95, 112, 114, 120
Spencer, Herbert, George Eliot and, 125
Stockton, Kathryn Bond, Brontë's tendency to take Romantic and Christian doctrines literally and, 35
Stone, Marjorie, *Aurora Leigh* and, 89
Subjection of Women (Mill), 151n3
Swedenborg, 23, 74, 85, 150
Swinburne, Algernon Charles: Brontë's hymn of visionary praise to her "mother nature" and, 147n7; "Hymn to Prosperine" and, 75

Tale of Two Cities (Dickens), 21
Taves, Ann: first-person narrative and, 22; Florence Nightingale and, 117
Taylor, Harriet, arguments for women's rights and, 98
Taylor, Irene, Brontë's use of a "Mighty Mother" and, 27
Taylor, Jeremy, manual for Christian living and, 29
Taylor, Mary, 34
Taylor, Olivia: *Aurora Leigh* and, 82; Browning on poetry and, 73
Thormählen, Marianne: Brontë's treatment of religion and, 25; heroism of the pilgrim and Brontë, 26; Victorian religious life and, 2

Trismegistus, Hermes, 102, 111, 129; Florence Nightingale and, 129
Trudgill, Eric, Madonna and, 8
Tuveson, Ernest L., millenarianism and, 18

Ullathorne, William Bernard, 54, 61; divine image of the mother and, 69; Mary as type of womanhood and, 150n4; Mary's ambiguous sexuality and, 58; Mary's virginal integrity and, 59
UNA: a paper devoted to the elevation of woman (1855), potentiality for divine womanhood and, 61
utopian feminists' depiction of Adam and, 66; millenarians and, 14–23. *See also* radical feminists; socialist feminists

Valéry, Paul, mastery of language and, 14
Vanita, Ruth, Protestant Victorian women writers and, 61
Vargish, Thomas, fictional inscriptions of providence and, 6
Villette (Brontë), 29, 49
Vindication of the Rights of Woman (Wollstonecraft), 124
Virgin Mary, 19, 22–23, 118 (*see also* Madonna); ambiguous power of, 8; *Aurora Leigh* and, 82; conflation of Romola with, 128; disagreement and, 49; Eliot's *Romola* and, 142; Florence Nightingale and, 116–17, 120; George Eliot and, 132; Kristeva's male-defined Virgin Mary and, 139; male dread of the emasculating Madonna and, 119; Nightingale's radical grandmothers and, 100; pagan alter egos and, 68; unrealized ideal for women and, 64

Wedderburn, Robert, 17
Wesleyan-Methodist Magazine, Immaculate Conception and, 52
Westminster Review, patronizing attitude toward Eliot and, 141
Whitfield, H. J., "rude sublimity" of Druid worship and, 9
Willcocks, M. P., Charlotte Brontë and, 147n7
William of Thierry, love and divine knowledge, 4
Wollstonecraft, Mary, 137; Nightingale's "Cassandra" and, 99; Nightingale's overdetermined commitments to feminist spirituality and, 120; *Vindication of the Rights of Woman* and, 124
Woman in the Nineteenth Century (Fuller), 124
Wooler, Margaret, 34
Woolf, Virginia, 92; Nightingale's "Cassandra" and, 99
Wordsworth, William, Mother Nature and, 7
Wright, Frances, 77; modern Eves and, 34; revision of Christian Fall and, 20; society's aim to keep women ignorant and, 137; symbolic female divinities and, 2

Yeast (Kingsley), 8
Yeazell, Ruth, social problem novel and, 33

Zonana, Joyce, Aurora's description of her mother and, 84

LITERATURE, RELIGION, AND POSTSECULAR STUDIES
Lori Branch, Series Editor

Literature, Religion, and Postsecular Studies publishes scholarship on the influence of religion on literature and of literature on religion from the sixteenth century onward. Books in the series include studies of religious rhetoric or allegory; of the secularization of religion, ritual, and religious life; and of the emerging identity of postsecular studies and literary criticism.

Victorian Women Writers, Radical Grandmothers, and the Gendering of God
    Gail Turley Houston

Apocalypse South: Judgment, Cataclysm, and Resistance in the Regional Imaginary
    Anthony Dyer Hoefer

www.ingramcontent.com/pod-product-compliance
Lightning Source LLC
Chambersburg PA
CBHW030112010526
44116CB00005B/211